Unless otherwise noted, all scriptural citations are from the New King James Translations 1990, 1985, 1983, Thomas Nelson, Nashville, Tn.

ISBN 978-0-9799337-8-3

Produced by
JaDon Management Inc.
1405 4th Ave. N. W. #109
Ardmore, Ok. 73401

Original Cover Art by:
Kim Lester
P. O. Box 33741
Amarillo, Tx. 79120

PRESTON - SIMMONS FORMAL WRITTEN DEBATE

SUBJECT:

THE PERFECTION OF SALVATION AND PASSING OF THE OLD COVENANT

SOME BACKGROUND ON THIS DEBATE

Kurt Simmons and I have been friends for years. I was honored to be invited by him to participate in a formal public debate with Mac Deaver, in Carlsbad, NM, in 2008.[1]

While Kurt claims to be a preterist, he no longer espouses *Covenant Eschatology* as he once did.[2] As a result of his rejection of Covenant Eschatology, Kurt has, for some years, been on a campaign against this view of preterism. In 2009 Kurt challenged me to debate the issue of the resurrection and the passing of Torah. To be honest, I was reluctant to engage in this debate since my observations to that point indicated to me that Kurt would simply use the debate as a campaign against Max King and that he would not actually engage my arguments. My concerns were fully justified. And many correspondents who contacted me commenting on the debate have expressed disappointment with Kurt's refusal to actually engage my arguments. Several have expressed amazement at Kurt's overt statements that he had no obligation to respond to my arguments and his denigration of the use of logic.

Nonetheless, I finally agreed to the debate and what follows is an extended discussion that is, I hope, helpful to the readers. A lot of ground is covered in the discussion.

For those unfamiliar with preterism, i.e. Covenant Eschatology, some of the arguments will seem presuppositional, and they are precisely that. Kurt and I are both in agreement that Christ's Second Coming, the judgment and the resurrection of the dead occurred in AD 70. As a result of this important mutual conviction many of our arguments may be a bit difficult for any reader not already convinced of the past fulfillment of Christ's parousia to follow. I hope this will not dissuade you from reading this important exchange. It is important to understand that *you need not be a preterist to follow the arguments on the passing of the Old Law.*

The subject of the time of the passing of the Law of Moses is critically important to anyone interested in Biblical studies. It matters not if one is a futurist, partial preterist or true preterist. This topic is not important simply and strictly for those of the preterist persuasion. Much of today's denominational confusion is based on mistaken concepts of the Law of

---

[1] That debate is available from me in MP3 format. Contact me through: www.eschatology.org or, www.bibleprophecy.com.

[2] Covenant Eschatology is the view that Biblical eschatology is about the end of the Old Covenant world of Israel in AD 70. Kurt affirms in this debate that the Old Covenant World of Israel ended at the cross. He claims to be simply a preterist, i.e. to believe that all predictions of the end of the age, Christ's parousia and the resurrection were fulfilled in AD 70. Kurt says AD 70 was totally "irrelevant soteriologically."

Moses. All futurist eschatologies share Kurt's (ostensibly preterist) view that the "ceremonial" aspect of Torah was removed at the cross, and yet, they– as well as Kurt-- then appeal to the Law of Moses to justify their eschatological views. In the final analysis, most views of the Law of Moses break it down into moral Laws, ceremonial laws and prophecy. I believe this is a false dichotomy.[3]

A comment here. Kurt agrees that the OT prophecies and promises made to Israel concerning the resurrection were fulfilled in AD 70. He asserts this repeatedly in his books. As the readers will see, I posed the issue of Israel and her promises to Kurt repeatedly in this exchange. I asked how God's covenant with Israel– *which included the eschatological promises*– could have been abrogated at the cross, and yet, Christ's coming, the judgment and resurrection did not occur until AD 70. Kurt never responded to my arguments on this issue, but it is fundamentally important. His refusal to deal with this issue puts him in common company with the futurist camps who likewise claim that the Mosaic Covenant and Israel passed at the cross, and yet, the Old Covenant promises made to Israel remain valid today.

Kurt may posit fulfillment in AD 70 while futurists say fulfillment of those promises remain unfulfilled, but the primary issue is the same– the continuing validity – *beyond the cross*-- of the Old Covenant promises made to Israel.

So, as you can see, the issue of Torah and eschatology is critical and inter-related. To restate, it does not matter if a person is a preterist, amillennialist, postmillennialist or dispensationalist, the issues covered in this debate are critical.

It is my hope, and Kurt's as well, that this debate will be a great benefit to the readers. While Kurt and I have pressed our points with vigor, we have tried to maintain Christian decorum and mutual respect.

A final note: I have not edited the presentations at all. I have simply "cut and pasted" them as I wrote them, and as received from Kurt. All "typos" grammatical *errata*, etc. have been maintained. No alterations of any kind have been made.

---

[3] See my book on the Transfiguration of Christ for a full discussion of the attempts to dichotomize Torah into three distinct classifications and then argue that part of the Law could pass while some would, and still does, remain valid.

Personal Information About The Disputants

Don K. Preston is the president of Preterist Research Institute of Ardmore, Ok. He has been in the ministry since 1975 and speaks at seminars around the world.

Preston has written over 19 books on Covenant Eschatology, including the first and only true preterist commentary on 1 Thessalonians 4, entitled We Shall Meet Him In The Air: The Wedding of the King of kings. He is also the author of Who Is This Babylon, The Elements Shall Melt With Fervent Heat, Like Father Like Son, On Clouds of Glory, and other popular titles.

Preston co-hosts a popular Internet radio program with William Bell every Tuesday night. The program is called Two Guys and the Bible. The program is available at www.AD70.net.

Mr. Preston was recently presented with an honorary doctorate degree from Vision International University of Ramona, California.

Don has engaged in numerous formal public debates as well as several formal written debates.
His websites are: www.eschatology.org; www.bibleprophecy.com

Kurt Simmons

Kurt Simmons resides in Carlsbad, NM, and is trained in the legal profession. He is president of Bimillennial Preterist Association.
He was co-sponsor with Bill Fangio of two preterist seminars in Carlsbad, 2007, 2008.

Kurt is the author of several books, including The Road Back To Preterism, The Consummation of the Ages, the first verse by verse full preterist commentary on Revelation, Revelation Explained (an abbreviated form of Consummation of the Ages, Adumbrations, a commentary on Daniel, and The Twilight of Postmillennialism, (co-written with Michael Fenemore).

Kurt's website is www.preteristcentral.com He also produces an E-Journal entitled "Sword and Plow."

SIMMONS-PRESTON FORMAL WRITTEN DEBATE
SUBJECT:

THE PERFECTION OF SALVATION
AND PASSING OF THE OLD COVENANT

FIRST AFFIRMATIVE BY DON K. PRESTON

It is an honor to discuss this important topic with my good friend Kurt Simmons. I know that this will be a friendly debate that all readers may profit from. It is likewise an important issue. Was the salvation process perfected and completed at the Cross, as Kurt affirms, or, was the Cross the initiation of a process that was not consummated until the AD 70 parousia? The latter is, in my view, patently the correct Biblical view, and I will seek to vindicate that claim.

Here is my proposition:
Resolved: The Bible teaches that the coming of Christ for salvation in Romans 11:25-27-- occurred in AD 70 at the climax and termination of the Mosaic Covenant Age.

Affirm: Don K. Preston

Deny: Kurt Simmons

Let me state now what this debate is not about:
Kurt and I both agree that Christ's second coming occurred in AD 70. Kurt and I both agree that the resurrection occurred in AD 70. We have some differences in regard to the nature and framework of the resurrection– differences that will be noted as we proceed, but, we both affirm the reality of the resurrection in AD 70.
This debate is not in way about whether the Cross of Christ is all sufficient for the salvation of mankind.

This debate is whether the salvation that is *dependent on the Cross was finished* at the Cross, or, whether the Cross was part of a complex of events. The Cross *initiated* the salvific process, the parousia (Christ's second coming), *finalized* that process.

Let me say at the beginning that Kurt does not believe–cannot believe– what he will affirm. He will affirm that the coming of Christ for salvation occurred at the Cross, and that no other events were necessary to perfect

1

that salvation. That is patently false. Here is why. Kurt believes, as I do, that *Jesus had to ascend to the Father and into the Most Holy Place,* there to "prepare a place for us" (Hebrews 9:24). *But, that event was forty days after the Cross!* Thus, Kurt's own position affirms that salvation was not completed at the Cross.

Kurt may respond that the amount of time is insignificant. *It is not.* Admitting that Christ had to enter the MHP–forty days after the Cross– is to admit that the Cross– as a stand alone event- did not complete salvation. It is to admit my position, that the obtaining of salvation was a process *begun at the Cross*, but perfected through a series of related events– specifically the parousia.

The question is: "Why did Jesus have to ascend and enter the MHP?" The significance of this cannot be overlooked, and Hebrews 9:6-10 holds the key: "These preparations having thus been made, the priests go continually into the outer tent, performing their ritual duties; but into the second only the high priest goes, and he but once a year, and not without taking blood which he offers for himself and for the errors of the people. By this the Holy Spirit indicates that the way into the sanctuary is not yet opened as long as the outer tent is still standing (which is symbolic for the present age). According to this arrangement, gifts and sacrifices are offered which cannot perfect the conscience of the worshiper, but deal only with food and drink and various ablutions, regulations for the body imposed until the time of reformation." (RSV. See also the NASV).

The RSV and NASV in contrast to other translations, properly render the present active indicatives of the text. Paul was undeniably speaking of the contemporary cultic practice in the temple. Note that Paul affirms that the entire cultic world "is a figure for the time now present" (*kairo ton enestekota.* Paul says the still on-going Temple practices were symbolic (parabolic) of *his present time*. He did not affirm that those typological practices and sacrifices had been nullified! This is *critical*!

Note that the Old Law, including the washings and sacrifices would stand imposed, "until the time of reformation." Kurt says that the time of reformation arrived at the Cross. This is a clear-cut violation of the present active indicatives of Hebrews 9, and Paul's statement that those things were, *when he wrote* "a figure for the present time." Kurt has Paul saying, "Those things were a figure for the past, they are no longer a figure for the present." This turns Paul's words on their head.

Paul says that as long as the Old Law– with its sacrifices and washings– stood imposed, there was no access to the Most Holy Place. *The reader must catch the power of this!*

My good friend says that the souls in Hades did not enter heaven until AD 70 (**KS**– "I believe that the general resurrection was the time when the dead were released from Hades" S-P, Sept. 2009).

But, Kurt says the Old Mosaic Law-the sacrifices of Hebrews 9, DKP-- was removed at the Cross!

Let me frame the argument using Kurt's position:

The sacrifices symbolized and foreshadowed entrance into the MHP

As long as the sacrifices (The Mosaic Covenant) were imposed there was no entrance into the MHP.

There was no entrance until AD 70– Kurt Simmons

Therefore, the sacrifices (and the Mosaic Covenant) were imposed until AD 70.

This is logically inescapable, and fully establishes my affirmative concerning the end of the age.

The reader needs to know what Kurt has to say about Revelation 15:8 and its relationship to Hebrews 9: "The way into heaven was not opened until God's wrath upon Jerusalem is fulfilled. The way into the holiest was not yet manifested while the first tabernacle was yet standing (Hebrews 9:8)."*(Consummation of the Ages*, 2003, p. 292).

So, from Kurt's own pen, Revelation 15 and Hebrews 9:6-10 are directly connected. Both speak of the same time, and the same event. But, this demands that *the Mosaic Law remained imposed until AD 70.*

Kurt will need to specifically and exegetically address this issue, and not ignore it.

Let me build on this material:

As long as the Mosaic cultus stood imposed, man (including the souls in Hades), could not enter the MHP (KS, *Consummation*, 293).

The Mosaic Cultus would be imposed until the time of reformation.

The time of reformation is when man (including the souls in Hades), could enter the MHP.

The time of reformation arrived at the Cross (KS).

Therefore, man (including the souls in Hades), could enter the MHP beginning at the Cross.

But no, Kurt says this is not true! The general resurrection and time when the souls in Hades could enter the MHP was not until AD 70.

Furthermore, as we have seen from Kurt's own keyboard, entrance into the MHP is related to two things: the abiding standing of Torah and the completion of the Wrath of God.
Kurt applies both Hebrews 9 and Revelation 15 to AD 70!
This *demands*, logically, that the Mosaic Law remained imposed until AD 70.

Let me build on this.
In Revelation 15:8, John saw the vision of the heavenly temple with the Ark of the Covenant visible. This means of course, that the MHP was now visible! However, note that it says that no one could enter the MHP, "until the seven plagues of the seven angels were fulfilled." These seven angels held the vials of God's wrath. So here is my argument:

No one could enter the MHP until the wrath of God contained in the seven vials was fulfilled.
But, the seventh vial would be poured out, and God's wrath fulfilled, in the judgment of Babylon (i.e Old Covenant Jerusalem, as KS and DKP agree, Revelation 16:17-20).
Therefore, no one could enter the MHP until the judgment of Babylon, i.e. Old Covenant Jerusalem).

Now, since Hebrews 9 says there would be no entrance into the MHP *while the Mosaic Law remained imposed*, and since Revelation 11-16 says there would be no access to the MHP until Jerusalem was judged, then of logical necessity, *the Mosaic Law remained imposed until the judgment of Old Covenant Jerusalem in AD 70.*

We must ask Kurt to answer some very important questions.
1.) Since you will affirm that salvation was completed, perfected at the Cross, and since salvation is directly related to entrance into the MHP, why is it that man, including those in Hades, could not enter the MHP, at the moment of the Cross? Please tell us specifically.
2.) If the time of reformation came at the Cross and that is when Torah was removed, as my friend insists, then why could not the souls in Hades enter the MHP from the time of the Cross? Paul is emphatic that it was the abiding imposition of Torah that prevented access to the MHP! Imposition of Torah– no access to the MHP. No Torah– Access to the MHP at the time of the reformation.

So, if the coming of the Lord for salvation in Romans 11:25f occurred at the Cross, and if Torah was abrogated at the Cross, then man, (including

4

the souls in Hades) could enter the MHP from the time of the Cross. But remember, that Kurt himself denies that man, (including the souls in Hades), could enter the MHP until AD 70. This is a fatal logical self contradiction.

You cannot on the one hand affirm that that which kept man from the MHP was removed at the Cross, and then claim that man still could not enter the MHP until AD 70! Do not forget that removal of Torah and completion of vengeance were *equal conditions* for entrance into the MHP. Kurt cannot focus on the vengeance aspect and deny what Paul has to say about the continuing imposition of Torah *until man could enter the MHP at the parousia.*

Here is a related affirmative argument:
The coming of Christ for salvation (Hebrews 9:28) would be the consummation (completion) of the typological Day of Atonement process, that was not ever considered completed until the return of the High Priest from the MHP.

The coming of Christ would bring man, including the souls in Hades— (KS)– into the MHP.

Thus, the coming of Christ would be the time of reformation– and it was not at the Cross.

Kurt admits that entrance into the MHP was at the second coming in AD 70.

But the time of reformation is when man could enter the MHP.

Thus, the time of reformation did not arrive until the second coming AD 70.

This means that Torah remained imposed until AD 70.

If man could not enter the MHP until the AD 70 parousia, as Kurt and I agree, then Torah– which prevented man from entering the MHP until the time of reformation– remained imposed until the parousia in AD 70.

If the praxis of the HP was typological of Christ's actions, then man could enter the MHP at Christ's parousia in AD 70.

If Christ's second coming finalized the salvation initiated at the Cross, then man could not enter the MHP until the parousia. And Kurt repeatedly says that man could not enter the MHP until the parousia in AD 70!

Remember that I noted that Kurt will agree that Christ had to enter into the MHP in order to fulfill the typological actions of the High Priest under Torah. Let the reader observe that Kurt's position on this demands that the "ceremonial commandments" of Torah were not completed at the Cross.

5

Christ's death and entrance into the MHP fulfilled those "ceremonial commandments" (typological actions) of Torah, thus, Torah remained as a type and shadow *at least until Christ entered into the MHP*.

This means that Kurt cannot argue that salvation was completed at the moment of the Cross.

The question is, how can Kurt deny *the absolute necessity of Christ's second coming* to fulfill those typological actions of the High Priest? Kurt wants to short circuit the Atonement process and have it complete while Jesus was on the Cross. But wait, no, he will insist that Jesus *did* have to enter the MHP *forty days after the Cross!* But then he will deny that Christ had to "come again the second time, apart from sin, for salvation"to complete that very atonement process! But wait, no, that is not correct, for Kurt says that Christ had to come again (AD 70) for man to enter the MHP!

In Hebrews 9 it is the so-called "ceremonial commandments," the sacrifices and cultic actions that Paul affirmed were types and shadows imposed until the time of reformation when man could enter the MHP. Paul said those things were, *when he wrote*, typological of the coming better things, the time of reformation.

Thus, the ceremonial commandments had not been annulled at the Cross, and were still imposed when Paul wrote.

Kurt wants to argue that the ceremonial aspect of Torah was abrogated, but that the prophecies could remain valid until AD 70. Hebrews 9 falsifies this, for, it was the typological *ceremonial commandments* that were still "symbolic for the present age" according to Paul.

Those ceremonial laws were "still standing," and would be until what they signified / predicted was realized at the time of reformation, and man could enter the MHP.

Unfortunately, Kurt's paradigm has those typological ceremonial commandments nullified at the Cross, before what they typified was fulfilled. This clearly violates Hebrews 9.

But, note again, that the Hebrews author cites the typological actions of the High Priest, and Jesus' fulfillment of those actions. The HP would slay the sacrifice, and Christ had appeared to put away sin by the sacrifice of himself. The High Priest entered the MHP, and Christ had entered the MHP (Hebrews 9:24). And while the author does not specifically say the HP came out, Hebrews then says "And to those who eagerly look for him he shall appear a second time, apart from sin, for salvation. Now, take note of Hebrews 10:1: "For, the Law having a shadow of good things about to come..." Note the connective particle "gar" translated as "for" in 10:1.

This word ties 9:28 to 10:1, and explains *why* Christ had to appear the second time. He had to appear the second time *"for* the law, having a shadow of good things (about) to come." *Christ's second coming was to fulfill the typological, ceremonial commandments and practices of the law!* That "for" cannot be ignored, and proves that Christ's second coming was the fulfillment of the typological commandments of Torah. The Day of Atonement is clearly the context. The author has compared Christ's sacrifice and entrance into the MHP with those types. The *"for"* demands that Christ's second appearing is the fulfillment of the Atonement typology. This cannot be ignored, and it means that the end of the Mosaic Covenant world did not come until Christ's parousia in AD 70!

Note also that 10:1 says that the good things typified by "the law" (note again the *present indicatives* in 10:1), were "about to come." For the Hebrews writer, the better things typified by the Atonement cultus-- entrance into the MHP-- were "about to come (from *mello*)." (Note that Kurt agrees that *mello* means "about to be, about to come" (*Consummation*, p. 1). This is the salvation of 9:28. It is the time of reformation anticipated by the typological, ceremonial commandments.

So, Christ's second appearing was to finalize the Atonement process. This logically demands that *salvation was not completed at the Cross*. If it were, man could enter the MHP at the moment of the Cross!
This means that the coming of the Lord for salvation in Romans 11 was Christ's coming to finalize the atonement complex of events. Salvation was totally *dependent on the Cross*, but was not *finalized* at the Cross.
To negate this argument Kurt must prove that while the death of Jesus was the fulfillment of the Atonement typology, and while his entrance into the MHP was the fulfillment of the Atonement typology, his reappearing was unrelated to the Atonement practices of the High Priest. Kurt cannot do this.

In two articles challenging my position on Romans 11 Kurt essentially surrendered his position. He said of Christ's betrothal / marriage, "We agree that the full benefit of Christ's atonement was *held in partial abeyance* until the consummation of the Lamb's marriage with the bride. The church was *betrothed* to Christ beginning at Pentecost, but did not enjoy the fullness of the New Testament intimacy until the consummation

7

in AD 70." (Sword and Plow, Sept., 2009– hereafter *S-P*. His emphasis). Now, clearly, a person *betrothed* is not "fully married" and simply awaiting the manifestation of that marriage. What is being held in "abeyance" is *the finalization of the marriage*. The betrothal is the *initiation* of a process, the marriage is the *consummation* of the process, just like the Cross and parousia.

If the body of Christ was *waiting for salvation* and "the fullness of New Testament intimacy" then those things were not yet completed. Paul himself said, ""He who has begun a good work in you will complete it until the day of Jesus Christ" (Philippians 1:6). Had the work of salvation begun? Unequivocally! Was it perfected and finished? Clearly not. It was an on-going process when Paul wrote.

I am going to ask Kurt to *very specifically* define the fuller blessings, the more intimate relationship, etc.. What is *"the full benefit of Christ's atonement"* that was being held in abeyance until AD 70? *According to Hebrews 9:28 it was salvation itself!* It was the very thing that Christ would come to bring as foretold in Romans 11! *It was in fact, the completion of the Atonement process, begun at the Cross. It was access to the presence of God!*

Note theses excellent quotes from *Consummation of the Ages*, (p. 1): "It is a well established point of scripture that *the redemptive work of Christ was held in abeyance* until the consummation at Christ's return when faith would be made sight...the connection between God's redemptive and eschatological purpose is essential to a proper understanding of Revelation." (My emphasis, DKP). Commenting on Romans 8:15f and the redemption of creation, Kurt then says: "Paul is here talking about the coming spiritual justification and regeneration in Christ that Jew and Gentile would receive at the time of the consummation in AD 70" (*Consummation*, 2). So, salvation, redemption, justification and regeneration were all future when Paul wrote Romans!

Well stated *indeed*. What Kurt fails to notice is that in Revelation we find the salvation of Israel– the salvation foretold in Romans 11– *at the parousia*. There is to be sure a referent back to the Cross, they had washed their robes in the blood of the Lamb, but, they were awaiting their imminent salvation, when they could enter the MHP!

I have proven that entrance into the MHP is inseparably related to the end of the Torah.

Stated simply, Hebrews 9 proves this:

Torah standing valid– no access to the MHP. This is irrefutable.

Torah removed– access to the MHP (the time of reformation). This is undeniable.

I have proven– and Kurt agrees– that entrance into the MHP did not take place until AD 70. This is *prima facie* validation of my proposition that the full end of the Mosaic Covenant age was at Christ's parousia in AD 70.

I cannot fail to note an extreme irony here. Kurt's proposition says the full end of the Mosaic Covenant age arrived at the Cross. Yet, his book, *Consummation of the Ages*, (2003, available from me) is dedicated to proving that the end of the age *arrived in AD 70!* Here is one quote of several that could be given: "Christ tied the judgment to the end of the Mosaic age and the destruction of Jerusalem" (*Consummation*, 229). Furthermore, Kurt is on record emphatically agreeing with my assessment of Hebrews 9 and access to the MHP.

In his latest book, (*Adumbrations*, 2009, p. 220, available from me) Kurt comments on Hebrews 9: "The writer of Hebrews says that the two compartments of the tabernacle (temple) stood for the two covenants: the first compartment, the Holy Place, for the Old Testament in which were offered gifts and sacrifices that could not make the worshipper soteriologically perfect; the second compartment, which he calls the *Holiest of all*, for the New Testament wherein the worshipper is made complete (Hebrews 9:1-10)....The saints 'entrance' into the *Holy of Holies* (that is, their legal and covenantal admission into the presence of God, cleansed by the blood of Christ) *did not occur until the second coming."* (My emphasis, DKP).

Let me offer my argument, utilizing Kurt's own excellent statements:
The "first tabernacle" of Hebrews 9:6f symbolized the Mosaic Covenant (KS).
As long as the "first tabernacle" stood imposed (binding) there was no access to the presence of God (Hebrews 9:8).
"The saints 'entrance' into the Holy of Holies (that is, their legal and covenantal admission into the presence of God, cleansed by the blood of Christ) *did not occur until the second coming"* (KS).
Therefore, the "first tabernacle" the Mosaic Covenant, stood imposed (binding) until the second coming (AD 70, DKP).

And yet, Kurt has signed a proposition to affirm that the full end of the Mosaic age occurred at the Cross! And, he has signed a proposition to *deny* the very thing that he says in his books!

9

To say the least, this is a *huge* and *fatal* self contradiction. You cannot affirm on the one hand that the Mosaic Covenant age ended at the Cross, and then affirm that the end of that age did not arrive until AD 70!

Thus, Kurt cannot argue that Romans 11 posits salvation as completed at the Cross and that man fully possessed that salvation, for that would demand *that man could enter the MHP from the Cross onward.* Kurt himself denies this. Kurt Simmons has established my affirmative proposition for me!

Having definitively proven my proposition about the end of the Mosaic Covenant age, let me turn now to Romans 11 and offer corroborative proof that the coming of the Lord for salvation in Romans 11 occurred in AD 70.

The Prophetic Background of Romans 11 Proves That the Coming of the Lord Paul Anticipated Was the AD 70 Coming of Christ

When Paul spoke of the coming of the Lord for salvation to take away Israel's sin, he cites three OT prophecies: Isaiah 27:9f, Isaiah 59:20 and Jeremiah 31:29f. (Another text, Daniel 9:24f clearly lies behind Romans 11 as well. I will *try* to get to that in this debate). For the moment, we will focus on the two prophecies from Isaiah.

In an article responding to Kurt's assessment of Romans 11 I noted that the time of Israel's salvation according to Isaiah 27:9f would be when YHVH took away her sin, in the day that the altar was turned to chalkstone, God would forget the people He had created, and have no mercy on them. I further noted that according to the antecedent references to "in that day" that this would be when YHVH would come and avenge the blood of the martyrs. (See my articles at: http://www.eschatology.org/index.php?option=com_content&view=article &id=685:a-response-to-kurt-simmons-on-romans-1125-27&catid=73:enga ging-the-critics&Itemid=61).

Here is the argument I made:
The coming of the Lord to take away Israel's sin would be the coming of the Lord foretold in Isaiah 27:9f.
The coming of the Lord in Isaiah 27:9f would be the coming of the Lord in judgment of Israel for shedding innocent blood (Isaiah 26:20f).
Therefore, the coming of the Lord of Romans 11:26 would be the coming of the Lord in judgment of Israel for shedding innocent blood.

My friend responded that "there have been many days of the Lord, and that to avenge innocent blood" (S-P, p. 2). He rightly notes that the Babylonian invasion was to avenge the martyrs' blood in the sixth century (2 Kings 24:1-4; Jeremiah 2-4:13).

Simmons is correct in his *basic* thought. What he fails to honor is that Jesus said that all of the blood of all the righteous, *all the way back to creation*, would be avenged in his generation (Matthew 23:29-37). Jesus' statement includes the *comprehensive and consummative* avenging of the blood of the martyrs that were in measure "avenged" in the Assyrian and Babylonian invasions! So, while those judgments came as a result of Israel's bloodguilt, there is no question that in the mind of Jesus the bloodguilt of Jerusalem was not *fully* avenged in those judgments. And Kurt Simmons agrees with this. See *Consummation*, 346.

Please catch this: my friend admits in a footnote (S-P, July 2009, p. 2), "We do not disallow the possibility that there is a *plenior sensus (fuller meaning, DKP),* to Isaiah 26:21 that may look beyond its historical setting to Christ's second coming." Well, if this is true, then Paul *could*, after all, be citing Isaiah to speak of the AD 70 judgment, *could he not? If not, why not?* We will see if my friend will answer the question this time, since he ignored it in our earlier exchange.

When I took note of my friend's admission that Isaiah 26-27 could refer to AD 70, in his second response (Sept., 2009, S-P), he then switched horses and *denied that Isaiah 27 was Messianic! He said it referred exclusively to the Assyrian invasion of the eighth century BC!* Why did Kurt do a 180% reversal and deny that Isaiah 27 could refer to AD 70? *Because that admission is fatal to his view of Romans 11.*

If Isaiah 27:9f has nothing to do with AD 70– in spite of the fact that Kurt initially admitted that it might– then it most assuredly has *nothing to do with the Cross! Catch the power of this!*

Kurt cannot argue that Isaiah 27 has no Messianic application, without destroying his own argument that Paul is speaking of the Cross! You cannot say that Isaiah 27 referred exclusively to the Assyrian invasion without saying that Paul was utilizing Isaiah 27 in a manner that was 100% unrelated to his discussion!

Why would Paul, in discussing the salvation of Israel- either the Cross or AD 70-- cite a prophecy that had *absolutely nothing* to do with either the

Cross or AD 70?

I am going to ask, no, I will *insist*, that my friend answer this question directly, without evasion or obfuscation. This is a critical issue of hermeneutics. Paul was either saying that Isaiah 27:9f had been fulfilled at the Cross, or, he was saying that Isaiah 27 would be fulfilled at the AD 70 parousia. Yet, Kurt says Isaiah 27 had *nothing to do with either one*!

There is not one word in Isaiah 27 about the Cross. If Kurt differs with this, let him give us "book, chapter and verse!" He cannot do it. Isaiah 27 is a judgment coming of the Lord, to avenge innocent blood.

Jesus' first coming, including the Cross, *was not a judgment coming*. Jesus said: "And if anyone hears My words and does not believe, I do not judge him; *for I did not come to judge the world but to save the world"* (John 12:47, my emphasis). Furthermore, his first coming was as the Suffering Servant, and "a bruised reed shall he not break" (Isaiah 42:3-6)–not as Judge and Avenger

Note that this coming of the Lord in Isaiah 26:20f / 27:9f is also *the time of the resurrection* (Isaiah 26:19). So, here is my argument:
The coming of the Lord of Romans 11:26 is the coming of the Lord of Isaiah 26-27.
The coming of the Lord of Isaiah 26-27 is the coming of the Lord at the time of the resurrection (Isaiah 26:19-21).
The time of the resurrection at the coming of the Lord was in AD 70 (Kurt Simmons and Don K. Preston agree).
Therefore, the coming of the Lord in Romans 11:26f was the AD 70 coming of the Lord.

It will not do for Kurt to ignore this. This is a question of *hermeneutics*. How can Kurt insert into Isaiah 26-27 a prediction of the Cross *when it is not there*, and then insist that Paul had the Cross in mind when he cited Isaiah, *a text that does not mention the Cross? So, again, Kurt, where in Isaiah 26-27 do you find the Cross?* Give us the verses! If you cannot find them, your view of Romans 11 is surrendered, for Paul most assuredly was citing Isaiah 26-27 as the source for his discussion of the coming of the Lord. The same is true of Isaiah 59.

Isaiah 59
The prophecy of Isaiah 59 breaks itself down very naturally into three headings:

Accusation – YHVH accused Israel of shedding innocent blood, of violence and unrighteousness (v. 1-8).

Acknowledgment – Israel admitted her guilt, but, it is clear that there is no true repentance in the text (v. 9-15).

Action – The Lord saw Israel in her sinful condition and, "His own arm brought salvation for Him; and His own righteousness, it sustained Him for He put on righteousness as a breastplate, and a helmet of salvation on His head; He put on the garments of vengeance for His clothing, and was clad with zeal as a cloak. According to their deeds, accordingly He will repay, Fury to His adversaries, Recompense to His enemies..."

So, just like Isaiah 27, this chapter is concerned with the coming of the Lord in judgment of Israel for her guilt in shedding innocent blood. Three times this sin is mentioned (v. 3, 6-7)! And yet, not a word about the Cross!

Notice that the Intercessor puts on the garments of a *Warrior*. He would clothe himself with the garments of vengeance to recompense his enemies. This is the promise of the coming of the Lord from Zion in verse 20: "The Redeemer will come to Zion, and to those who turn from transgression in Jacob" Verse 20 is not a different coming from that in verses 16-19! It is one and the same coming, and again, it is the coming of Christ in judgment of Israel for shedding innocent blood.

So, here is the argument:

The coming of the Lord for the salvation of Israel in Romans 11:26-27 is the coming of the Lord predicted in Isaiah 59.

But, the coming of the Lord predicted in Isaiah 59 is the coming of the Lord in judgment of Israel for shedding innocent blood.

Therefore, the coming of the Lord in Romans 11:26-27 is the coming of the Lord in judgment of Israel for shedding innocent blood.

Isaiah 59 presents the identical hermeneutical challenge as Isaiah 26-27. If Kurt claims that Isaiah 59 had nothing to do with AD 70, then it assuredly does not predict the Cross.

If he claims that the Cross is in Isaiah 59 he must produce the verse.

If he claims that in spite of the fact that the Cross is not mentioned in Isaiah 59 that we must see it there, this is *eisegesis. That is imposing a theological presupposition on a text.* When we begin doing this, we can prove any position that we want! Our theology must flow from text, not presuppositions.

The challenge for Kurt is simple: Explain why Paul cites two Old

Testament prophecies of the coming of Christ in judgment of Israel for shedding innocent blood, when in fact, according to Kurt, Paul was not concerned *in any way* with the fulfillment of those prophecies of Christ's judgment coming.

Even worse, Kurt must explain exactly why Paul would even *mention* Isaiah 27 in his prediction of either the Cross or AD 70, when according to Kurt, *Isaiah 27 had nothing to do with either event!*

And, if Kurt is so bold as to say that Isaiah 59 has nothing to do with AD 70, then how can he say that it predicted the Cross when the Cross is not in the text?

Why would Paul cite two prophecies that had nothing, *absolutely nothing*, to do with his subject matter, in order to prove his point about the salvation of Israel, either at the Cross or in AD 70?

Now, should Kurt once again admit that: "We do not disallow the possibility that there is a *plenior sensus (fuller meaning, DKP),* to Isaiah 26:21 (or Isaiah 59, DKP) that may look beyond its historical setting to Christ's second coming" then this opens the door for the AD 70 fulfillment.

There are many OT prophecies of the Passion of Jesus. Why did Paul not cite a single one of them if he had that in mind?

When I presented these arguments in my initial article, Kurt responded: "The solution is quite simple: When did God provide the remedy for sin? At the fall of Jerusalem or at the Cross? The Deliverer came to Zion and brought forgiveness of sin when Jesus died on the Cross, not when Jerusalem was destroyed." So, Kurt *completely ignored the context of Isaiah 27 and 59* and imposed his presuppositional theology onto those prophecies– all the while claiming that Isaiah 27 at least, is not even Messianic!

Am I denying that Christ died to take away sin? Patently not! Am I denying that the Cross is the foundation of our salvation? Not for a moment! What I *am doing* is utilizing proper hermeneutic in honoring the indisputable fact that both of the prophecies of the coming of the Lord for salvation, cited by Paul, are prophecies of Christ's judgment coming. And I am insisting that it is improper eisegesis to deny that context, and import into Paul's discussion something that is not there.

14

Paul cited two major OT prophecies that foretold the coming of the Lord in judgment of Israel for shedding innocent blood. *He did not cite prophecies of the Passion of Christ!* Now, for my friend to find the Passion of Christ in Romans 11, *he must find it in Isaiah 26-27 or Isaiah 59. It is not there!* Simmons must therefore *import it into prophecies that do not mention it*, and then *assume* that Paul likewise *imported it in Romans 11!* What is the hermeneutical justification for this? Is this not, *prima facie, eisegesis* (reading *into* the text), and not exegesis (drawing *out* of the text *what is there*)?

Remember one of the primary rules of hermeneutic: "A text cannot mean what it never meant!" So, if Isaiah 26-27 and 59 did not predict Christ's Passion then my friend cannot apply Isaiah's prophecies of the *judgment* to Jesus' *incarnation without importing those concepts into the text.*

Both Isaiah 27 and Isaiah 59 are Messianic and Paul's citation of them in Romans 11 means that Paul has the judgment coming of Christ in mind in Romans 11.

Summary and Conclusion
I have demonstrated, *prima facie*, that the end of the Mosaic Covenant age did not occur until Christ's AD 70 coming.
Kurt Simmons specifically states the truth of my affirmative in both of his books.
Does Kurt now reject and renounce what he has so eloquently written concerning the end of the Mosaic Covenant age?

I have proven from the prophetic context of Romans 11 that the coming of the Lord of Romans 11 was to be– and was– the AD 70 judgment of Israel for shedding innocent blood.

Scripture, logic and Kurt's own words have fully established my proposition.

PRESTON- SIMMONS DEBATE

The Perfection of Salvation and Passing of the Old Covenant

FIRST NEGATIVE BY KURT SIMMONS

He that is first in his own cause seemeth just; but his neighbor cometh and searcheth him out. Proverbs 18:17

Don is a wonderful brother and good friend. His work defending Preterism is unsurpassed. I am sure we will all learn a great deal from this exchange. I am thankful that we can have this sort discussion in a spirit of brotherly love and affection.

I should say at the outset, that Don offers quotes from my books to substantiate his case. But, these do not really help Don. As I informed Don when we entered this discussion, although at one time I shared many of his views, *I no longer do.* I repudiate all things Max King! It is because I have learned *better* that we are having this discussion at all. Here are the issues of this debate:

- To what *event* does scripture attach man's salvation, the death of Christ upon the cross, or his coming in wrath upon the Jews and Romans?

- Was the law *fulfilled* and the legal efficacy of the Old Testament *end* at the cross, or did it remain valid and binding until the second coming?

- Was remission of sins and fulness of grace *available* from and after the cross, at Pentecost when the gospel was first preached were sins remitted and washed away, or was salvation from sin postponed until Jerusalem fell?

Every Christian knows that the Bible places salvation at the cross. The cross was *the* defining event of salvation history that makes resurrection possible. Paul said, "God forbid that I should glory save in the cross of our Lord Jesus Christ" (Gal. 6:14). Paul told the Colossians God had "*forgiven* you all trespasses;" Christ's blood had "*blotted out*" the handwriting of ordinances that was against us;" Jesus "*took it* out of the way, *nailing* it to his cross, *triumphing* over principalities and powers in it" (Col. 2:14, 15). These are the very essentials of the gospel; everything of redemptive significance from

16

sin happened at the cross. There are no more basic doctrines to the faith delivered "once for all" to the saints than these. The cross is bedrock Christian stuff.

Yet, Don finds himself on the *wrong end* of every one of these propositions. Don places salvation from sin at the fall of Jerusalem in AD 70 rather than Calvary AD 33. Don denies that the law was fulfilled (satisfied) at the cross. He believes instead that the Old Testament was valid and binding until AD 70; he affirms that man continued under *bondage to sin* until Jerusalem fell, and that then, and not before, was man justified and restored to a full and perfect relationship with God. My study of Don's books and articles leads me to conclude that under his system man is not saved by the *addition of grace* at the cross, but by *removal of the law* at the fall of Jerusalem.

Consider: If the cross triumphed over the law, if Jesus paid the debt of sin in his death, the law could have no further power over Christians. A debt paid is extinguished forever. But if the cross did not *triumph* over the law at Calvary, if man had to wait until the law was *removed* to be justified from sin, then *nothing* happened at the cross.

Let us repeat that lest it be missed. *If the cross did not <u>triumph</u> over the law at Calvary, if man had to wait until the law was <u>removed</u> to be justified from sin, then <u>nothing</u> happened at the cross.* This is the long and short of Don's teaching: nothing happened at the cross.

Historical Background to this Discussion – Understanding Our Positions

It will be helpful to the reader to understand Don's and my respective positions if we pause briefly to survey the history of Preterism over the last 40 years and the different schools that have grown up. If you have read Don's books, you may have noticed that Don refers to his particular version of eschatology as "Covenant Eschatology." Covenant Eschatology is *not* Preterism. Preterism merely assumes a *"contemporary-historical"* interpretation of New Testament prophecy regarding Christ's second coming; it affirms that the second coming, including the general resurrection, occurred in the events culminating in the destruction of Jerusalem in AD 70. Covenant Eschatology affirms all this and more.

Covenant Eschatology is the brain-child of Max King, a Church of Christ preacher who came to the front of the modern Preterist movement with the publication of his book *"The Spirit of Prophecy"* (1971. Warren, OH). The phrase "Covenant Eschatology" was coined by King's father-in-law, C.D. Beagle. Covenant Eschatology sees Biblical eschatology in terms of *covenantal transformation* from Moses to Christ. The two identifying features of Covenant Eschatology are King's *spiritualized* view of the resurrection and the notion that the Old Testament was *valid* and the saints *under the debt of sin* until AD 70.

According to King, Judaism was a "power or system of death", and "became a 'body of death' by the old law.[4] For King, the "resurrection of the body or the church" applies to the raising up of the church "from the Jewish body...at the fall of Judaism."[5] "One must look to the Jewish system as the state and power of death to be destroyed by the reign of Christ."[6] "Paul is conscious that death's defeat hinges upon sin's defeat, and that *the defeat of sin is tied to the annulment of the old aeon of law*...For Paul, *death is abolished when the state of sin and the law are abolished*."[7] "When the 'ministration of death written in tables of stone' was finally destroyed, death was swallowed up in victory."[8]

Of course, this is all perfectly frivolous. The Gentile churches of Athens, Colossae, Thessalonica, Rome, and Ephesus in the "grave of Judaism?" "Raised from the Jewish body" at Jerusalem's fall? The sheer fantasy and nonsensical nature of the teaching aside, the sum and substance of King's spiritualized view, then, is that mankind was in bondage to sin by virtue of the Mosaic law, but was justified from sin by removal of the law at AD 70. Therefore, for King, "resurrection" equals "justification" and justification results from removal of the law. *"The defeat of sin is tied to the annulment of the old aeon of law...death is abolished when the state of sin and the law are abolished."*

The idea that the general resurrection was in AD 70 is perfectly sound. All Preterists are agreed in this. However, once the spiritualized view is adopted and resurrection is equated with justification, the cross is *displaced* by the second coming; justification is *moved* from Calvary to the fall of Jerusalem. However, Covenant Eschatology doesn't stop there; it does not merely change the *timing* by which justification accrued to the church. No, it goes much, much further, and actually changes the *means* of justification itself.

---

[4] . King, *The Spirit of Prophecy* (Warren, OH, 1971),145

[5] Ibid, p. 195

[6] Ibid, p. 144

[7] Max R. King, *The Cross and the Parousia of Christ*, p. 644 (emphasis added).

[8] Max R. King, *The Spirit of Prophecy*, p. 145

Covenant Eschatology affirms that it is *only by removal of the Old Law that justification is possible.* In other words, the very *substance* of our salvation becomes removal of the law, rather than the addition of grace. Paul said, "Where sin abounded, grace did much more abound" (Rom. 5:20). *Grace overcomes law!* Paul places grace at the cross; the idea that the law had to be removed is totally foreign to Paul's soteriology (theology of salvation). The grace inherent in Christ's cross *triumphs* over sin and the law. However, Covenant Eschatology says "where grace did abound, the law did much more abound." The cross does not triumph over law; bondage to sin *survives* the cross, and is only taken away in AD 70! Thus, the cross is totally negated and annulled. It has *no part* in salvation. If it does, Don should please tell us what that part is, for I confess I cannot find or understand it in his system.

Don, like many others, came under the early influence of King. King was at the front of Preterism in the 70's, 80's and 90's until his system of eschatology led him into Universalism. We believe that King's system is *inherently* Universalistic, but that is not a matter we can take up here.[9] Don has not followed King into Universalism, but otherwise embraces King's views. In fact, it was King who first (so far as I know) asserted that Rom. 11:25-27 referred to the second coming (which is Don's affirmative in this debate).[10] Don is very explicit that "forgiveness of sin did not arrive until AD 70". Don is also very explicit that it is *only* by removal of the law that man is justified: "The destruction of the temple signaled that God's covenant with Israel was now fulfilled. He had kept his Word and, 'brought life and immortality to light through the gospel' (2 Timothy 19f). The 'law of life in Christ Jesus' (Romans 8:13), now stood triumphant over the law that was *'the strength of sin,'* (Romans 7:7f)[11]" (emphasis Don's). PLEASE NOTE: Don says the law had to be removed before sin was defeated! What Paul

---

[9] Consider this syllogism: *All men were under the debt of sin by the law (where there is no law, there is no transgression Rom. 4:15; all have sinned and come short of the glory of God Rom. 3:23). No man could be justified from sin until the law was removed. But the law was removed for all men for all time in AD 70. Therefore, all men were justified from the law.* Notice that the cross and obedience of faith logically are not required under King's system for justification. Men are not saved by responding to the gospel one-by-one, but corporately by removal of the law, hence, Universalism.

[10] *The Spirit of Prophecy*, pp.215; McGuiggan –King Debate (Warren, OH), pp. 250-253; 268.

[11] Don K Preston, *Like Father, Like Son, On Clouds of Glory* (Ardmore OK, 2006), p. 109.

places at the cross, Don moves to AD 70! Here is another quote: "You cannot logically affirm the fulfillment of the resurrection in AD 70... and not affirm the end of whatever law it was that held the condemning power over man." Thus, according to Don, we are saved by the removal of law, not the addition of grace. The cross accomplished *nothing*, for it is not until AD 70 when the law is removed that sin is defeated. The cross has vanished from Don's soteriology.

Max King's Soteriology and Eschatology

Resurrection = Justification = Removal of Old Law (AD 70)

*"death is abolished when the state of sin and the law are abolished"*WHERE IS THE CROSS?

This brief review should help the reader understand the origin of Don's and my differences and what is at stake. Reduced to its simplest form, it is a question of Covenant Eschatology versus Cross-based Soteriology. Did justification obtain at the cross, or at the fall of Jerusalem? *Did the cross fulfill the law and cancel the debt of sin, or did it not?* That is the question.

What Don Must Prove

Don has the affirmative, therefore the burden of proof is his. His proposition states,

"The Bible teaches that the coming of Christ for salvation in Romans 11:25-27 occurred in AD 70 at the climax and termination of the Mosaic Covenant Age." We have already seen that Rom. 11:27 involves salvation from sin. Hence, Don must prove:

1) The coming referred to is the second, not first, advent of Christ.
2) The judgment and sentence associated with sin hung over the saints until AD 70; *viz.*, the cross did not cancel sin's debt.
3) AD 70 represented the *legal* climax and termination of the Mosaic Covenant age; *viz.,* the law, including circumcision, animal sacrifices, the priesthood, dietary restrictions, etc, was valid and binding until AD 70.
4) The judgment and sentence associated with sin were set aside in AD 70 by annulment of the law.

20

Don must prove *each* of these to carry his burden of proof. I need only negate *one* of these to prevent him from carrying his proposition. It is like a trial where the prosecution must prove *each element* of the crime, but the defense need only negate *one element* to win acquittal. Don therefore has the heavier, more onerous task. We would ask the reader to PLEASE NOTE that Don has not and cannot produce even ONE VERSE that states the saints were under the debt of sin until AD 70. NOT ONE. I can, and when it is my turn to be in the affirmative will, produce *dozens* of verses that expressly state that justification was a present possession of the saints, that they had forgiveness of sins and fulness of grace before AD 70. I will produce some in this negative. But Don has not and cannot produce EVEN ONE. His whole ability to keep men under the debt of sin until AD 70 is based upon argumentation from faulty assumptions to wrong conclusions. You know the type I mean.

Jehovah's witnesses say "The Bible prohibits eating blood. People who are sick are fed intravenously. What is introduced into the body intravenously is therefore equivalent to eating. Blood transfusions are conducted intravenously. Therefore, blood transfusions are equivalent to eating blood and unlawful." Seems logical, right? But there is not one verse in the Bible that actually teaches against blood transfusions. The whole thing is built upon deductive reasoning. Don is a MASTER of deductive reasoning; his books are saturated with logical syllogisms. But virtually anything can be proved this way. "All crows are black. This bird is black. Therefore, this bird is a crow." Really? Are crows the *only* birds that are black? Might not this bird be a raven or some *other* species? What we need are not syllogisms, but VERSES! And Don has NONE. He cannot produce even one verse that says New Testament saints were under the debt of sin until AD 70. His whole ability to make you *think* the saints were under the debt of sin until AD 70 is based upon faulty argumentation. Don builds exegetical paradigms in the sky. But since Jehovah's Witnesses can prove by logic and argumentation that blood transfusions are unlawful, that you can't celebrate birthdays, you can't vote, and Christ isn't God, this sort of thing really proves NOTHING. Here is a box. Let Don put in it all the verses he can that expressly state the saints were under the debt of sin from and after the cross. At the end of this discussion the box will still be empty and Don will not have carried his proposition.

Don's Box
Verses?

I can produce PAGES OF VERSES that make salvation, justification, grace, and forgiveness of sin the *present possession* of the saints. Don cannot produce even one verse. What does that tell you about Don's system of eschatology? The most important, single topic in the WHOLE BIBLE and Don does not even have ONE VERSE. Startling isn't it? This is a wake up call for those that embrace the Corporate Body View![12] Your whole edifice is built upon a supposition that does not have a single verse to support its most basic supposition! Don't believe me? Just try and find one to put in the box!

I am sure Don would like me to take the bait and use up my allotted space following him down all sorts of rabbit trails, answering questions, and interacting with his affirmative. Why should I? He has not produced a single verse to substantiate the most important topic of this discussion, if not the whole Bible. Why should I involve myself in discussion about the proper exegesis of Isaiah 26, 27 and 59 and what light that may or may not throw on Rom. 11:25-27 if Don cannot produce even ONE VERSE to show the debt of sin still hung over the saints from and after the cross? I do not say this to embarrass or belittle Don. I am sure Don does not even realize that he doesn't have a single verse he can produce. I am hoping to save my brother from what I deem a dangerous system of theology, a system of theology that negates the cross, by now calling it to his attention. As the quotes Don produces from my earlier works show, I too was at least partly under similar misapprehensions at one time. But I have studied and have disabused myself of them, and I thank God I have seen my error. I pray God will grant that I may see and repent all my errors! Imagine the culpability of impugning the cross of Christ, even unintentionally! Don, for your own sake, take the challenge; bring forward your verses. And when you can't produce *even one,* awake as from a trance out of the system of teaching you have become enmeshed in; renounce Max King's Covenant Eschatology. Preterism is completely sound. But this? Never!

I have now used up just over five pages. I could stop here and not write another word. The burden of proof is Don's. He never has and never will produce even one verse stating that the saints were under the debt of sin by the law until AD 70. But, since I have the space, I will *gratuitously* continue on. Since, I only need to negate one of the points of Don's proposition, I will focus upon what matters most: 1) when justification accrued to the saints,

---

[12] "Corporate Body View" is a term describing King's notion that the church/mankind were "corporately" justified ("resurrected") by removal of the law in AD 70.

and 2) when the Old Covenant was *legally* abrogated and nullified. We will deal with the last first.

Don's favorite proof text for extending the validity of the law until AD 70 is probably Matt. 5:17, 18. This is a favorite Preterist proof text, and it is horribly abused. So, let us begin here. Jesus said, *"Think not that I am come to destroy the law, or the prophets: I am not come to destroy but to fulfill. For verily I say unto you, Till heaven and earth pass, one jot or one tittle shall in no wise pass from the law, till all be fulfilled."* Three points need to be discussed: 1) the meaning of "heavens and earth" – metaphoric or parabolic? 2) Fulfillment of the law; and 3) Nullification of the law.

Heavens & Earth Normal Preterist misuse of this passage proceeds upon the assumption that Jesus uses "heavens and earth" in a mystical, metaphoric sense, a hidden double meaning where they are symbols for the Old Testament temple and system. Don does this all through his books. He argues that the Jews viewed the temple as "heaven and earth" and that Jesus is mystically referring to it here. Don believes that the "heavens and earth" of Matt. 24:35 mystically refer to the temple complex. He believes the "heavens and earth" of Heb. 12:26, 27 and II Pet. 3 are the Old Testament law and system, the "covenantal world of the Jews." This is wrong; it contradicts the established usage of the prophets whereby the "shaking" of the heavens and earth in times of national and world judgment had no covenantal significance whatever (Isa. 13:-13; 34:1-10; Ezek. 32:7, 8; Joel 3:16, 17; Hag. 2:6, 7, 21, 22). Don is aware that the prophets' use of the heavens and earth to describe times of judgment upon the world and various nations, and that they carry *no covenantal significance.* He cites them in his books. In fact, he cites N.T. Wright, who says that the prophets employ imagery of shaking the heavens and earth, not covenantally, but socio-politically and militarily.[13]

Indeed, Don makes identical statements himself.[14] There is not one single occasion in the whole Bible where the heavens and earth refer to the Old or New Testaments – not one. They are *always* socio-political, *never* covenantal.

---

[13] *"This language denotes socio-political and military catastrophe."* N.T. Wright, Jesus the Victory of God (Minneapolis, Fortress, 1996), p. 361.

[14] "It is emotive language, hyperbolically expressing the catastrophic end to a social order, the end of a kingdom." Don K Preston, *Like Father, Like Son, On Clouds of Glory* (Ardmore OK, 2006), p. 33.

More to the point, Jesus does not use "heaven and earth" in Matt. 5:18 metaphorically in any event. Rather, Jesus evokes the heavens and earth *parabolically*. He compares the word of God to the heavens and earth as things divinely permanent, immutable, and irremovable to show that, as the cosmos has been established by God's word and cannot fail or be removed, so the promises and prophecies contained in the law and prophets cannot fail, but must surely be fulfilled. What Jesus is actually saying, then, is that it is *easier* for heaven and earth to pass than that a single dot or stroke of the law to pass without first being fulfilled. And, in fact, he says this very thing in Luke 16:17: *"And it is easier for heaven and earth to pass, than one tittle of the law to fail."* This parallel saying therefore controls our interpretation and precludes making more out of Matt. 5:18 than the Lord himself intended. A simple comparison of similar passages will prove that the permanence and immutability of the heavens and earth are evoked parabolically to show that it would be easier for them to fail than God's purpose and word to fail; there is nothing "covenantal" intended at all. (See Matt. 24:34; Lk. 16:17; Jer. 31:35, 36.)

Law Fulfilled   This is the very heart of the matter. Don urges that Jesus has his *second coming* in view in Matt. 5:18 and that the law was therefore not fulfilled until that time; Don argues that the law was valid, binding and obligatory until AD 70. This is wrong. Jesus is speaking about his *earthly mission*, not second coming, telling the Jews why he was come. Matt. 5:17 establishes this fact beyond dispute: "Think not that I am come to destroy the law and prophets; I am not come to destroy but to fulfill."

What coming is in view? The second? No! The first. When would Jesus fulfill the law? At his second coming? No! His first! He did not say, "I will come again and then fulfill," but "I AM COME TO FULFILL!" Jesus fulfilled the law at his *first coming*. There is simply no avoiding the obvious meaning of the text. From the Nativity to Calvary, Christ fulfilled the law. Over and over again we encounter the evangelists' testimony "now all this was done, that it might be fulfilled" (Matt. 1:22); "Then was fulfilled that which was spoken" (Matt. 2:17); "But all this was done, that the scriptures of the prophets might be fulfilled" (Matt. 26:56). Matthew alone makes statements of this sort 13 times. (Matt. 1:22; 2:15, 17, 23; 4:14; 8:17; 12:17; 13:35; 21:4; 26:54, 56; 27:9, 35) Mark makes similar statements twice (Mk. 14:49; 15:28); Luke twice (4:21; 24:44); John eight times affirms "these things were done that the scripture should be fulfilled" (Jn. 12:38; 13:18; 15:25; 17:12; 19:24, 28, 36, 37). Thus, *twenty-five* times in the gospels we are informed Jesus fulfilled the law and prophets. Acts adds to this four more (Acts 1:16; 3:18; 13:27, 29). Indeed, Jesus, before he died, cried out from the cross "It is finished!" (Jn. 19:30; *cf.* Matt. 27:50), showing that he had *completed* the work his Father gave him to do. Luke even states "And when they *had fulfilled* all that was written of him, they took him down from the tree, and laid him in a sepulchre" (Acts 13:29). And when all was fulfilled regarding Jesus' *life,* God fulfilled the remainder when he raised him from the *dead* (still first coming)!

> "And we declare unto you glad tiding, how that the promise which was made unto the fathers, God hath fulfilled the same unto us their children, in that he hath raised up Jesus again" (Acts 13:32, 33).

GOD HATH FULFILLED! First coming, not second! The gospels abundantly prove that Jesus fulfilled the law and prophets in his first coming beginning with the Nativity. However, it is at the cross that the *debt of the law* was paid, terminating the Old Covenant. The end and object of the whole law was the cross of Christ. The temple, the ceremonies, the priesthood, and untold other incidentals and minutia of the Mosaic law all stood as one grand object lesson, one great prophetic type pointing to Christ and his all-sufficient sacrifice upon the cross. Jesus' death fulfilled the law of sin and death, which required blood sacrifice in atonement for sin. "For the life of the flesh is in the blood: and I have given it to you upon the altar to make an atonement for your souls: for it is the blood that maketh atonement for the soul" (Lev. 17:11). The blood of bulls and goats could not take away sins (Heb. 10:4). But the blood of Christ could and did. Jesus was the greater and more perfect sacrifice, which the priesthood, temple service, and animal sacrifices looked to.

> "Wherefore when he cometh into the world, he saith, Sacrifice and offering thou wouldst not, but a body hast thou prepared for me: In burnt offerings and sacrifices for sin thou hast had no pleasure. Then said I, Lo, I come (in the volume of the book it is written of me,) to do thy will, O God." Heb. 10:5-7)

Notice what the writer states, "When HE COMETH INTO THE WORLD." What coming is this? Clearly, it is the first coming. "I COME TO DO THY WILL, O GOD." What was God's will? That Jesus fulfill the law, providing redemption. Fulfilling the law was a first coming event, not second. Any question is resolved by what the writer of Hebrews says next.

> "Above when he said, Sacrifice and offering and burnt

25

offerings and offering for sin thou wouldest not, neither hadst pleasure therein; which are offered by the law; then said he, Lo, I come to do thy will, O God. He taketh away the first, that he may establish the second. By which will we are sanctified by the offering of the body of Jesus Christ once for all" (Heb. 10:8-10).

Here is unequivocal evidence that the sacrifice of Christ fulfilled the law. The writer says "HE TAKETH AWAY THE FIRST, THAT HE MAY ESTABLISH THE SECOND." What is the first? The Old Testament! When would the Old Testament be taken away? When the law of blood sacrifice was once for all fulfilled. What is the "second" Christ came to establish? The New Testament! God's will that Christ satisfy the debt of sin becomes for us THE NEW TESTAMENT! We are SANCTIFIED ONCE FOR ALL by the offering of the body of Jesus. The writer of Hebrews thus continues: "For by one offering he hath perfected forever them that are sanctified." HATH PERFECTED FOREVER. When? At his second coming? No! His first coming.

Don wants our perfection to be put off to AD 70; he wants to keep the debt of sin hanging over the saints until the second coming when they are "resurrected" (justified) by removal of the law. Don embraces a "cross-free" salvation; his eschatology demands it. You cannot place justification at the cross and have a spiritualized resurrection in AD 70! But the writer of Hebrews uses the perfect tense, saying the work was *already accomplished.* "HATH PERFECTED FOREVER." Jesus has perfected us forever by the addition of grace, not removal of the law. Memorize that: WE ARE SAVED BY THE ADDITION OF GRACE, NOT REMOVAL OF LAW! GRACE TRIUMPHS OVER LAW! The second coming added *nothing* to the cross. It was a complete irrelevancy in terms of man's redemption from sin. (If you doubt that, just go back and look at Don's empty box!)

The writer of Hebrews said above that in Jesus' death the first covenant was taken away and the second was established. He calls this second covenant a "will." We have all heard of a "last will and testament." When does a testator's will attain legal authority and power? The Hebrew writer answers: "A TESTAMENT IS OF FORCE AFTER MEN ARE DEAD" (Heb. 9:17). This verse is dispositive of the issue when the gospel brought justification to man; it is conclusive of the issue when the New Testament came into force and effect: At Jesus' death, not AD 70! This same lesson is set out in Rom. 7:1-4 (emphasis added):

> Know ye not, brethren, (for I speak to them that know the law,) how that the law hath dominion over a man as long as he liveth? For the woman which hath an husband is bound by the law to her husband so long as he liveth; but IF THE HUSBAND BE DEAD, SHE IS LOOSED FROM THE LAW OF HER HUSBAND. So then if, while her husband liveth, she be married to another man, she shall be called an adulteress: but if her husband be dead, she is free from that law; so that she is no adulteress, though she be married to another man. Wherefore, my brethren, YE ARE BECOME DEAD TO THE LAW BY THE BODY OF CHRIST; that ye should be married to another, even to him who is raised from the dead, that we should bring forth fruit unto God.

Paul here uses the law of marriage as an analogy for Israel and the Old Testament. The "woman" is Israel; her "husband" is the Lord; the law of the marriage union was the Old Testament (*cf.* Jer. 2:2; Ezek. 16:8). Paul says that the Mosaic law was binding upon Israel *while her husband lived*, and that she would be an adulteress if she married another while her first husband was alive. In Rev. 18:7, national Israel, under delusion that the Old Testament was still in force, boasts "I sit a queen, and am no widow, and shall see no sorrow." But she was indeed a widow, for she had murdered her husband in the person of the Son of God, when she caused him to be crucified. Jesus' death ended the law of Israel's husband. Under Paul's analogy, "marrying another" means entering into another covenant, here obeying the gospel of Christ. However, Paul says there is no fear of adultery, because "YE ARE BECOME ARE DEAD TO THE LAW BY THE BODY OF CHRIST"! Could it be clearer? The Old Testament had dominion over Israel; its obligations were as indissoluble as the marriage bond; while it continued in force the debt of sin remained unpaid; man was not justified. But by the death of Jesus, that covenant had been annulled and the saints were justified and freed to marry another; they were loosed from the Old Testament that they might be married to Christ under the gospel. Paul thus says "For the law of the Spirit of life in Christ Jesus hath made me free from the law of sin and death" (Rom. 8:2).

Notice the verb tense: "HATH MADE ME FREE" – this is the perfect tense - "FROM THE LAW OF SIN AND DEATH." The perfect tense shows completed action. The first century saints had been *freed from the law* of sin and death by marriage to Christ under the New Testament. AD 70 does not figure in the equation at all! No waiting until AD 70 to be acquitted from the debt of sin! It is true that the consummation of the marriage did not occur

27

until the eschaton (Rev. 19:7). But the consummation was merely the time when husband and bride cohabited together and shared sexual intimacy. It is NOT the point at which the marriage contract became binding or of legal force and effect. The marriage contract was fully effective under Old Testament law from and after the betrothal. A woman found to have engaged in sexual relations with another man during the betrothal period was guilty of adultery and subject to the penalty of death (Deut. 22:23, 24. Matt. 1:28, 29). Paul said he had betrothed the church to Christ by the gospel (II Cor. 11:2). By Don's argument, the bride was impure and defiled, stained with sin until AD 70 when Christ consummated the marriage with her. But Paul says "not so!" The gospel had washed and purified the bride from sin – justified her from the debt of the law – *during the betrothal period* that Christ "might present it to himself a glorious church, not having spot, or wrinkle, or any such thing; but that it should be holy and without blemish" (Eph. 5:25-27).

Jesus justified the church from sin that he might present it to himself *at the consummation* not having spot, or wrinkle, or any such thing. It could not be more plain or clear. AD 70 is simply nowhere in sight. Don's argument makes the church an adulteress, for she has contracted marriage to another while the law of her first husband was still valid and binding; he has Jesus a polygamist with two wives at one time, Old Testament Israel and the New Testament church, and he has Jesus consummate the marriage before his wife is washed and made pure! (See I Cor. 6:11 for confirmation when the washing occurred.)

A last text and we shall conclude this part: "For sin shall not have dominion over you: for ye are not under the law, but under grace" (Rom. 6:14). NOT UNDER THE LAW. Clearly, the notion that the law was valid and the saints were under the power of sin until AD 70 cannot be sustained. There are just too many texts that directly contradict that proposition. What does this mean? It means that Max King's Covenant Eschatology and spiritualized resurrection are false; worse than false, they are found to destroy the cross of Christ. It is a dangerous doctrine and must be *fully rejected.*

Nullification of the Law   Don's reading of Matt. 5:18 has it that no part of the law or prophets would pass until all parts were fulfilled; if a single prophecy remained to be fulfilled, then the whole law was still valid, binding, and obligatory. To quote Don himself: "*There is no escape from this fact: If* *any Old Testament prophecies remain unfulfilled, then the Old Testament remains in force."[15]*

In other words, it all goes out at once, or not at all. But this is not what Jesus meant or even what he said. He did not say, "verily I say unto you that no part of the law or prophets will pass until all parts of the law and prophets are fulfilled." How could he? Micah prophesied Jesus could be born in Bethlehem (Mic. 5:2). That prophecy was fulfilled and passed away. Isaiah prophesied Jesus would be born to a virgin (Isa. 7:14). That prophecy was fulfilled and passed away. There are hundreds of prophecies that came and went before AD 70. But by Don's argument, there can be no progressive fulfillment of scripture, no progressive fulfillment of the law. All parts remain valid as long as even one part is unfulfilled. This simply makes no sense at all. What Jesus actually is saying in Matt. 5:18 is that "not the least part of the law will pass except it first be fulfilled." The idea that *all* must be fulfilled before *any* of it passed away is a misreading of the text.

Don says the whole law goes out at once, or not at all. Until all the law was fulfilled, all was valid and binding. Thus, by Don's own admission, if I can show that even *one law* was nullified, if I can show that the disciples were free to ignore even *one law*, then they were free to ignore the *whole law* (exclusive of the moral law, for it will never be nullified). Here there can be no doubt. The New Testament shows that long before AD 70 the disciples were loosed from the sacrificial law, the dietary laws, the laws prohibiting them to eat or keep company with Gentiles, and they were loosed from circumcision. Israel's dietary laws, laws against marrying and keeping company with Gentiles, and law of circumcision served primarily to keep Israel *separate* from the nations around her. These laws were tied to the *land promises* and were inter-related. The laws of the temple also separated the Jews from the Gentiles, who were compelled to worship in the outer court. However, Paul says all these laws were abolished by Christ:

> "For he is our peace, who hath made both one, and hath broken down the middle wall of partition between us; having abolished in his flesh the enmity, even the law of commandments contained in ordinances; for to make in himself one new man, so making peace" (Eph. 2:14, 15).

---

[15] Don K. Preston, *Like Father, Like, Son, On Clouds of Glory* (JaDon Productions, Ardmore, 2006), pp. 190.

The "middle wall of partition" refers to the wall in the temple that separated the court of the Jews from the court of the Gentiles. The temple and wall, of course, stood until AD 70. But Paul says that the *legal* separation represented by this wall was done away at the cross. This wall being legally abrogated and done away, the laws and ordinances related to it were abolished as well, including dietary restrictions (Acts 10:9-15; cf. Mk. 7:14-23; Rom. 14:14; I Tim. 4:3-5), laws against keeping company with Gentiles (Acts 10:28-48), the Sabbath and feast days (Col. 2:16); and circumcision (Gal. 5:2, 11). Notice the verb tense of the passage above, "HATH ABOLISHED IN HIS FLESH...THE LAW OF COMMANDMENTS." This is the perfect tense, showing completed action.

The laws Moses set in place to separate Jew and Gentile were abolished in Jesus' flesh upon the cross. Thus, we find Peter and other disciples keeping company and table fellowship with Gentiles (Gal. 2:11, 12). But when certain false, Judaizing brethren came down from Jerusalem saying (like Don) that the law was still binding and valid, Peter withdrew table fellowship. But Paul rebuked Peter *to the face* for his duplicity to the truth of the gospel. The issue of circumcision also came up, and the Jerusalem Counsel decided that these laws were no longer binding (Gal. 2:1-10; Acts 15). Don agrees. Don says the land promises were tied to circumcision, but that Paul taught "circumcision was invalid" and that he "unequivocally condemned the religious practice of circumcision." According to Don, "If God removed circumcision, the sign and seal of the Abrahamic land promise, then the Land Covenant was null and void."[16] Don says "When Paul wrote...circumcision no longer availed, God had abrogated that mandate."[17]

Don says that *no law* would pass until all was fulfilled; he says no law would pass until all passed together; *all were valid until none were valid.* Yet here is unequivocal evidence that a *vast body* of laws integral to the temple service and daily life of the Jews was ABOLISHED IN JESUS' FLESH. The law of the temple service imposed and enforced the rite of circumcision (Acts 21:28, 29). If circumcision was abrogated, then so was the temple service. Paul made no distinction between circumcision and the feast days and other observances of the Jews; his repudiation of circumcision applied equally to them all (Gal. 4:10; *cf.* Col. 2:16). The land covenant, the law of circumcision, the dietary laws, the feast days, the temple ritual, and laws against keeping company with Gentiles were swept away by the cross!

---

[16] Don K. Preston, *Like Father, Like, Son, On Clouds of Glory* (JaDon Productions, Ardmore, 2006), pp. 134, 135.
[17] Ibid, p. 180.

Therefore, by Don's argument all was fulfilled and the law abolished before AD 70. Consider:

> No law would pass until all was fulfilled; all were valid until none were valid.
> But Jesus abolished and rendered invalid in his flesh (cross) the law of commandments contained in ordinances.
> Therefore, in Jesus' flesh (cross/crucifixion) the law was fulfilled.

The Cross, The Time of Reformation, and the Age to Come

But if the law was fulfilled and was abrogated at the cross, what about verses like II Cor. 3:11, 13, 14 which states the Old Testament was still "being annulled" or Hebrews 8:13, which says "that which decayeth and waxeth old is ready to vanish away?" What about verses that mention the "age to come?" What about Heb. 9:9 which mentions the "present time" during which sacrifices were still offered? Don't these teach that the law somehow remained? Did the two covenants *overlap*, so that *both were valid* at the same time? Rom. 7:1-4 teaches that the Old Testament terminated in Jesus' death that his people might enter a new marriage relationship under the New Testament. If the Old Testament was still binding, the saints would be guilty of adultery for entering a second marriage contract while the law of their first husband was still valid. Therefore, we may safely reject the view that the covenants were both legally valid at the same time. Any lawyer will tell you it is a legal impossibility to have two testaments in force at one time. The only way to have two valid wills, whose terms are conflicting, is for one to be deemed a codicil or amendment of the other. But Jesus was very clear that the gospel was not a piece of new cloth to be added to the tatters of the Old Testament (Mk. 2:21); the two covenants would not co-exist side-by-side or be valid at the same time. What then is the solution?

The answer lies in the distinction between the *legal efficacy* of the law and its *outward forms*. The Emancipation Proclamation ostensibly freeing the slaves was made Sept. 22, 1862. It became effective Jan. 1, 1863. Yet, it was not until April 9, 1865, that Lee surrendered and the war concluded. Thus, despite the legal proclamation freeing the slaves, the *institution* of slavery continued for at least two more years, if not longer. The outward forms continued even though their legal efficacy and validity was gone! The two covenants were similar.

31

Although Jesus abrogated the Old Testament at the cross, the outward forms of the law – the temple and ritual, the Jewish polity and nation – continued for almost 40 years. The Old Testament was like a tree whose root was severed and dead. The trunk and branches did not immediately wither and fall over, but decayed and waxed old over time, and were ready to vanish at the end of 40 years (Heb. 8:13). The writer of Hebrews shows that the Old Law was not valid when he says, "then verily the first covenant had also ordinances of divine service, and a worldly sanctuary" (Heb. 9:1). His use of the *past tense* to show its validity was gone. "The first covenant had," not the "first covenant has." The fact that the trunk of the Mosaic tree remained for a time did not mean its root was alive, no more did the fact that the temple and ritual continued to linger on mean that it was valid or approved of God. Just the opposite, God called the temple ritual an *abomination* because it stood as an implicit denial of Jesus' Sonship and atoning sacrifice.

> "Thus saith the Lord, The heaven is my throne, and the earth is my footstool, where is the house that ye build unto me?...He that killeth an ox is as if he slew a man; he that sacrificeth a lamb, as if he cut off a god's neck: he that offereth an oblation, as if he offered swine's blood; he that burneth incense, as if he blessed an idol. Yea, they have chosen their own ways, and their soul delighteth in their abominations." Isa. 66:1-3

Stephen quoted this prophecy before the Sanhedrin in defense against the charge he blasphemed the temple (Acts 7:49, 50). Thus, from at least as early as Acts 7 (AD 34), the church recognized that Jesus' sacrifice on Calvary had supplanted the temple service and that it was rejected by God. However, according to Don the ceremonial law was still valid and binding. How can something God abominated have been valid and binding?

Don says "One reason we must see the transition from the Old to the New as an on going process *empowered by the Cross but not consummated at the Cross* is because that transformation was a 'last days' work of the Spirit, and the work of the Spirit did not begin until after the Cross."[18]

I would challenge Don again to please show us how the cross figures in his system, how it empowered anything at all. According to Don, the cross did not triumph over the law, it did not satisfy and annul the debt of sin, it did not justify the saints. No, Don makes all of these things happen at the second

---

[18] Ibid, p. 212 (emphasis in original).

32

coming and then only by removal of the law at the fall of Jerusalem. The cross *does* nothing, *accomplishes* nothing, *is* nothing under King's system. If we are wrong in this, we welcome correction and look forward to Don's answer.

But to return to the matter more immediately at hand, according to Don, the *transition period* equals the *transformation period* that began at the cross. But what is the time of transformation if not the "time of reformation" mentioned Heb. 9:10-11? In that passage, the writer states that the ceremonial law was imposed *until the time of reformation*. Don makes the time of reformation begin in AD 70. But as reformation and transformation mean the same thing, it is clear that the time of reformation began at the cross. The gifts of the Holy Ghost led the apostles into all truth for the specific purpose of affecting reform (Jn. 16:13). When the gifts ceased, the time of reformation was *over*, not begun. Don therefore has it backward; he makes the ceremonial law valid and the time of reformation begin where the gifts of the Holy Ghost end! But the ceremonial law pointed to Christ; they foreshadowed Jesus' work on the cross. Therefore, they were fulfilled in AD 33, not AD 70. Consider:

The ceremonial law was imposed until the time of reformation.
The time of reformation was marked by the ministry of the Spirit
But the ministry of the Spirit began immediately following the cross.
Therefore, The ceremonial law was imposed only until the cross.

Don argues that the Atonement ritual was not fulfilled, the shadow and typology of the Old Law was still valid, and the law therefore binding and obligatory until AD 70. We deny this emphatically.

Don assumes that Christ's ascension equals the High Priest entering the Most Holy Place, thus postponing completion of the Atonement ritual until Christ emerged at his second coming. Don forgets that the High Priest entered the Most Holy Place *twice* (Lev. 16:14, 15). Yes, TWICE! There were *two sacrifices* in the atonement ritual: a bull and a goat; blood was carried in twice, *once for each sacrifice*. But Jesus died only *once*; he made a *once-for-all* sacrifice when he died on the Calvary. We believe that the typology of sprinkling the blood before the Mercy Seat was fulfilled when Jesus died. The Hebrew writer agrees, saying that Jesus opened the way into the Most Holy Place through his FLESH (Heb. 10:20). That is, in his death Jesus pierced the legal veil separating man from God. This is why the veil was "rent in twain" from top to bottom when Jesus died, showing that the way was *now open* and the atonement COMPLETE (Matt. 27:51). The Hebrew writer thus urges Christians to ENTER the presence of God within the Most Holy Place – before AD 70! (Heb. 10:19-22; *cf.* 6:19). In other words, the legal barrier separating men from God was totally removed in the cross, almost 40 years before AD 70. Isn't that what Colossians says, that Jesus blotted out the debt of sin, took it out of the way, nailing it to his cross, triumphing over the law in it? (Col. 2:14, 15).

Don wants us to believe that Jesus stood sprinkling his blood for FORTY YEARS (seems long!). But the writer of Hebrews does not portray Jesus standing, offering his blood, but SITTING at God's right hand waiting for his enemies to be put beneath his feet (Heb. 1:3; 2:8; 8:1; 10:11-14). Jesus being *seated* is set in opposition to the priests who *stood* daily ministering. His being seated is specifically cited as proof that the atonement was COMPLETE and man was PERFECTED. *"But this man, after he has offered one sacrifice for sins for ever, sat down on the right had of God...for by one sacrifice he hath perfected forever them that are sanctified."* In the verses that follow, the writer urges believers to ENTER where Don says they could not go – the Most Holy Place, the Presence of God! (Heb. 10:19-22). Regardless of what interpretation DON may want to place upon Heb. 9 to postpone atonement, God spoke decisively when he caused the veil symbolizing the debt of sin to be rent in twain at the cross. God deemed the Atonement ritual FULFILLED and the way into his presence OPENED in JESUS' DEATH.

> Man could not enter the Most Holy Place until the
> atonement was complete and the law fulfilled;

But the veil was ripped in two in Jesus' death, and the Hebrew writer urged Christians (pre-AD 70) to enter the Most Holy Place through the blood of Christ. Therefore,
The atonement was complete and the law fulfilled in Jesus' atoning sacrifice!

Perhaps we can interact with some of Don's material in our next negative, assuming he can produce a verse (even one) expressly stating the saints remained under bondage to sin from and after the cross. Don has a *heavy* burden of proof to show that the cross did not cancel the debt of sin or triumph over the law. Let's see if Don can put any verses in that box.

Meanwhile, here are a couple questions for Don.

1) Did the cross cancel the debt of sin under the law?

2) Does the cross (grace) triumph over law, or did law have to be removed for man to be justified?

These are two very simple gospel questions that we may all use as a standard to measure Max King. If Don says, NO the cross did not triumph over the law or cancel the debt of sin he will have repudiated the cross of Christ (a dangerous deed I hope Don will not do!). If he says, YES, then Don will have repudiated Max King, Covenant Eschatology, and the Corporate Body View. Which will it be? Let us all labor with Don in prayer that he chooses aright.

PRESTON- SIMMONS DEBATE
SUBJECT:
THE PERFECTION OF SALVATION
AND PASSING OF THE OLD COVENANT

SECOND AFFIRMATIVE BY DON K. PRESTON

My worst fears have been realized. I shared with some close friends that I was concerned that my friend Kurt would not actually engage in a debate, following my affirmatives as a negative is pledged to do, but, would simply use this to promote his personal agenda. Lamentably, this is precisely what has happened. Kurt spent *five pages* presenting material that is *totally irrelevant* to responding to my affirmative arguments, in spite of the fact that he signed rules not to introduce material not "directly relevant to proving or disproving the respective positions!" *Five pages of irrelevant material!*

Take note that each of us signed rules for the debate. One of those rules reads: "Each man agrees to answer the other man's arguments directly, without obfuscation or evasion, to the full extent of their ability and knowledge." What does my friend do? He gave an *affirmative presentation*, that has the appearance of being *pre-prepared. He did not follow my arguments!* Then he says: "I am sure Don would like me to take the bait and use up my allotted space following him down all sorts of rabbit trails, answering questions, and interacting with his affirmative. Why should I?"He even asks: "Why should I involve myself in discussion about the proper exegesis of Isaiah 26, 27 and 59 and what light that may or may not throw on Rom. 11:25-27 if Don cannot produce even ONE VERSE to show the debt of sin still hung over the saints from and after the cross?"

Well, Kurt, here are just a *few* of the reasons you should follow my affirmative arguments:
1.) *You gave your word to do so!* Is that not enough?
2.) Because my arguments– in spite of your declarations to the contrary– prove my position!
3.) Because your failure to follow my arguments will demonstrate irrefutably your *inability* to answer my arguments.
Why should my friend involve himself, "in discussion about the proper exegesis of Isaiah 26, 27 and 59 and what light that may or may not throw on Rom. 11:25-27"? Well, he should do so, because if he does not properly exegete Isaiah 27 / 59, and I do, then I have proven my point in regard to Romans 11, and at the same time falsified my friend's entire rejection of Covenant Eschatology!

36

With that in mind let me offer here *three more affirmative arguments* from the prophetic source of Romans 11. We will see if Kurt will ignore these new arguments.

#1– ISAIAH 26-27 AND THE SALVATION OF "ISRAEL"

Re: Romans 11:26f– The coming of the Lord to take away Israel's sin is the coming of the Lord to take away Israel's sin foretold by Isaiah 26-27 / Isaiah 59. But note this...

Kurt claims that Romans 11:26f predicts the salvation of individual Jews, via obedience to the gospel, throughout the entirety of the endless Christian age. This *demands* that Isaiah 26-27 / 59 predicted the salvation of individual Jews, via obedience to the gospel, throughout the entirety of the endless Christian age.

But, Isaiah 26-27 /59 *does not predict* the salvation of individual Jews, via obedience to the gospel, throughout the entirety of the endless Christian age. Isaiah 26-27 / 59 predicted the salvation of Israel at the coming of the Lord in judgment of Israel for shedding innocent blood. This is irrefutably true, and Kurt has totally ignored it.

Therefore, the prediction of the coming of the Lord in Romans 11:26f is not the prediction of the salvation of individual Jews, via obedience to the gospel, throughout the entirety of the endless Christian age.

Kurt simply must deal with this! He pledged himself to follow my arguments. This argument alone proves my affirmative. But there is more.

#2– ROMANS 11:26-27 AND THE SALVATION OF THE *REMNANT*

When Paul discusses the salvation of "all Israel" he actually has *the salvation of the remnant* in mind (see Romans 11:1-11). This is affirmed in the prophetic passages he cites (cf. Isaiah 27:12-13; 59:18-20). Now watch this! Romans 11:26-27 is *the salvation of the remnant of Israel* (Kurt, is it the salvation of only *a remnant of the church*?) at the coming of the Lord foretold in Isaiah 26-27 / 59.

In Romans 9:25-28 Paul (citing other OT prophecies of the salvation of the remnant of Israel) says: "Though the children of Israel be as the sand of the sea the remnant will be saved. For He will finish the work and cut it short in righteousness because the Lord will make a short work on the earth."

Here is the argument:

The salvation of Israel in Romans 11:26f is the salvation of Israel in Romans 9:28.

But, the salvation of Israel in Romans 9:28 would be finished in a short time.

Therefore, the salvation of Israel in Romans 11:26f would be finished in a short time.

37

But this can't be, per Kurt, for he demands that Romans 11:26f is the continuing salvation of Jews *throughout the entirety of the endless Christian age!*

Kurt's position denies what Paul (and Isaiah) had to say about the salvation of the remnant.

Unless Kurt can prove that the salvation of "all Israel" is to be divorced from Paul's discussion of *the salvation of the remnant of Israel*, then my affirmative is established beyond dispute. And of course, Kurt cannot prove this.

#3– ROMANS 11--ISAIAH 27 AND THE SALVATION OF THE REMNANT AT THE SOUNDING OF THE GREAT TRUMPET AT THE RESURRECTION

Please follow this carefully.

The coming of the Lord to take away Israel's sin in Romans 11:26f is the coming of the Lord at his coming in judgment of Israel foretold by Isaiah 26-27, when He would call the dead–those scattered to the four winds-- to Him (i.e. the *resurrection*) *by the sounding of the Great Trumpet* (Isaiah 27:13). Jesus said that the calling of the remnant, those scattered to the four winds– would be at his coming in judgment of Israel– *at the sounding of the Great Trumpet*– (Matthew 24:30-31) the time of the resurrection per my friend Kurt Simmons– in AD 70.

Therefore, the coming of the Lord to take away Israel's sin of Romans 11:26 was to be (it was) at the coming of the Lord in judgment of Israel– the time of the resurrection at the sounding of the Great Trumpet-- per my friend Kurt Simmons– in AD 70. (The coming of the Lord in Romans 11 is not the individual conversion of Jews throughout the endless Christian age).

I proved that the coming of the Lord in Romans is the coming of the Lord of Isaiah 26-27, which is the coming of the Lord at the *resurrection*. Kurt says the resurrection was in AD 70. Therefore, the coming of the Lord in Romans 11 was in AD 70. I likewise proved that Isaiah 27 (thus Romans 11) foretold the defeat of Satan at the parousia. Kurt admits the defeat of Satan was in AD 70! Therefore, Romans 11 must be AD 70. *Kurt ignored these arguments!* My affirmative is established.

I have proven beyond any doubt that Isaiah 26-27 / 59 and thus Romans 11:26-27 fit, *very firmly*, in Kurt's box.

As I pointed out several times in my first affirmative, this debate is about *proper hermeneutic*. Kurt, proper exegesis of scripture is *the only way that you can prove your point*, and negate mine! Thus, refusal to even mention my arguments about the prophetic background of Romans 11 is a tacit surrender of your negative. You have virtually admitted that you cannot deal with the exegetical material I presented. You refused to answer my questions based directly on the text (Yet, interestingly, you asked me questions, *expecting an answer)*! And you question what relationship proper exegesis of those prophetic texts would have on this discussion!

THE ABIDING (VALIDITY) IMPOSITION OF TORAH UNTIL AD 70

Let me now prove my point about the continuing validity of Torah until AD 70. I will prove this from both scripture and Kurt Simmons' own statements. In my first affirmative, *I asked Kurt eight questions that he totally ignored*. The last question was at the end of my affirmative. I specifically asked my friend to answer the question in his first negative. He refused to do so until I pressed him to do so in private email. Here is that final question: "If a law or covenant has been abrogated, are any of the provisions of that covenant, i.e. its mandates, its promises or penalties (positive or negative) still binding and valid (imposed)? Please answer specifically, clearly, without evasion."

I can establish the truth of my affirmative on the *correct* answer of this question. Sadly, Kurt refused to give the correct answer to the question! Here is his answer: "I guess that would depend upon the terms and conditions of the covenant and which party was in violation. The breaching party forfeits the benefit of the bargain. The non-breaching party is still entitled to the benefit of the bargain; the penalty provisions, incidental and consequential damages, etc, are therefore still valid. If a king made a covenant with another nation or kingdom that the latter would pay tribute, and the latter then broke that covenant, the former would be entitled to come and lay siege against the breaching kingdom..."

Somebody call the fire department! I have never seen so much *smoke*! (That is my attempt at a bit of levity, DKP). My friend's lawyerese came shining through on this, *didn't* it? Now, the observant reader will realize *immediately* that *Kurt did not answer the question directly, without evasion or obfuscation*! In fact, he ignored *the real question*. My friend knows full well that to answer this question *directly and correctly* establishes that the Torah remained valid until AD 70!

Kurt says that the "non-breaching party is still entitled to the benefit of the bargain." But that is only true if the bargain (covenant) *is still in effect*! Likewise, per Kurt, if a nation broke the covenant then the king would come and "lay siege against the breaching kingdom," But again, this would only be *true if that covenant was still in effect*! *The entirety of Kurt's "answer" assiduously avoids my question!* Kurt *knows* that provisions of a covenant can only be applied *if that covenant is still binding*. I know it, and every reader of this debate knows it! Let me illustrate.

The law of East Berlin ended in 1990 when the Wall and government came crashing down. But, suppose someone arrested a former member of East Berlin– although they were now living in West Berlin– and charged them with violation of the former (dead) Communist government law. What would happen? The case would summarily be dismissed, and everyone knows it! Why? Because the law of East Berlin has no continuing validity! This is beyond dispute. But, let's take a look at Torah shall we?

Kurt says the Torah legally *died* at the Cross. But, if Torah died at the Cross, and no longer had legal power, *how in the world could the provisions of Torah be imposed and fulfilled in the fall of Jerusalem in AD 70*, as Kurt Simmons, and most importantly scripture, affirms?

Kurt tells us he no longer holds to some of the positions in his books. So, I will give the citation from Kurt's books. If he no longer believes what he wrote, *he will have to formally recant that position for us*. The trouble is, if he renounces the positions that I will cite, *he will be rejecting the truth!*

In his comments on Revelation 15:8, Kurt says: "The angels emerge from the tabernacle of the testimony with *the covenantal curses and plagues*" (*Consummation*, 292, my emphasis). As he comments on the judgment of Babylon he says: "The threefold judgments of death (pestilence) mourning, and famine were foretold by Moses: And I will bring a sword upon you, ***that shall avenge the quarrel of my covenant***: and when ye are gathered within your cities, I will send the pestilence among you; and ye shall be delivered into the hand of the enemy...(Leviticus 26:25, 26, 29-32)." In addition, commenting on Revelation 16:19, and how Babylon was "remembered" before God, Kurt says, "'Remembrance' is a uniquely covenantal term" (*Consummation*, 313, my emphasis, DKP). Well said, my friend!

So, what do we have? We have Kurt affirming that the Mosaic Covenant provisions of wrath (*for violation of Torah*), *were still alive in AD 70!* He has the covenantal provisions of wrath applied 40 years after the violations of that Covenant, and 40 years after that Covenant supposedly died!
Now, Kurt's statements about Revelation and the covenant provisions of wrath are true beyond dispute, but, nonetheless, we will ask Kurt: **Do you**

still affirm these statements? Yes of No? Let me frame my argument like this:

The provisions of a covenant are only applicable while that covenant remains binding.

But, the provisions of wrath found in the Mosaic Covenant were still applicable in AD 70 (Kurt Simmons, Revelation 15-18).

Therefore, the Mosaic Covenant remained binding in AD 70.

This argument establishes my affirmative *100%, and it means that the coming of the Lord in Romans 11 was the AD 70 coming of Christ!* As we have shown, Romans 11 was the coming of the Lord in AD 70, in application of Covenantal wrath on Jerusalem! It thus goes in Kurt's box, along with the rest of the passages I have discussed. That box is filling up!

THE TRANSFIGURATION AND THE END OF MOSAIC COVENANT

Building on the argument above, let me offer another affirmative argument. The Transfiguration of Jesus is one of the most incredible events in the Bible. It unequivocally identifies the time of the passing of the Torah, *and it was not the cross! Please* pay close attention to this material.

The Transfiguration was a vision of the second coming of Christ. This is what Peter affirms in 2 Peter 1:16f: "For we have not followed cunningly devised fables, when we made known unto you the power and coming (parousia, DKP) of our Lord Jesus Christ, but were eyewitnesses of his majesty. For he received from God the Father honour and glory, when there came such a voice to him from the excellent glory, 'This is my beloved Son, in whom I am well pleased.' And this voice which came from heaven we heard, when we were with him in the holy mount."

Let me recount that marvelous scene. If I say anything in error, I will expect Kurt to correct it with *text and context.* Simple denials will not suffice, however.

On the mount, Moses and Elijah appeared with Jesus.

Moses and Elijah represented the Law and the Prophets– i.e. *the Mosaic Covenant.*

Peter wanted to build three tabernacles, one for each of the three, but, Moses and Elijah *disappear*, and the Voice of God says of Jesus, "This my beloved Son in whom I am well pleased, hear him!"

The Transfiguration is therefore a vision of the transformation from the Mosaic Covenant glory to the New Covenant glory of Jesus! (And remember that Paul said in 2 Corinthians 3:16f that the transformation was taking place in his ministry! It had not already happened!). The implications of this are

41

astounding.

If the Mosaic Covenant was abrogated at the cross, as Kurt claims, then *the Transfiguration should have been a vision of the cross.* But, the Transfiguration was patently not a vision of the cross. And this is what is so critical.

Peter undeniably said that the Transfiguration was a vision of the *parousia* (2 Peter 1:16f)!

Let me express my argument like this:

The Transfiguration was a vision of the Second Coming of Christ (2 Peter 1:16f).

But, the Transfiguration was a vision of the end of the Mosaic Covenant and the establishment of the New Covenant of Christ.

Therefore, the end of the Mosaic Covenant was at the Second Coming of Christ (which Kurt agrees was in AD 70!

Kurt, my friend, I am going to ask that you address this argument directly, without evasion, without obfuscation. Deal with it contextually, hermeneutically and logically, if you can.

KURT'S ALL OR NOTHING ARGUMENT

Kurt makes some very illogical statements. Here is one of them: "But if the cross did not *triumph* over the law at Calvary, if man had to wait until the law was *removed* to be justified from sin, then *nothing* happened at the cross." I must say, I was shocked at the profound illogic of this claim. Let me illustrate the problem, by simply changing the story a bit.

If Israel did not fully receive her deliverance from Egypt *at the very moment* of the slaying of the Passover lamb, then *nothing* happened at the slaying of the Passover lamb!" Or...

If Israel did not *fully receive her inheritance* at the *very moment* she left Egypt, then "*absolutely nothing* happened the night of the crossing of the Red Sea!" Or...

If a *temple* is not completed, at *the very moment* the foundation is laid, then *absolutely nothing* happened when the foundation was laid. (Compare Ephesians 2:19f; 1 Peter 2:4f!). Or...

If the adoption of a child is not completed *at the very moment* of the declaration of the intent to adopt then *absolutely nothing* has happened when the declaration to adopt is made. (But, take a look at Romans 8:14-23)! Or...

If the marriage is not completed at *the very moment* of the betrothal, then *absolutely nothing* happened at the moment of betrothal!

The logical fallacy of such claims is clear to *anyone*. And, given that the NT story is based on the Passover / Exodus i.e. Christ was the Passover (1 Corinthians 5:5f, and the Second Moses (Hebrews 3-4), and that the first century saints were still waiting on their "redemption" (Luke 21:28; Ephesians 4:30– a word taken directly from the Exodus / Passover story), perhaps Kurt can tell us why he can justify such an illogical claim. Kurt's claim is specious at the very least.

KURT'S BOX CHALLENGE– GLADLY ACCEPTED!

Kurt denies that forgiveness was still a future hope prior to AD 70. No less than six times he says I did not produce "one verse" affirming the futurity of redemption, salvation, atonement, forgiveness.

This is a smoke screen and nothing else. Let me illustrate how proper logic works by means of a hypothetical syllogism:

If it is the case that the coming of Christ to take away sin in Romans 11:26 was the AD 70 coming of Christ, then it must be true that forgiveness was not an objective, fully given reality in Romans 11:26.

It is the case **that the coming of Christ to take away sin in Romans 11:26 was the AD 70 coming of Christ (Isaiah 26-27 / 59, Hebrews 9:15-28, and more).**

Therefore, it must be true that forgiveness was not an objective, fully given reality in Romans 11:26.

Kurt has *totally ignored* my affirmative evidence. Having ignored it, and *petitio principii*, (assuming without proof) that he is correct, he claims that I cannot offer "one single verse" to prove my case! The truth is that *every verse I presented proves my case!* Kurt's box is *full, and getting fuller*!

ON THE MHP...AGAIN AND STILL

You simply must catch what Kurt has done. He has entangled himself even deeper in contradiction.

On the one hand, in both of his books, he affirmed that entrance into the MHP was not until AD 70.

Now, he claims that the saints *could* enter the MHP prior to AD 70!

It seems my friend has forgotten *Revelation 15:8!* Or, perhaps he has renounced his position on Revelation 15. If he has, we will insist that he tell us. The trouble is, if he has renounced his statements on Revelation 15:8 *he has renounced the Truth*!

Remember that Revelation 15:8 affirms unequivocally that entrance into the MHP could not take place until God's wrath on Babylon (Jerusalem) was fulfilled (in AD 70). And here is what Kurt said about Revelation 15 and Hebrews 9: "The way into heaven was not opened until God's wrath upon Jerusalem is fulfilled. The way into the holiest was not yet manifested while the first tabernacle was yet standing (Hebrews 9:8)"*(Consummation*, 2003,

43

p. 292).

Kurt, which part of that quote do you now renounce as false doctrine, and what is your exegetical justification? Could man enter the MHP before God's wrath was completed? If so, *prove it!*

Revelation 15 and Hebrews 9:6-10 undeniably speak of *the same time, and the same event*- entrance into the presence of God. Kurt himself made these events synchronous!

Yet, now, Kurt affirms that the saints did in fact enter into the MHP prior to AD 70! Kurt, how could the saints enter the MHP before the judgment (*the time of reward*) and completion of wrath on the "ministration of death"? (The reader will note that Kurt *totally ignored my material* on the indisputable fact that AD 70 was the judgment of the Old Covenant and its failure to justify). Kurt, tell us plainly, **did the saints enter the MHP before God's wrath was completed in the destruction of Jerusalem? YES or NO? Do not evade or ignore this question!**

Furthermore, in our negotiations for this debate, *in November, 2009*, my friend wanted to affirm the following (remember that this was only *a couple of months ago!*):

"**Resolved:** The general, eschatological resurrection consisted exclusively in the release of souls/spirits from Hades to their eternal reward in heaven/Gehenna."

Let the readers take careful note of the following: Just *one month* before drafting that proposition, my friend wrote (*Sword and Plow*, Oct. 2009, p. 2)– "The soul could not enter the presence of God in heaven without the atoning sacrifice of Christ, so, the dead were sequestered in Hades until the general resurrection." So, *just a few months ago* Kurt argued that the saints could not enter the MHP until AD 70 because they did not have the forgiveness of their sins. This absolutely affirms that salvation was not perfected at the cross. Kurt, *actually wanted to affirm that as his proposition!*

Let me frame my argument based on Kurt's comments:

The souls in Hades could not enter heaven until they received the benefits of Christ's atoning blood (Kurt Simmons, October, 2009– Is this true or false, Kurt?)

But, the souls in Hades could not enter heaven until the resurrection in AD 70 (KS, November, 2009– True or False, Kurt?).

Therefore, the souls in Hades did not receive the benefits of Christ's atoning blood until AD 70.

AFFIRMATIVE ARGUMENT ON HADES

Hades was the place of separation from God, even for the righteous, until the time of the resurrection when sin would be overcome through forgiveness and salvation (1 Corinthians 15:54-56; Revelation 20:10ff). ***The only reason Hades existed was because there was no forgiveness of sin.***

Kurt believes that Hades was not destroyed until AD 70, and the souls in Hades did not enter their reward until AD 70.

The existence of Hades until AD 70 as Kurt affirms, is *prima facie* proof that *neither the living or the dead entered the MHP until the resurrection.* After all, the living saints could not bypass Hades when they died before the resurrection. So, until the resurrection in AD 70 neither the living or the dead saints could enter the MHP, and Kurt's assertions to the contrary are falsified.

But since Hades existed until AD 70 then Torah remained binding until AD 70! **Remember that Paul said there could be no access to the MHP while Torah remained binding!**

The destruction of Hades is when man could enter the MHP. *Hades and Torah were coexistent!* Remember Luke 16– "They have Moses and the prophets, let them hear them"! As long as Torah stood valid there was *no forgiveness* and thus, no entrance into MHP. As long as Hades–which existed because of *no forgiveness*-- remained there was no entrance into the MHP. Kurt Simmons says that Hades was not destroyed until AD 70. Therefore, Torah remained binding until AD 70. (*Because Torah could not provide forgiveness!*)

Make no mistake, Kurt affirms repeatedly that the resurrection, *when Hades was destroyed*, occurred in AD 70. So, here is what we have.

Kurt affirmed, *October / November 2009,* that the saints could not enter the MHP "without the atoning sacrifice of Christ, so, the dead were sequestered in Hades until the general resurrection." (Notice that highly significant "**so**" in Kurt's comments). He still affirms– ***don't you, Kurt?***– that the dead saints could not enter heaven until AD 70 and the "general resurrection"? **Don't fail to answer this, my friend!** *This is crucial!* You owe it to the readers of this debate to address this argument **without evasion or obfuscation**, as you promised to do when you signed the debate rules.

You have stated that the dead saints could not enter the MHP without the atoning work of Christ, and *you unequivocally tied that entrance to AD 70!*

There could not be a clearer *demonstration of my affirmative*, or rejection of Kurt's new theology. **Kurt, do you now renounce as false teaching, what you wrote in October of 2009, and the proposition that *just last November* you wanted to affirm concerning the resurrection and Hades?**

We will eagerly await your response. But we are not done. We are going to fill Kurt's box to overflowing!

HEBREWS 9, TORAH, REMISSION OF SIN, HADES AND THE MOST HOLY PLACE

"And for this reason He is the Mediator of the new covenant, by means of death, for the redemption of the transgressions under the first covenant, that those who are called may receive the promise of the eternal inheritance." (Hebrews 9:15).

Notice what the text says:
Christ died for the remission (redemption) of sins committed under Torah. *I affirm this!* The Cross was *for* redemption! It does not, however, say that redemption occurred *at* the Cross. Follow closely:

Those under the first covenant were dead Old Covenant saints that Jesus died to give forgiveness.
But, remember that Kurt wanted to affirm *in this debate* that the resurrection was *exclusively* the entrance of the souls in Hades into the MHP, i.e. *the dead Old Covenant saints!*
But, if the dead OT saints could not enter the MHP until AD 70, then it is undeniably true that they did not yet have the remission of sins that Jesus died to give them. The *one thing– and the only thing* –that kept man out of the MHP was *sin*!

If, as my friend affirms, remission of sins was objectively applied from Pentecost onward, then those OT saints *should have* entered the MHP at the moment of the Cross. But no, Kurt wanted to affirm *in this debate* –that the dead saints could not enter the MHP until AD 70!
Thus, they were still awaiting their forgiveness purchased through Christ's death. They would not have the benefits of Christ's atoning blood until the resurrection. ***Kurt, do you now affirm that the OT saints entered the MHP at the time of the Cross / Pentecost? Yes or No?***
Do you affirm that those in Hades entered the MHP before Hades was conquered in AD 70? Yes or No? If you so, **you are in denial of Revelation 15:8 and Revelation 20!**

Hebrews 11:40 relates to this issue. Paul, speaking of the dead OT saints said, "They without us cannot be made perfect." Kurt claims (by misusing Hebrews 10:19f) that the living saints were able to enter the MHP from Pentecost onward. Yet, he wanted to affirm in this debate that the OT saints could not enter until AD 70! That would mean that the living NT saints could

46

enter the MHP *before the OT saints*. But there is a problem! *Paul said that the New Covenant saints would not precede the OT saints* (1 Thessalonians 4:15f)!

According to Paul, the OT saints could not enter into the "better resurrection" (Hebrews 11:35f, without the NT saints, and, the NT saints could not enter before the OT saints. *In other words, OT and NT saints would enter into the MHP together, at the same time!* So, the proposition that Kurt wanted to affirm in this debate, that the dead saints would enter the MHP in AD 70, winds up proving my proposition, and destroying Kurt's!

Kurt believes that the resurrection was in AD 70. He believes the resurrection was exclusively the raising of the dead out of Hades into heaven. But this demands that the OT saints remained in Hades, *unforgiven*, until AD 70! And if those in Hades could not enter the MHP until AD 70, it is irrefutably true that *the living could not enter until AD 70!* The living, when they died, had to go to Hades, before the time of the resurrection!
If the dead OT saints were objectively forgiven at Pentecost onward *there was no reason for them to remain in Hades.* This is especially true if, as Kurt claims, AD 70 had *no redemptive relevance!* If AD 70 had no redemptive significance, and if forgiveness was an objective reality prior to AD 70, then again, *there was no reason whatsoever for the dead saints to remain in Hades.*

Kurt's insistence that the saints entered the MHP before AD 70 demands that Hades was emptied before the resurrection, or that the resurrection occurred at the time of the Cross / Pentecost, since per Kurt, forgiveness and redemption was completed at that point. Remember *the living and the dead would receive their reward at the same time* (Matthew 16:27-28; 1 Peter 4:5).

Yet, Revelation 15:8 is unequivocal. There was no entrance into the MHP until the supposedly "irrelevant event" of the judgment of Old Covenant Babylon! This is why Kurt's statement–whether he now recants it or not-- stands true: "Christ tied the judgment to the end of the Mosaic age and the destruction of Jerusalem" (*Consummation*, 2003, p. 229).

Jesus said he was coming in judgment "to reward every man" (Matthew 16:27-28; Revelation 22:12). The reward Jesus was going to give was the incorruptible inheritance and salvation (1 Peter 1:3f; Hebrews 9:28; 10:35f, etc.). But, Kurt is now arguing that the saints received their reward (entrance into the MHP / salvation) *before Christ came in judgment to give the reward!* This is clearly untenable.

47

THE HOLY SPIRIT– THE EARNEST OF THE REDEMPTION--AD 70

Let me introduce some more affirmative arguments based on the work of the Spirit. Remember that Kurt admits that the charismata were given as the earnest (guarantee) of the finished work of Christ (i.e. redemption, Ephesians 1:13-14). The truth is that the Spirit was the guarantee of *all* of the still future promises contained in the NT! (Note how Kurt *ignored* my referent to Philippians 1:6f).

Paul said that the Spirt– the charismata– was given as an Earnest of the Inheritance / Resurrection (2 Corinthians 5:5; Ephesians). This means that the Earnest of the Spirit was given to *living people*, who, according to Kurt, already had the very thing that the Spirit was given to guarantee– Salvation, redemption, forgiveness! *Why did living people need to be given the Earnest (the guarantee) of what they already possessed?*

The Spirit was given to guarantee the *resurrection*. Deliverance from Hades. The resurrection was exclusively for the dead (per KS). Thus, the charismata was given to the living, but had no redemptive significance for them. It did not guarantee *them* anything. It simply guaranteed the dead something that had no redemptive significance! (*As if release from Hades into the presence of God had no redemptive significance!*)

I must be brief, but I want to make an affirmative in regard to the Spirit and resurrection.
The promise of the Spirit was made to Israel *to raise her from the dead* (Ezekiel 37:10-14).
This "death" from which Israel was to be raised was not physical death, but *covenantal death* (Isaiah 24:4f; Hosea 5-6; 13:1-2). Living people were called *dead*, but they continued to "sin more and more" (Hosea 13:1-2). Biologically dead people cannot do this! This is *spiritual death*- alienation from God– as a result of sin (Isaiah 59:1-2--The sin that needed to be removed at the coming of the Lord, Isaiah 59:20f--Romans 11!). Sin brought death. Thus, forgiveness would bring resurrection (cf. Acts 26:17-18)!
This resurrection, *guaranteed by the Spirit*, would be Israel's salvation (Isaiah 25:8-9). This is the resurrection promise of 1 Corinthians 15 when sin, *the sting of death*, would be overcome (1 Corinthians 15:54-56– *Romans 11:26-27*). In other words:

1 Corinthians 15 foretold the resurrection (when sin would be put away), predicted by Isaiah 25.
The resurrection of Isaiah 25 is the resurrection of Isaiah 26-27 (and thus, Romans 11:26-27), which would occur at the coming of the Lord

in judgment of Israel for shedding innocent blood.
But, the coming of the Lord -- at the resurrection to put away sin-- of Isaiah 25-27 / 1 Corinthians 15-- would be the coming of the Lord in judgment of Israel for shedding innocent blood.
Therefore, the coming of the Lord of Romans 11 to take away Israel's sin-- to bring her salvation-- is the coming of the Lord at the time of the resurrection, in judgment of Israel for shedding innocent blood, i.e. AD 70.

You cannot divorce the resurrection of 1 Corinthians 15 from that in Isaiah 25-27. But again, the resurrection of Isaiah 25-27 is the coming of the Lord *for the salvation of Israel* in Romans 11. Therefore, the coming of the Lord for the salvation of Israel in Romans 11 is the time of the coming of the Lord for the resurrection (the salvation of Israel), in 1 Corinthians 15. This is inescapable.

Let me express this simply:
The resurrection is when sin, the sting of death was to be overcome, (1 Corinthians 15:54-56).
The miraculous gifts of the Spirit were the guarantee of that resurrection (2 Corinthians 5:5; Ephesians 1:13).
Therefore, the miraculous gifts of the Spirit *were the guarantee of the overcoming of sin!*

This proves, *prima facie* that while the cross was the power for the putting away of sin, that the work of the cross was not completed until the parousia / resurrection in AD 70. It proves that AD 70 was redemptively *critical.*
Since the Spirit was the guarantee of the resurrection, (in AD 70 per KS!), the time when sin, the sting of death would be overcome, it therefore follows that the coming of the Lord to put away sin in Romans 11:26f was the time of the resurrection in AD 70. Thus, these verses go in Kurt's box.

THE TIME OF REFORMATION AND KURT'S ATTEMPT AT LOGIC

My friend has a difficult time dealing with logical syllogisms. He *refused to comment on even one of my seven syllogisms.* (Refutation of a syllogism demands that a person analyze and refute the *major premise*, or *the minor premise*, proving with *evidence* that they affirm something that is untrue. One can also show that the conclusion does not follow from the premises. *Ignoring a syllogism* does not refute the arguments, and Kurt did not offer a syllable *of analysis!*

I took note, in *over six pages of argumentation*, with careful attention to the

49

Greek tenses and the actual wording of the text, that the time of reformation would fully come at Christ's AD 70 parousia. *Kurt ignored all of this.* Go back and refresh your memory of what all I wrote, and then carefully consider Kurt's total silence.

He ignored the present tenses of Hebrews 9:6f (insisting on the other hand that we consider some of the past tenses as the final word, forgetting the proleptic nature of those statements and the work of the Spirit *to guarantee the completion*). He ignored the grammar of the text that declares Jesus' coming to be necessary to fulfill the typological nature of the OT which was, when Paul wrote, still a shadow of good things about to come (Hebrews 9:28-10:1). *He ignored all of this!*

I offered the following:
Kurt admits that entrance into the MHP was at the second coming in AD 70. (Of course, he wants now to deny this, except in regard to the dead saints, but, as proven above, this does not help him).
But the time of reformation is when man could enter the MHP (Hebrews 9:10).
Thus, the time of reformation did not fully arrive until the second coming AD 70.
This means that Torah remained imposed until AD 70, because Torah would stand "until the time of reformation" (Hebrews 9:10).

I noted that in 2 Corinthians 3-6 Paul affirmed that the work of the Spirit, in and through his ministry, was the transformation from the Old Covenant glory to the New (2 Corinthians 3:16f). Thus, the work of the Spirit was the guarantee of Covenant transformation! Kurt insists however, that this transformation, the time of reformation allowing man into the MHP, was at the Cross / Pentecost. Trouble is, Paul said the ministry of Covenantal transformation was his ministry!

In a vain attempt to counter my arguments, Kurt offered a syllogism that is rife with error:
The ceremonial law was imposed until the time of reformation.
The time of reformation was marked by the ministry of the Spirit.
But the ministry of the Spirit began immediately following the cross.
Therefore, the ceremonial law was imposed only until the cross.
Kurt is guilty of the "law of the excluded middle." In other words, he left out a bunch of critical stuff! He is likewise guilty of *anachronism*. The ministry of the Spirit did not begin for *40 days after the cross*. Yet, Kurt says that the law ended *before the Spirit even began his work*! The reformation did not

come at the cross! (Note also that he limits definition of "the law" to the "ceremonial law." This is a false dichotomization of Torah, and we will prove this as we proceed).

Kurt's syllogism is fundamentally flawed because of the "Law of Excluded Middle." He leaves out several significant facts. He claims that the time of reformation fully arrived at the moment of the *initiation* of the Spirit's work of reformation–actually *before*. See above! This denies Paul's statement that the Spirit was working through his ministry to bring about Covenant transformation. Thus, Kurt's "conclusion" fails to honor *the on-going work of Covenant transformation– the work that was not finished when the Spirit was given*! Kurt even admits this, but then tries to deny it (or wrongly apply it) all at the same time! Read what he said in his first negative: "It is clear that the time of reformation began at the cross. The gifts of the Holy Ghost led the apostles into all truth for the specific purpose of affecting reform (Jn. 16:13). When the gifts ceased, the time of reformation was *over*, not begun." My friend keeps contradicting himself, and scripture.

The time of the reformation– at the end of Torah-- is when man could enter the MHP. Kurt says the time of reformation was at the cross / Pentecost, and was "over, not begun" when the gifts ceased (i.e. in AD 70). Well, my friend, if the time of reformation was over (terminated, not perfected), then the time when man could enter the MHP *ended in AD 70!* Your position demands that the time of reformation– when man could enter the MHP– only lasted forty years and then "was over, not begun!" **Where does that leave us today?** We all know that you believe the believer enters the MHP today, thus, the forty year transformational work of the Spirit was *to bring the time of reformation to perfection!* The *only solution* to your self contradiction is to accept my affirmative and return to the position you have abandoned: the work of the Spirit *initiated the time of reformation, the parousia perfected the time of reformation*. Your view of Hades, the resurrection and the charismata logically demand this.

So, *the time of reformation was not completed when the Spirit was given, as Kurt claims*. You cannot have the time of reformation completed before Paul (and the Spirit through Paul) began his work of Covenant transformation. *The time of reformation fully arrived when the Spirit finished His work, and that was when man could enter the MHP, which by Kurt's own admissions was in AD 70!* So, just as we have affirmed from the beginning, the work of salvation was a process *begun at the Cross*, and *consummated at the parousia*. The next point confirms this even more.

51

MORE ON THE ATONEMENT AND KURT'S AMAZING ARGUMENT

I offered a number of arguments based on the actual text and the present tenses of the Greek– all ignored by Kurt– on the necessity for Christ to fulfill the typology of the Day of Atonement, when the high priest *killed the sacrifice*, entered the MHP, and then came out to announce salvation to the worshipers. I must admit that I was staggered by Kurt's attempt at refutation. I have never read or heard anyone, in any commentary, at any time, make such an argument! Here is what he said:

"Don assumes that Christ's ascension equals the High Priest entering the Most Holy Place, thus postponing completion of the Atonement ritual until Christ emerged at his second coming. Don forgets that the High Priest entered the Most Holy Place *twice* (Lev. 16:14, 15). Yes, TWICE! There were *two sacrifices* in the atonement ritual: a bull and a goat; blood was carried in twice, *once for each sacrifice*. But Jesus died only *once*; he made a *once-for-all* sacrifice when he died on the Calvary. We believe that the typology of sprinkling the blood before the Mercy Seat was fulfilled when Jesus died. The Hebrew writer agrees, saying that Jesus opened the way into the Most Holy Place through his FLESH (Heb. 10:20)." No, Kurt, the Hebrews writer does not agree with you! But, does the reader of this debate catch what Kurt has done? This is simply amazing!

Notice just some of the problems with Kurt's proposal.

1.) Kurt argues that since, under Torah, the High Priest had to enter the MHP TWICE, Jesus likewise had to do so. *This is unbelievable!* Why did the high priest have to enter the MHP TWICE? Why were there *two sacrifices*, Kurt? Answer: The priest had to enter twice because *the first time* was when **he offered blood for his own sins** (Leviticus 16:1-6; Hebrews 5)! Kurt, my friend, your insistence on Christ entering the MHP TWICE, means that Christ offered his own blood *to atone for his own sin*. That is the *only* reason why Christ would have to enter the MHP TWICE That is the typology that you are appealing to!

But once again, we have the refutation of Kurt Simmons from Kurt's own keyboard! In *Adumbrations*, (2009, p. 168) Kurt wrote: "At his resurrection Jesus made it very plain to Mary that he had 'not yet ascended' unto the Father in heaven" (John 20:17). Peter expressly states that Jesus was in Hades prior to his resurrection (Acts 2:22-32)." So, Jesus did not enter the MHP on the Cross, or while in Hades! Kurt's argument is destroyed.

2.) The sacrifice was always killed *outside the MHP* and then *offered* in the MHP (Leviticus 16)! Yet Kurt says Jesus entered the MHP while he was on the cross! *The mercy seat was within the veil,* not outside. Your argument violates the type / antitype, and your own words.

3.) Of course, Kurt then violates his own argument by admitting (tacitly of course), that Jesus did enter the MHP at his ascension! Okay, so Kurt has Jesus entering the MHP while on the cross. Then, he has Jesus entering the MHP when he ascended! There is no logical harmony here.

4.) Notice Hebrews 9:12– Christ "entered the Most Holy Place *once for all by his own blood*." Per Kurt, the author should have said Jesus had entered *twice*!

All of this establishes the point I made earlier. The cross, *as stand alone event*, did not complete salvation. I argued that Kurt's own position demanded that Jesus enter the MHP to fulfill the Atonement typology. Now, *he has tacitly admitted it*, while seeking desperately to deny it! He claims, without a syllable of proof, that Jesus entered the MHP while hanging on the cross, but then, while arguing for Jesus to enter the MHP TWICE, admits that Jesus had to enter the MHP at his ascension! This proves my point that the typological aspects of Torah were not fulfilled at the cross, and nullifies Kurt's claims, *prima facie*!

KURT'S QUESTIONS TO ME

Although Kurt refused to answer any of my questions, he posed two questions to me and in private correspondence said that he would only answer my final question if I answered these:

1) Did the cross cancel the debt of sin under the law?

Response: Kurt's problem is that he reads "**at** the cross" into the texts that speak of the Cross initiating the redemptive process! But those texts speak of Christ cancelling the debt *(not the law itself!) through the cross*. Kurt's questions are based on faulty premises and presuppositions.

2) Does the cross (grace) triumph over law, or did law have to be removed for man to be justified?

Response: The cross did triumph over law. However, Kurt fails, sadly, to differentiate between the *process begun*– that I have demonstrated definitively in my comments on Hebrews 9:15– and process *finished*. Likewise, Kurt fails to consider the difference between the objective passing of the Law itself– which did not happen at the Cross (Hebrews 8:13), and what happened when a person *died to the law by the body of Christ,* receiving the earnest of the Spirit as the guarantee of the transformation from the Old Covenant glory to the New.

This last point is critical. *The Law itself was not nullified at the cross.* As believers came into Christ, "the veil was taken away" (2 Corinthians 3:10f). Yet the *Law itself*, not just an outer manifestation of the law, as Kurt falsely claims, was "ready to vanish away" (Hebrews 8:13). Remember, it was the

Spirit's work to bring that covenantal transformation to completion. *It was the Spirit's work to apply the power of the cross and bring that foundational work to completion.*

As noted above, Kurt, in violation of the rules he signed, engaged in an affirmative presentation, which I am under no obligation to even mention since I am in the affirmative. He spent a good long time on Matthew 5:17-18 claiming to falsify the preterist paradigm in regard to that text. I am going to ask my friend to *please use that argument* in his affirmative presentations! I promise to demonstrate, *definitively*, the fallacy of the argument.

In this second affirmative I have totally rebuffed all of Kurt's few attempts to negate my arguments. I have buttressed my arguments with solid exegesis, sound hermeneutic and logic. I have added new arguments that prove, *prima facie* that Torah was not nullified at the cross, and that salvation was perfected at Christ's parousia in AD 70. My affirmative is established beyond any ability of Kurt to rebut, but, we will see what he has to offer.

A final question: Kurt, tell us plainly, What was "the *__power__* of the holy people" mentioned in Daniel 12:7? Please, do not ignore this. Clearly define Israel's *__power__*.

Second Negative by Kurt Simmons

A Vindication of Christ Cross against the Errors of Covenant Eschatology

I always smile when I recall the folksy saying the Texas preacher used after stepping on someone toes in a Sunday sermon: throw a rock at a bunch of dogs; the one that screams is the one that hit. Apparently, Don has been hit because he sure is screaming! Accusations are flying! Don protests I am not keeping to the terms of the debate. He says my first negative has five pages of irrelevant material! Really? What could be more relevant to a debate about Covenant Eschatology than to provide the reader with facts about the origin of the doctrine and the man who authored it? What could be more relevant in a debate about Covenant Eschatology than to tell the reader that this doctrine has led its author into the false gospel of Universalism? What could be more relevant to a debate in which Don affirms that sin was *not* blotted out at Calvary than some explanatory material about how Covenant Eschatology denies the cross of Christ? In his first affirmative, Don said his debate is not about the cross. But as we have seen, that is EXACTLY what this debate is about! If Don asserts the debate is not about the cross, am I not entitled to show the reader that in fact it is? Of course I am!

Don complains I have not answered his arguments about Isaiah 26, 27, and 59. Really? Did I sign a proposition to negative Don *arguments*? No! I signed a debate to negative Don *proposition!* I am under NO obligation to answer even one of Don arguments. If I can negative Don proposition by marshaling dozens of verses showing the debt of sin was paid at the cross, if I can negative Don proposition by marshaling dozens of verses showing the law was fulfilled and abolished at the cross, is there any reason I should withhold these verses? Of course not! And if I can negative Don proposition by simply producing verses (and pointing out that he can marshal *none*) is there any reason I should waste time discussing Isaiah 25-27? Of course not. Even so, in this article, we will deal with many of Don arguments. We will show there is not *one particle* of credibility to his argument that Isaiah 27:7-11 is about AD 70. We also address his arguments based upon his misrepresentations of what I have said. Four times in his last affirmative he misrepresents me. He sets up straw-man arguments by putting words in my mouth then proceeds to tear them down. We will address these and other arguments of Don in their proper time and place. But first, let us make certain the reader understands exactly what this debate is about. The TWO most basic and important issues in this discussion are:

- When did the legal validity of the Old Testament cease? and
- When did the legal efficacy of Christ blood justify the saints? AD 33 at Calvary, or AD 70 at the fall of Jerusalem?

Dear reader, this is what this debate is about! Not the proper exegesis of Isaiah 25-27! Issues of Isaiah 27:7-11 are a distraction at best. They enter at all only because Don proposed the debate be framed around Rom. 11:25-27, and I accepted lest there be no debate at all. Even so, we have signed the proposition and are willing to discuss all matters connected with Rom. 11:25-27, but issues of Isaiah are collateral at best compared with questions about the efficacy of Christ cross. My charge is that Covenant Eschatology *denies* the cross of Christ! I have shown that when you *spiritualize* (figurine the resurrection and make it equal to *justification*, that when you argue justification occurred in AD 70 by *removal of the law rather than the addition of grace*, you OVERTHROW the cross of Christ. When you say that the saints languished under the *debt of sin* until the second coming, YOU OVERTHROW THE CROSS OF CHRIST! I said in my first negative,

> If the cross did not triumph over the law at Calvary, if man had to wait until the law was purportedly removed in AD 70 to be justified from sin, then nothing happened at the cross.

Don claimed in his last affirmative that my argument was illogical, that my logic here is bad. Alright then, Don, tell us what happened at the cross! You *deny* that atonement was made there, that redemption happened there, that reconciliation happened there. You *deny* that salvation happened there, that the debt of sin was then and there blotted out. Tell us, please, what did happen at the cross? I said I could not find the cross in your system of soteriology/eschatology. I charged that the cross had dropped out of your theology of salvation. I charged that in a system which claims the law continued to hold man under the debt of sin until it was separately removed in AD 70, the cross cannot rationally be said to have triumphed over any thing. I invited you to explain to us where the cross fits in and what happened at Calvary, but you absolutely have not told us. So, I renew the invitation; tell us what *did* happen at the cross?

Don Gives Away the Debate

We asked Don two questions at the end of our first negative. Since the cross has come up, we might as well address this now, before moving on to Don argument about Isaiah. Here are the questions: 1) Did the cross cancel the debt of sin under the law? 2) Does the cross (grace) triumph over law, or did law have to be removed for man to be justified? I found Don answer to the second question particularly interesting: Here, in pertinent part, is what Don said: response: The cross did triumph over law.

Don affirms that the cross triumphed over the law! Good, that is the correct answer. But if the cross triumphed over the law, how could the law continue to hold the saints under bondage until AD 70? Fair question, right? If the Persians triumphed over the Babylonians, would Babylon still have power over the nations of its former empire? No, of course not, Persia would! If the Greeks triumphed over the Persians, would the Persians still have power over the nations of its former empire? No, of course not, the Greeks would! Yet, Don says the cross triumphed over the law, but the law still had power to keep the saints under condemnation until AD 70! Don, please explain to us how the cross can triumph over the law and not triumph over the law at the same time!

Dear reader, Don has given away the debate. Don argues that the law was valid, binding, and obligatory until AD 70. He argues that not until the law was taken out of the way in AD 70 could the saints be justified. Yet, here he admits the cross triumphed over the law! SOME TRIUMPH! A triumph that leaves the adversary still holding all the power! A triumph in which all the captives are still under the enemy command! But that is not what Paul said. NO! Paul said that *hen he ascended he led captivity captive* (Eph. 4:8). Notice that Christ ascension was not to make the atonement and then return a second time to release the captives as my brother says. NO! Jesus led the captives of sin in triumph *at his ascension!* In other words, the victory was already won and the atonement complete! The triumphal parade was at the ascension, not the second coming! (Some affirm that the reference here is to the souls in Hades, but we do not share their view. Hadean death was the last enemy and the resurrection was not until AD 70.)

The imagery in Ephesians is similar to the time when the Amalekites raided Ziklag and captured David wives and children and those of the men who were with him. David went, conquered the Amalekites, and led the captives back again. (See II Sam. 30.) That is what Paul says Jesus did at his ascension; he led those formerly under dominion to sin in triumphal procession! The victory was at *Calvary,* the triumphal parade at the *ascension.* AD 70 was a total irrelevancy in terms of redeeming man from sin.

Don Boxes

In our first negative, we made the charge that Don could not produce even one verse that plainly states the saints were under the dominion of sin until AD 70. We put a box on a page for Don to fill with *any verse* he could find that plainly taught that the saints were under the debt of sin from and after the cross.   Let the record reflect that Don could not produce even ONE VERSE! We produced dozens of verses that plainly teach that the saints were fully and freely justified from and after the cross. We noted the verb tenses, and that the perfect tense, showing completed action in the past, occurred with stunning frequency. We said that when it was our turn to be in the affirmative we could produce *pages of verses*. Don could not produce even one! Don pretended three times to fill the box *with arguments*, but he never once produced a single BOOK, CHAPTER, AND VERSE.

Don's Box No. 1
Verses?

It pains me to point this out for Don sake, it really does. I find this very distasteful; this debate would be easier if Don were a stranger rather than a beloved brother and friend. But the cross is too important to allow my love for Don to prevent me from pointing out his utter inability to sustain his case with a single verse. How many debates have there been when one party could not produce even one verse to establish his case? Arguments there are in abundance; logical syllogisms grow on trees. But verses! That is the foundation of our teaching, not argument. Every error in Christendom is build upon argument, deduction, and syllogisms. We all understand the plain testimony of verses, but when men start building doctrine based upon deductions, look out! If this, then that. And if that, then this, and this, and this! Before you know it we wake up to find that we cannot have blood transfusions, celebrate birthdays, Christ's Nativity, or, what is more serious, the cross has dropped out of our soteriology!

Imagine, if you will, a man who says want to affirm in debate that the world 's sin was atoned for when the Moabite king offered his son upon the wall (II Kings 3:26, 27). A strange proposition to be sure, but we accept the challenge. The man then argues for 14 pages why the Moabite sacrifice of his son paid the world debt of sin. Then he argues for 18 pages more. He uses all sorts of wonderful, mystifying syllogisms and logical arguments. He often seems very persuasive! But after all is said and done, he *never can and never does* produce even one verse to sustain his position. We on the other hand have pages and pages of verses saying that the debt of sin was paid in full at the cross; we have pages and pages of verses saying the law was fulfilled and abolished in Jesus death. Our opponent has not one verse he can bring forward. Has he sustained his proposition? Would you be willing to accept his view when he cannot even produce one verse in his own support? Of course not. Yet that is what Don is asking you to do.

Since we have given Don one box and he could not produce a verse to put in it, perhaps there is no point in giving him a second box to fill. Even so, here it is. I do not do this to rub Don's nose in it, but to help the scales fall from his eyes. Don, it is your position that the law was valid, binding, and obligatory until AD 70 and that being so, the saints were purportedly under its condemnation until that time. It is therefore essential to your position to show that the saints were under obligation to *keep and observe* the whole law until AD 70, including the animal sacrifices, dietary restrictions, circumcision, and laws against keeping company with Gentiles. This is the logical implication of your position, and it is what you expressly state over and over again in your books. Based upon Matt. 5:18, you say *all the law was valid until none of the law was valid.* Therefore we are giving you another box to fill. Please provide us with any verse, even one, that plainly and expressly states that the saints (Jewish or Christian) were *bound and obligated* to keep the ceremonial law, the dietary law, circumcision, the laws forbidding associating with Gentiles, or *any other law* announced and enjoined by Moses (exclusive of the moral law, laws against idolatry, and eating of blood, etc., which never have and never will be annulled). Do not evade or obfuscate by trying to fill the box with arguments, just give us BOOK, CHAPTER, AND VERSE, if you please.

Don's Box No. 2
Verses?

We predict that as before Don will be unable to bring forward even one verse that plainly teaches the Christians were obligated to keep the ordinances of the Torah. But if they were not obligated to keep the Torah, the Torah could not be valid or binding. And if the Torah was not valid or binding, then the saints most certainly could not be under its power or the debt of sin from and after the cross. Therefore, Don proposition is lost and Covenant Eschatology falsified.

59

Don's Fail-Safe Question

Don made much ado about the question he asked at the end of his first affirmative. He whipped up a zinger of a question and thinks that there is no answer that can be given but that it must prove his case. Here is Don's question:

"If a law or covenant has been abrogated, are any of the provisions of that covenant, i.e. its mandates, its promises or penalties (positive or negative) still binding and valid (imposed)?"

Don says, "my friend knows full well that to answer this question *directly and correctly* establishes that the Torah remained valid until AD 70!" If the Torah was valid until AD 70, Don should have no problem putting one verse, only one, in our box, should he? But since he will invariably fail to bring forward a verse, we can rest assured that his question can be correctly answered without giving away the debate. I answered Don's question.

Here is my answer in pertinent part, including the part Don withheld (Don mentioned the "entirety" of my answer, but did not publish all of it):

"If a king made a covenant with another nation or kingdom that the latter would pay tribute, and the latter then broke that covenant, the former would be entitled to come and lay siege against the breaching kingdom. But isn't it true that in this case we are dealing, not with the abrogation of a covenant, but its fulfillment? Jesus did not come to abrogate, but to fulfill, and, having fulfilled, took out of the way the types and shadows pointing to his work on the cross, and the sundry incidental laws related thereto. The New Testament is the fulfillment of the Old Testament, so whatever benefits were promised under the old find fulfillment in the new, including remission of sins and eternal life."

Did you notice that Don does not want to deal with the fact that the New Testament is the fulfillment of the Old Testament, that whatever was promised under the Old is fulfilled in the New? Don argues that Old must be fulfilled before the New can come! He says that if there is even one promise still unfulfilled, then the Old Law is still valid. He even says that the resurrection had to happen under the Old Law before it could pass away! Yes, he says that!

"The Old Covenant could not pass away until it all was fulfilled. The resurrection was a part of the Old Covenant, as Paul expressly says. Therefore, unless the resurrection has happened, the Old Law has not yet been taken away." (*Elements*, p. 115)

So, based upon Don's interpretation of Matt. 5:18, resurrection had to occur BEFORE the Old Testament passed away! Resurrection UNDER THE LAW? But there could be no resurrection without forgiveness you said, and no forgiveness until the law was taken away. Here is what you said in our exchange last summer: "You cannot logically affirm the fulfillment of the resurrection in AD 70... and not affirm the end of whatever law it was that held the condemning power over man." So, which is it? In one place Don says that resurrection had to occur BEFORE the law was taken away, in another he argues resurrection could not happen UNTIL it was taken away. Which is it? Both cannot be true.

Does the law being fulfilled and thus abolished prevent God from executing wrath upon Jerusalem in AD 70? Don thinks it does. He argues that God could not execute the "quarrel of his covenant" (**Leviticus 26:25, 26, 29-32**) **if the covenant was no longer valid and binding.** Don says, Kurt says the Torah legally *died* at the Cross. But, if Torah died at the Cross, and no longer had legal power, *how in the world could the provisions of Torah be imposed and fulfilled in the fall of Jerusalem in AD 70?*"Don assumes without proof that the quarrel of God's covenant means the covenant is still valid! Don assumes the very point to be proved!

Don, provisions of wrath recited in Leviticus are not proof the covenant is still valid when wrath is poured out. God called his covenant with Israel a marriage covenant (Jer. 2:1; 3:2; Ezek. 16:8). When God divorced Israel the covenant was broken, the marriage was ABOLISHED, NULLIFIED, NONEXISTANT. God, because of his promise to Abraham and his purpose to bring Christ into the world through Abraham's seed, would renew the covenant by taking Israel back again for his wife, but while she was divorced the covenant was annulled. Did the fact the covenant was annulled stop God from punishing Israel and sending her into captivity in enemy lands? Of course not! A king makes a treaty with another king or kingdom. The terms say the latter will pay tribute; in exchange, the former covenants to protect and defend the latter. If the latter breaks the terms of the covenant, the former is certainly entitled to come and lay siege to the other kingdom. His making war in no way depends upon the continuing validity of the covenant. Just the opposite, it is because it is broken that the latter is entitled to make war! So with the Jews, they broke the covenant and God cast them away. They were no longer under his protection, but became his enemies. Hence, he came and avenged the violation ("quarrel") of his covenant. Don says the very same thing himself:

"Here is the principle that that any destruction of Israel was proof that she was out of covenant relationship with Jehovah" (*Like Father, Like*

Son, p. 175). "The old city had not only served its purpose, it had also become the enemy of God, by holding onto the Old Covenant" (*Ibid*, p. 193).

Thus, according to my brother, the very fact Israel was destroyed shows that the covenant was no longer valid! Yet, according to Don, God could not destroy Jerusalem unless the covenant was still in place! What a quandary Don has created for God! He cannot destroy the city unless the covenant is valid, but to destroy it the covenant must first be invalid! It is a good thing God does not subscribe to this logic and argumentation, or the Jews would be immune to wrath for there is no scenario according to Don that permits God to act! But there is more! Don says the law was valid, binding and obligatory until AD 70. Yet, here we have Don telling us that in keeping the law Israel became God's enemy! So, God imposed the law until AD 70 per Don, but the Jews' obedience to what God imposed made them his enemies! I think we are beginning to get the picture that Don has involved himself in endless contradictions through Covenant Eschatology.

Don's Arguments from Isaiah
Don has several arguments from Isaiah. The first argument, the only one that really matters, is based upon Isa. 27:7-11. This passage is commonly (though not universally) believed to have been cited by Paul in Rom. 11:25-27. If Don cannot prove his point here, he cannot prove it anywhere and we will be free to pass on to other things. Don's argument goes like this: The salvation of Israel in Isa. 27:7-11 would be when God made all of the altar stones like chalk. But God made Israel's altar stones chalk in AD 70. Therefore, the salvation of Israel in Isa. 27:7-11 was in AD 70. Do you see the error in Don's reason? This argument is like the one we put forward about crows: "All crows are black. This bird is black. Therefore, this bird is a crow." The mistake in this syllogism is that it ignores or overlooks the fact that crows are not the only birds that are black! If the conclusion had been, "this bird MAYBE a crow" then it would at least be valid reasoning. But, like Don, it concludes with a positive identification where none is logically permitted or required. Don's argument assumes that "making the altar stones like chalk" refers to AD 70. He assumes the very point to be proved. And guess what? NOT ONE COMMENTATOR AGREES WITH HIM! Don proves the case for me himself. In his book *"Like Father, Like Son, On Clouds of Glory,"* Don makes use of his argument from Rom. 11:25-27 and Isaiah 27:7-11. Endnote 104, on page 89, states *"Many commentators believe this judgment refers to the Assyrian destruction of 721 B.C."*

There you have it. Many commentators, indeed, *every commentator* I have ever read, considers this a prophecy of the coming national captivity under the Assyrians and Babylonians. The Pulpit Commentary states "Judah's chief smiters were Assyria and Babylon" (*in loc*). Homer Haley states, "The fruit or achievement of the severe judgment will be the abolition of idolatry: through the judgment he maketh all the stones of the altar as chalkstones that are beaten in sunder, pulverized and completely destroyed. Idolatry must be destroyed in Jacob as among the heathen…After the captivity, idolatry never appeared again among the people" (Homer Hagley, Commentary on Isaiah, *in loc*). We could go on, but the result would be the same in the end. Nobody agrees with Don in applying Isa. 27:7-11 to AD 70. Here is a box for Don. We will ask him to produce any commentator (except Max King) that agrees with him that AD 70 in is view in Isa. 27:7-11.

```
Don's Box No. 3
Commentators?
```

In this case, Don may have more success. It is at least *possible* some commentator somewhere has once opined that Isa. 27:7-11 refers to AD 70. I don't think there is, but we'll let Don try. But even if he should find someone who agrees with him, that would no more prove the case than Don's belief about the passage does. The historical context of the passage is inescapable. In fact, the very verses that follow (vv. 12, 13) actually mention the re-gathering of the nation from Assyria and Egypt after the scattering, captivity, and destruction (see below)! Rome and AD 70 are nowhere in sight.

What about typological significance? Could there be a double meaning so that the "purging of Jacob's iniquity" looks ahead typologically to AD 70 and redemptive salvation from sin? NOT A CHANCE! The salvation Don is trying to prove in Rom. 11:25-27 is clearly redemptive; he says it is the atonement for sin that is completed and occurs when Jesus comes out of the Most Holy Place in AD 70. But the "purging" of Jacob's sin in Isa. 11:25-27 is not redemptive, but retributive justice! There is a huge difference! Redemptive salvation comes from Jesus' substitutionary death and atoning sacrifice. Retributive justice and purging of Jacob's sin was in punishment for iniquity, by annulling the covenant and sending the nation into captivity. Israel and Judah would "pay double" for their national sins (Isa. 40:2). When the 70-years captivity was fulfilled, God would then bring Judah and Israel back into their land and renew the covenant until it was done away once and

63

for all in the cross of Christ. Redemptive salvation simply is not part of Isaiah 27:7-11 and no amount of argument by Don can put it there. We hasten to point out that if redemptive salvation was somehow mysteriously wrought through retributive justice in AD 70, then national Israel should be restored, just like Isaiah promises! National Israel was re-gathered after the captivity in Assyrian and Babylon. If this is a type of AD 70, then Israel *must* be re-gathered after destruction by Rome. This is Premillennial Dispensationalism, not Preterism! If Don is correct, he has just won the debate for McArthur and Ice!

More from Isaiah

In Don's argument #1 – Isaiah 26-27 and the Salvation of "Israel," Don states, *"Kurt claims that Romans 11:26f predicts the salvation of individual Jews, via obedience to the gospel, throughout the entirety of the endless Christian age."* Don then goes on to argue in his #2 that since God would make a "short work" on the earth and save only a remnant, that therefore I am wrong in saying Rom. 11:26 predicts the salvation of individual Jews throughout earth's continuing history. Don has one problem. *I have never said any such thing!* His claim is totally false. Don, produce the quote where I say this. You have set up a straw-man argument, innocently mistaking me I am sure, but a straw-man nonetheless. I agree with Don that the "short work" in Rom. 9:27-29 refers to national Israel. God gave the nation a 40 year grace period in which to obey the gospel, and then destroyed the nation for rejecting the Messiah and clinging to the law. However, I deny that Israel in Rom. 11:26 ("so all Israel shall be saved") refers to national Israel. Rather, it is true, spiritual Israel that is in view here.

Paul uses the imagery of a cultivated olive tree. Jesus is the root that sanctifies and sustains the whole. Unbelieving Jews are like branches broken off. Believing Gentiles are grafted into the tree in their place. Together, believing Jews and Gentiles constitute "true Israel." Paul thus concludes, "And so all Israel shall be saved." "So" here has the meaning of "in this way." That is, through the process of breaking off the unbelieving and grafting in Gentile believers, all spiritual Israel will be saved. Now, let us ask, Does the olive tree of God's faithful still exist? Of course it does! Are people still being grafted into the tree, saved and sanctified by the "Root of Jesse"? Of course they are! Will true Israel ever cease to exist? No, of course not. As long as time continues, "in this manner, all Israel shall be saved." Nowhere at anytime did I say that national or ethnic Jews down through the ages would be saved or that Rom. 11:26 has them in view. They were cut off and the nation destroyed. Don's charge is reckless, and his argument is completely invalid.

64

Still More from Isaiah

What about Don's argument #3? In this case, Don argues that the resurrection of Isa. 26:19 was in AD 70 and therefore the coming of the Lord in Isa. 27:7-11 must be in AD 70. Don states: "The coming of the Lord to take away Israel's sin in Romans 11:26f is the coming of the Lord at his coming in judgment of Israel foretold by Isaiah 26-27, when He would call the dead–those scattered to the four winds-- to Him (i.e. the *resurrection*) *by the sounding of the Great Trumpet (Isaiah 27:13)."*

That is Don's major premise (notice his spiritualized resurrection). Here is his minor premise:

Jesus said that the calling of the remnant, those scattered to the four winds would be at his coming in judgment of Israel *at the sounding of the Great Trumpet– (Matthew 24:30-31) the time of the resurrection per my friend Kurt Simmons– in AD 70."*

Here is his conclusion:

"Therefore, the coming of the Lord to take away Israel's sin of Romans 11:26 was to be (it was) at the coming of the Lord in judgment of Israel– the time of the resurrection at the sounding of the Great Trumpet."

Do you spot the logical fallacies in this argument? First, Don assumes without proof that the coming of the Lord in Rom. 11:25-27 is in judgment upon Israel. He has no proof, he just asserts this as fact. Second, he asserts without proof that Rom. 11:25-27 equals the resurrection of Isa. 26. Don is building exegetical paradigms in the sky! He has not established ANY CONNECTION between Rom. 11:25-27 and Isa. 26. NONE. He just asserts it! Third, he assumes Isa. 27:7-11 refers to AD 70. **Yet, we have already disproved this premise!** NOT ONE COMMENTATOR AGREES WITH HIM! For this argument to have ANY validity, Don must first find some commentator who agrees that Isa. 2:7-11 refers to AD 70. Don needs to put some references in the box first; otherwise he is building arguments upon unproved premises. The context of the passage is clearly the Assyrio-Babylonian captivity. The great trumpet is when God called them back from captivity, beginning with the decree of Cyrus in 539 BC:

"The great trumpet shall be blown, and they shall come which were ready to perish in the **land of Assyria** and the outcasts in the **land of Egypt,** and shall worship the Lord in the holy mount at Jerusalem." Isa. 27:13.

Plainly, this is NOT AD 70! Roy Deaver once quipped, "Don Preston could find AD 70 in Genesis 1:1!" There was no malice in Brother Deaver's comment. His point is valid. We must be careful not to let our hermeneutic drive our interpretation of scripture (and who hasn't been guilty of that one time or another?). When we set out to prove something, we tend to press into our service passages that do not really teach what we employ them for. (This is especially true when we heap up deductions.) Don has done this very thing in the instant case. Don has completely ignored the plain language of the passage that establishes the historical context and has built his case on thin air. His major premise is totally unfounded. Isa. 27:7-11 is about the Assyrio-Babylonian captivity, not AD 70!

Don's minor premise is also unfounded. The assumption underlying this premise is that the trumpet in Matt. 24 is the SAME TRUMPET in Isa. 27:13. But as we have just seen, Isa. 27:13 is specifically about the captivity in Assyria and Babylon! There is no evidence that can possibly make these the same trumpet. Trumpets were widely used in Israel to announce feasts and assemblies and holy convocations of all sorts, particularly the Jubilee, which seems to be the allusion here – a time of freedom from the Assyrio-Babylonian captivity.

Trumpets were also used to announce battle and call the nation to arms. That trumpets occur in both passages in no way proves the same events are in view. There was a gathering after the captivity, and there would be a gathering of the saints when the gospel was carried to the known world. There was also a gathering into the kingdom by martyrdom (I Thess. 4:1 et seq. cf. Matt. 3:12; 13:30; Rev. 14:13-16). Clearly, the gathering in Isa. 27:13 is NOT the same gathering as Matt. 24:30-31 any more than it is the same as the gathering by martyrdom under Nero! Don's minor premise assumes the fact to be proved and is invalid. Since BOTH Don's major premise and minor premise are invalid and false, his conclusion is false as well.

Entering the Most Holy Place

Since the topic of Don misrepresenting me has come up, we might as well take these next. Don argues that I said the saints could enter actually and spatially heaven (the Most Holy Place) from and after the cross. Don charges that in both of my books I affirm, quote: That entrance into the MHP was not until AD 70. Now, he claims that the saints *could* enter the MHP prior to AD 70! It seems my friend has forgotten *Revelation 15:8!* Or, perhaps he has renounced his position on Revelation 15."

Don states Kurt affirms that the saints did in fact enter into the MHP prior to AD 70! Don then parades before the reader places where I have denied this very thing in the past and makes me seem to contradict myself. The problem with this argument is that **I never said any such thing!** I never said the saints entered heaven before AD 70! Don, produce the quote! You have misrepresented me to the reader and set up a straw-man argument. Don knows I do not believe the saints went to heaven before AD 70 and the general resurrection. I know he knows this because he says so himself. Here is his argument, cut and pasted from his second affirmative:

The souls in Hades could not enter heaven until they received the benefits of Christ atoning blood (Kurt Simmons, October, 2009 Is this true or false, Kurt?) But, the souls in Hades could not enter heaven until the resurrection in AD 70 (KS, November, 2009 True or False, Kurt?). Therefore, the souls in Hades did not receive the benefits of Christ atoning blood until AD 70.

Notice that Don puts question marks after his major and minor premises. By this Don admits that he knows I do not hold the view he alleges. He affirms one minute that I say the saints were actually entering the Most Holy Place, then he asks me if I believe it or not. If he has to ask if I believe this why did he assert moments before that I do? Yes, why? I know Don knows I do not believe and have never said the saints went to heaven before AD 70 because three sentences later he says so himself! *Kurt believes that Hades was not destroyed until AD 70, and the souls in Hades did not enter their reward until AD 70.* There you have it! Don knows very well I have never taught, said, or believed that the saints went to heaven before AD 70 and says so himself. So, why does he frame the argument pretending he believes I have changed? Yes, why? Here is what I said. You the reader may be the judge.

This is why the veil was rent in twain from top to bottom when Jesus died, showing that the way was *now open* and the atonement COMPLETE (Matt. 27:51). The Hebrew writer thus urges Christians to ENTER the presence of God within the Most Holy Place before AD 70! (Heb. 10:19-22; *cf.* 6:19). In other words, the legal barrier separating men from God was totally removed in the cross, almost 40 years before AD 70.

Now, did I ever say or even suggest that the saints entered heaven before AD 70? No! I said the HEBREW WRITER URGES Christians to ENTER! "Having therefore, brethren, boldness to enter into the holiest by the blood of Jesus" (Heb. 10:19). BOLDNESS TO ENTER! It is not I, but the HEBREW WRITER who told the saints to enter in! Don wrongly puts words into my mouth.

67

The Hebrews were alive on this side of eternity. Flesh and blood cannot inherit the kingdom of heaven (I Cor. 15:50). How then could they enter the holiest still being alive? Legally and covenantally, of course! Here is what I said in my commentary (the part Don withheld):

"Man is restored to the **legal presence** of God by the sacrifice of Christ and is given boldness to enter into that which is within the veil (Heb. 6:19; 10:19)."

There it is, dear reader! Man is restored to the LEGAL PRESENCE of God by the sacrifice of Christ. The Hebrew writer had just taught in the preceding chapter that under the Old Testament system the ay into the holiest of all was not yet made manifest, while as yet the first tabernacle had *legal standing* (Heb.9:8). The Jewish Christians were under persecution, and being pressured by Jewish authorities to turn back to the law (this proves, parenthetically, that they had left the law and it was no longer legally imposed!). The writer shows them the futility of that system to save. He urges them to persevere the persecution of unbelieving Jews and to forsake the temple ritual. Indeed, the ritual, which Don claims was still valid and imposed, stood in very denial of Christ's atoning sacrifice and was abominated by God as an apostate form of worship.

> Thus saith the Lord, The heaven is my throne, and the earth is my footstool, where is the house that ye build unto me?...He that killeth an ox is as if he slew a man; he that sacrificeth a lamb, as if he cut off a dog neck: he that offereth an oblation, as if he offered swine blood; he that burneth incense, as if he blessed an idol. Yea, they have chosen their own ways, and their soul delighteth in their abominations. Isa. 66:1-3

The following verses in Isaiah talk about the persecution of the church and the coming of the Lord to destroy the city and temple (Isa. 66:5, 6, 15), the very destruction that would shortly overtake the Jews and was held out to encourage the suffering Christian population of Palestine. This is the salvation Jesus would bring when he appeared second time without sin unto salvation (Heb. 9:28). He was not coming back to deal with sin; he did that when he died upon the cross! NO! He was coming back to put his enemies beneath his feet and to save his bride from her persecutors.

The Hebrew writer says that the blood of bulls and goats could not cleanse or make pure, but that they had been PERFECTED FOREVER by the sacrifice of Christ (v. 14), and should therefore boldly enter (legally and covenantally) the presence of God within the veil (v. 19). Don knows this is what this passage teaches but if he admits it, he forfeits his case because this passage PROVES that the way into the Holiest was opened in Jesus death and the saints were justified from sin long before AD 70.

Souls in Hades Justified by the Blood

Having set up his straw-man argument, Don concludes that the souls in Hades did not receive the benefits of Christ atoning blood until AD 70. My friend is wrong! The Hebrew writer says otherwise! He says that in the gospel they had come to the Judge of all and the spirits of just men made perfect (Heb. 12:23). THE SPIRITS OF JUST MEN MADE PERFECT! How were these souls in Hades made perfect? By the blood of sprinkling, that speaketh better things than that of Abel. (v. 24). This same lesson is shown in Revelation where the souls under the altar are given WHITE ROBES and told to rest a little while until the number of martyrs had reached its fill (Rev. 6:9-11). Don, what part of made perfect do you deny?

This also dispenses with Don's argument that if sins were atoned for at the cross, then the spirits in Hades should *then and there* have entered heaven. The Hebrew writer calls them the spirits of just men MADE PERFECT. The law could not make the dead souls or spirits in Hades perfect, so what did? Clearly, the blood of Christ, for it is the only thing that can! Why didn't they go to heaven then? God told them to rest a little space until the full number of martyrs was reached, then they would all be taken to glory together! This is what the Hebrew writer means when he says nd these all, having obtained a good report through faith received not the promise: God having provided some better thing for us, that they without us should not be made perfect (Heb. 11:39, 40). The promised eternal inheritance was not achieved by the Old Testament worthies, because it was God purpose that they without us not be complete! Death was the LAST ENEMY because it was also the ULTIMATE ENEMY. Sin was defeated at the cross. The resurrection waited until it did for no more reason than it pleased God that it should be the last enemy put beneath Jesus feet. Don's argument that they were made to remain in Hades because they were not yet justified is erroneous.

The Sprinkling of Blood and the Atonement Ritual

Max King invented the doctrine that justification was incomplete and the saints remained under bondage to sin until AD 70. One of his arguments for this was the atonement ritual, claiming (without warrant) that until the High Priest emerged from the Most Holy Place the atonement for sin was incomplete. I learned this error from King and repeated it in my commentary on Revelation, but I repudiate it now. (Contrary to what Don says, my commentary on Daniel does *not* teach this error, as when I wrote that book

I had already learned better.) The Hebrew writer says that the two courts of the temple or tabernacle answer the two covenants. The outer court, where the priests stood daily offering sacrifices that could never save from sin, answered the Old Testament. The Most Holy Place within the veil answered the New Testament. The scripture says that as long as the first tabernacle and covenant had legal standing (not physical standing) the way into God presence within the veil was foreclosed. (See Heb. 9:1-10.) As we have already seen, after the death of his Son, God abominated the continuing temple ritual as an apostate form of worship, perpetuated in defiance of Jesus priesthood and sacrifice. As we have also seen, first century Christians were already soteriologically perfected by the sacrifice of Christ and urged to boldly enter within the veil through Jesus blood. In the words of Paul e are complete in him (Col. 2:10).

Notwithstanding all this, Don argues that the temple ritual was valid, binding, and obligatory (imposed) until AD 70. He says redemption came *through*, not *at* the cross! Don thinks that Christ appearing second time without sin unto salvation is to save from sin, even though the passage expressly disclaims this very thing! Apart from sin means apart from the problem of sin or apart from sacrifice for sin. Jesus triumphed over sin in his cross and was not coming to address this problem a second time! Don says redemption could not happen at the cross because the blood had to be carried into heaven, and this he claims did not happen until the ascension. Even if this were true it would not help Don. The ascension was in AD 33, not AD 70. Thus, either way Don's argument can not carry him far enough. He can get from Calvary to the ascension, but not to AD 70! However, we do not believe that Jesus carried his blood into heaven at his ascension. Rather, we believe that the blood was *received* by God within the veil at Jesus death. This is why the veil was rent in twain when the Lord died (Matt. 27:51; Mk. 15:37). If this is not what the meaning of happened, then let Don explain what is. How he can argue that Christians were excluded from God's legal and covenantal presence within the veil until AD 70 is beyond me. Don, the Hebrew writer urges Christians to enter into the holiest. What does he mean? Please tell us.

We made the point in our first negative that the High Priest had to enter the Most Holy Place twice, once for himself and once for the sins of the people (Lev. 16:14, 15). Don, misrepresenting me yet a ***third time*** claims I said Jesus entered the Most Holy Place at his death. Did I ever say such a thing? Don, produce the quote! Here is what I wrote. You the reader be the judge:

> We believe that the typology of sprinkling the blood before the Mercy Seat was fulfilled when Jesus died. The Hebrew writer agrees, saying that Jesus opened the way into the Most Holy Place through his FLESH

70

(Heb. 10:20). That is, in his death Jesus pierced the legal veil separating man from God. This is why the veil was ent in twain from top to bottom when Jesus died, showing that the way was *now open* and the atonement COMPLETE (Matt. 27:51).

Did I say Jesus went into heaven? Of course not. I said Jesus pierced the LEGAL VEIL when he died. Does that mean Jesus personally went to heaven? No, of course not, and no reasonable person would draw that meaning from what I said. I am sure Don has a good explanation for repeatedly misrepresenting me to the reader, and we will look for him to explain in his next affirmative. Meanwhile, let us hasten on.

Was our observation that the High Priest had to enter twice amiss of the mark? Not at all! Jesus died a sinner death. Cursed is every one that hangeth on a tree (Gal. 3:13). The Lord hath laid on him the iniquity of us all (Isa. 53:6). This is why Jesus cried out upon the cross hy hast thou forsaken me? (Matt. 27:46). Bearing our sins upon the tree, the veil of separation came between Jesus and the Father and the horror of this isolation caused him to exclaim. Jesus could not carry his blood into the Holiest at his death because he was under imputation of sin. His entrance the first time therefore was *by and in* his own blood. Neither by the blood of goats and calves, but by his own blood he entered in once into the holy place, having obtained eternal redemption for us (Heb. 9:12). ENTERED BY HIS BLOOD. Not with but by his blood! Jesus blood entered at his death, he did not! Christ died a (righteous) sinner death and descended to Hades, but his blood was received by God within the veil, terminating the legal separation of man (including Christ) from God, making the reconciliation. Hence, God himself tore the veil in two, from top to bottom, showing the act was God , not man .

When Jesus entered heaven at his ascension, it was not to carry his blood there. NO! The atonement was already complete! We *never,* ever see an image of Christ carrying his blood into heaven nor are we shown images of him standing sprinkling his blood. Never! What we see instead is that Jesus receives the coronation as King and sits down at God right hand! What is the significance of Jesus sitting down? The Hebrew writer makes very clear that it shows the atonement is *complete*. The priests stood daily offering sacrifices, but Jesus sat down.

> Every priest **standeth daily** ministering and offering oftentimes the same sacrifices, which can never take away sins: But his man, after he had offered one sacrifice for sins for ever, **sat down** on the right had of God, from henceforth expecting till his enemies be made his footstool. For by one offering he **hath perfected for ever** them that are sanctified. Heb.

71

10:11-14.

Notice the verb tenses here. Don, what part of perfected for ever do you deny? Don, did the High Priest sit down in the Most Holy Place within the temple? Why is Jesus then shown seated and not shown standing sprinkling his blood? Please explain. But just to be sure there is no misunderstanding and that the atonement was complete before AD 70, Paul states:

> for if when we were enemies, we were reconciled to God by the death of his Son, much more, being reconciled, we shall be saved by his life. And not only so, but we also joy in God through our Lord Jesus Christ, by whom we have now received the atonement. Rom. 5:10, 11

Notice the verb tenses. WERE RECONCILED, BEING RECONCILED, HAVE NOW RECEIVED THE ATONEMENT. Don, what part of now received do you deny? You say the atonement was not complete until AD 70. Paul says otherwise. Please reconcile these claims.

The Resurrection of Jesus: God Objective Proof that Atonement was Complete

The quote above states we were reconciled by Jesus death, and saved by his life. What does this signify? What does he mean saved by his life Simply this, Jesus resurrection and ascension are God objective proof that the promises were all fulfilled. *And we declare unto you glad tiding, how that the promise which was made unto the fathers, God **hath fulfilled** the same unto us their children, in that he hath raised up Jesus again (Acts 13:32, 33).* Jesus died a sinner death upon the tree. For he hath made him to be sin for us, who knew no sin (II Cor. 5:21). *The bonds and fetters of sin having been clasped upon Christ, Jesus was as much under the law condemnation as any man, and therefore could not be raised and enter the presence of God in heaven unless and until he was justified from the sin imputed unto him by God on our behalf.* His resurrection therefore is God testimony that the sacrifice was *accepted,* the law *satisfied* (fulfilled), the debt of sin *paid,* its power *broken,* and the atonement *complete!* This is why Paul says Jesus was delivered for our offenses, but raised for our justification (Rom. 5:14). In raising Jesus, God showed that man was now justified. In declaring the debt of sin paid and freeing Jesus from its power, God freed all who come to Christ! Hence, Paul says if Christ be not raised, your faith is vain; ye are yet in your sins (I Cor. 15:17). But Christ was raised, therefore we are NOT in our sins, nor were any of the saints, living or dead, from and after the cross. To deny the saints were fully justified before AD 70, Don would have to put Jesus back in the grave.

72

Validity of the Law and the Time of Reformation

In my first negative, I showed how Don says the ministry of the Spirit marked the time of transformation following the cross. I noted that transformation is identical to reformation and that, therefore, the time of reformation mentioned by the writer of Hebrews was marked by the ministry of the Spirit following the cross. Don, misrepresenting me a *fourth time* (count them, four!), mocks and ridicules my attempt at logic saying that I argued that the time of reformation *concluded* at the cross. Yet, I did not say the time of reformation concluded at the cross, I said it *began* there. Don again falsely puts words into my mouth. Here is a cut and paste from his second affirmative: You be the judge what I said:

The ceremonial law was imposed until the time of reformation.

The time of reformation was marked by the ministry of the Spirit.

But the ministry of the Spirit began immediately following the cross.

Therefore, the ceremonial law was imposed only until the cross [when the transforming ministry of the spirit began]

I have added the bracketed information to make the syllogism more complete, even though it is not necessary to be correct. Recall that I equate the transforming work of the Spirit with the time of reformation. Although the law was terminated at the cross and the gospel was ratified and came into full force and effect, there was a period and process of transformation as the doctrine of the New Testament was revealed and the canon of scripture reduced to writing. Now here is what Don says I said:

"No, the time of reformation was not completed when the Spirit was given, as Kurt claims." Did I claim the time of reformation was completed when the Spirit was given? Did I not say it *began* when the Spirit was given? Don even quotes me "When the gifts ceased, the time of reformation was over, not begun." Thus, I say the time of reformation was *marked* by the gifts of the Spirit (though in reality it began at the cross, the gift of the Spirit was merely the objective evidence of that fact). When the gifts of the Spirit ceased, the time of reformation was complete and not before. How can Don claim I said the time of reformation was complete when the Spirit was given? Don has misrepresented me again. At least he is consistent!

But while I say the time of reformation began with the cross and outpouring of the Spirit, Don says that the time of reformation began when the gifts of the Spirit ceased! The gifts had ceased by AD 70, yet that is when Don says the time of reformation started up. How can that be? Did the Protestant Reformation begin when the transforming work Luther and others was

73

finished? NO! The Reformation began when the work of change and transformation began, not when it was complete. Don has it backward! But that the law was invalidated by the cross, that it was NOT valid when Hebrews was composed, and that the time of reformation was then and there a present fact virtually all commentators agree. Regarding Heb. 9:9, Franz Delitzsch (Epistle to the Hebrews, 1882) states:

> or though the present tense, *prospherontai*, certainly implies the continuance of the Levitical sacrifices in the writer own time, it is certain that he regarded them as ***no longer having any validity***. The Levitical priesthood was now ***virtually abolished***, and its symbolical office as ***no more***. (Emphasis added.)

Regarding Heb. 8:13 (that which decayeth and waxeth old is ready to vanish away), Delitzsch states:

> the temple service, though to continue it may be a few years longer in **outward** splendour, is only a bed of state, on which a **lifeless corpse** is lying.

Regarding Heb. 9:9, Hagner (New International Biblical Commentary, 1983, 1990) states (emphasis added):

> It is finally to be stressed that these regulations are only temporary, applying (lit. being imposed only until the time of the new order. It is clear from what he has already written that our author regards that new order as **already existing**. The time of fulfillment has **already come** through the work of Christ. If this is true, then the whole levitical system and Mosaic legislation upon which it rests has **come to an end**. This conclusion is indeed inescapable given the conclusions drawn in 8:13 he Old covenant stipulations are displaced when the new covenant with its new order comes into existence **The new era, the time of reformation and fulfillment, has arrived.**

II Peter & the Transformation of Christ

Don asked that I respond to his argument about the transfiguration. I consider this one of his weaker arguments and was not going to bother answering it. However, since I have a little space left here at the end, I will answer it briefly (we had agreed to a 14 page limit; Don took 17, so I suppose I am entitled to do the same).

74

Don argues that Peter appeals to the transfiguration of Christ as proof of his imminent return. For we have not followed cunningly devised fables, when we made know unto the power and coming of our Lord Jesus Christ, but were eyewitnesses of his majesty; etc (II Pet. 1:16-18). Don argues that the transfiguration is, therefore, a vision of the second coming. But as Moses and Elijah appeared with Jesus on the mount, the transfiguration is also a vision of the end of the Mosaic Covenant. Don thus concludes, if the Mosaic Covenant was abrogated at the cross, as Kurt claims, then *the Transfiguration should have been a vision of the cross*. But, the Transfiguration was patently not a vision of the cross."

Dear reader, do you see the second coming in the transfiguration? Do you see Jerusalem besieged, or the legions of Vespasian and Titus? Do you see the temple burning? What about the image in Nebuchadnezzar's dream? Do you see Christ striking Rome in the year of Four Emperors? What about the destruction of the fourth beast of Daniel, or the beast of Revelation 13? Do you see any of this in the transfiguration of Christ? No, of course you don't. These are the things that we are taught by scripture that the second coming consisted in. Yet, none of them are in the transfiguration, not even one. But the cross that Don says is not there…look again!

"And, behold, there talked with him two men, which were Moses and Elias: who appeared in glory, and spake of his decease which he should accomplish at Jerusalem."

There it is! Don says that the transfiguration is about the end of the Mosaic covenant and that it should therefore be impressed with images of that event. For Don, that means the second coming. But is the second coming anywhere in the transfiguration? No, of course not. Is the cross present, yes! **They spake of Jesus' decease which he should accomplish at Jerusalem.** Jesus was going to Jerusalem to die upon a Roman cross.

At the cross, the Savior bore our iniquity.
At the cross, God heaped upon him the sins of the world.
At the cross, the redeeming blood the Lamb was shed.
At the cross, the debt of sin was paid and blotted out.
At the cross, the handwriting of ordinances that was against us was taken out of the way.
At the cross, Jesus triumphed over the law.
At the cross, the law was fulfilled.
At the cross, Jesus cried out "It is finished!"
At the cross, the veil was rent in twain.

75

At the cross, not AD 70! The cross, YES, AD 70, NO!

Conclusion

Don cannot produce a single commentator who agrees that Isa. 27:7-11 refers to AD 70.

- Don cannot produce a single verse that plainly states or teaches the saints were under the debt of sin from and after the cross.
- Don cannot produce a single verse that plainly states or teaches the law was valid, binding, and obligatory until AD 70.
- Don cannot produce a single verse that plainly states or teaches that the saints were obligated to keep the law until AD 70.
- Don cannot produce a single verse that plainly states or teaches justification occurred in AD 70.

Don needs to concede the debate. Don is a great arguer, but the verses just are not there. Don should renounce "Covenant Eschatology" as a cross-denying doctrine that has served as a font and source of Universalism among Preterists. I did it; he can too.

PRESTON - V - SIMMONS DEBATE

SUBJECT:
THE PERFECTION OF SALVATION
AND PASSING OF THE OLD COVENANT

PRESTON'S THIRD (FINAL) AFFIRMATIVE

The discerning readers of this debate are aware of what Kurt is consistently doing. He virtually ignores every argument that I make (he did say a few words this time, and I will refute his arguments below) but then demands that I respond to him. He ignores my questions and yet, asks questions of me, asking that I respond. Then, my friend says he is under no obligation to respond to *anything* I say! Wow!

Kurt signed his name to rules of conduct that specifically said: "Each man agrees that no material or arguments shall be presented that is not directly relevant to the affirmation or negation of his or the other man's position.

Each man agrees to answer the other man's arguments directly, without obfuscation or evasion, to the full extent of their ability and knowledge."

Kurt, how can you claim that you have no obligation to respond to anything I say when _you gave your word of honor_ to respond to my arguments and to answer my questions? Are you saying that you have no obligation to keep your word?

Kurt's Disparagement of the Use of Logic

It was stunning to see my friend use almost a full page of text *to denigrate the use of logic*. He ridiculed my use of syllogisms, but of course, he later tried (again he failed) to offer a syllogism to present his case! He tells us we should beware of the "if- then" (*modus tollens*) form of argument. Hmm, Jesus and Paul seemed to like that form of logic and think it effective! Yet, Kurt tells us that we need to be wary of anyone having to appeal to this form of argumentation.

My supposed misrepresentations of Kurt's positions

I made the statement that, "Kurt claims that Romans 11:26f predicts the salvation of individual Jews, via obedience to the gospel, throughout the entirety of the endless Christian age."

Kurt responds: "*I have never said any such thing!* His claim is totally false."

Yet, Kurt proceeds to say: "Together, believing Jews and Gentiles constitute "true Israel.""... "Are people still being grafted into the tree, saved and sanctified by the "Root of Jesse"? Of course they are! Will true Israel ever

77

cease to exist? No, of course not. As long as time continues."

So, Kurt says that believing *Jews* and Gentiles constitute the salvation of all Israel– throughout the entirety of the Christian age.

Kurt, just how did you **not** say that the salvation of all Israel does not at least include *the conversion of Jews throughout the entirety of the endless Christian age?* While you did say, "all Israel" includes Gentiles, *you most assuredly did include believing Jews, didn't you!* Thus, I did not misrepresent your position. You do believe that Romans 11 speaks of the conversion of individuals (both Jew and Gentile) throughout the Christian age.

Kurt's position violates my argument on Romans 9, which Kurt dismissed, *with no proof whatsoever*. Paul, speaking of the salvation of the remnant, which is what he is discussing in Romans 11, says *the Lord would make a short work of that salvific work*. That means that the salvation of Romans 11:25f cannot speak of the salvation of individuals (Jews or Gentiles) throughout the entirety of the endless Christian age. What did Kurt say in response?

Kurt says: "I agree with Don that the "short work" in Rom. 9:27-29 refers to national Israel. God gave the nation a 40 year grace period in which to obey the gospel, and then destroyed the nation for rejecting the Messiah and clinging to the law. However, I deny that Israel in Rom. 11:26 ("so all Israel shall be saved") refers to national Israel."

What is Kurt's *evidence* for changing the definition of Israel in 11:26 from the definition used consistently in Romans 9-11? *He offers not a syllable of evidence.* So, my argument stands.

The Second "Misrepresentation": Entrance Into the MHP

I inadvertently misrepresented Kurt by saying that he says man could enter the MHP before AD 70, so I apologize for this. I evidently misunderstood what my friend was saying. However, my friend's position on this issue is still self contradictory.

He tells us that when the veil of the temple was rent while Jesus was on the cross, that this meant: "That the way was *now open* and the atonement COMPLETE (Matt. 27:51). (Matthew 27:51 says not a word about the atonement being complete, dkp). Kurt adds...

A.) "The Hebrew writer thus urges Christians to ENTER the presence of God within the Most Holy Place – before AD 70! (Heb. 10:19-22; *cf.* 6:19)."

B.) "The legal barrier separating men from God was totally removed in the cross."

C.) "I said the HEBREW WRITER URGES Christians to ENTER! "Having therefore, brethren, boldness to enter into the holiest by the blood of Jesus" (Heb. 10:19). BOLDNESS TO ENTER! It is not I, but the HEBREW

WRITER who told the saints to enter in!.."

Although Kurt is adamant that the saints **did not** in fact enter the MHP, I think the readers can see why I said what I did about Kurt believing that the saints *could* enter the MHP before AD 70.

Now, of course the Hebrews author urged the saints to enter! **But when could they enter, my friend?** If the Hebrews author urged them to enter, but they could not enter until AD 70 as you (and I!) affirm, *this is prima facie proof that* Torah remained valid, that the atonement was not perfected **until AD 70.** Christ had initiated the work of salvation, but would perfect it at his parousia. Kurt's claim that I know (but just won't admit) that the saints were objectively perfected before AD 70 is a mere debater's tactic. Kurt's own position that the saints could not actually enter the MHP until AD 70 is what proves that Christ had initiated the atonement, but did not perfect it at the cross.

The only thing, that prevented man from entering the MHP was *sin, and by extension, Torah because of its inability to forgive sin (Hebrews 9:6-10).* Kurt cannot deny this. **So, Kurt, if the separating barrier– sin and Torah-- was "completely removed" what** *prevented* **them from entering until AD 70?** I have repeatedly challenged my friend to answer this question, but he has **adamantly refused.** Why? Because the correct answer destroys his rejection of Covenant Eschatology. His words about Christ "leading captivity captive" are moot in light of this!

Now, consider again Revelation 15:8– There could be no entrance into the MHP until God's wrath was completed on Jerusalem. So, please watch.

Kurt tells us that the destruction of Jerusalem had *nothing, **whatsoever***, to do with man's spiritual justification. He says AD 70 had nothing to do with the passing of Torah and that Torah– which prevented man from entering the MHP due to its inability to forgiven– was removed at the cross.

But consider Luke 16, a text Kurt appeals to for his Hadean doctrine. There was a great gulf between Abraham and the lost. There was also, undeniably, a separation between Abraham and the MHP. **Abraham and the righteous were not in heaven!** My friend agrees with this.
But, according to Kurt, at the cross, the atonement was perfected, the separating barrier was "completely removed." Abraham and the righteous must have entered heaven, right?
No. They still don't get to enter the MHP. "Why?," they ask. They are told

that God must first destroy Jerusalem. They ask: "What does that have to do with us entering heaven?" "Nothing! The fall of Jerusalem is totally irrelevant to your entrance into heaven" they are told. "Then why can't we enter? **Why do we have to wait for God to judge Jerusalem if that has nothing to do with our entrance into heaven?**" they ask.

This is clearly an imaginary situation, but, it is based on my friend's current theological claims. So, Kurt, *we would truly and sincerely appreciate it* if you would answer that question. I think you owe it to the readers of this debate to candidly answer, without evasion, as you promised to do.

What was the relationship between the judgment of Jerusalem and entrance into the MHP, given the indisputable fact that **the only thing** that prevented man from entering the MHP was sin and Torah?

The combination of Hebrews 9 and Revelation 15 stands as an impenetrable wall against Kurt's rejection of Covenant Eschatology. He cannot explain why the saints could not enter the MHP until the supposedly irrelevant judgment of Jerusalem, although Hebrews 9 unequivocally posits entrance into the MHP at the end of that Old Covenant system. These are synchronous events, and Kurt's objections cannot overthrow these truths. Daniel 12 proves this beyond dispute and we will examine that just below. But first...

I must insert this significant thought: Kurt says the removal of Torah had nothing to do with man's justification, that salvation is simply the application of grace: "Grace overcomes law! Paul places grace at the cross; the idea that the law had to be removed is totally foreign to Paul's soteriology (theology of salvation). The grace inherent in Christ's cross *triumphs* over sin and the law."

You simply must catch the power of what I am about to ask Kurt. You will want to eagerly anticipate his response.

Kurt winds up arguing ***that removal of Torah was essential for man's justification after all!*** He says, "Grace triumphs over Law." The Law was removed at the cross (KS). "The grace inherent in Christ's cross triumphs over sin and the law." Do you see what he has done? ***He has affirmed that removal of Torah was essential for the entrance of Grace!***

Here is the key question: If the removal of Torah was irrelevant for the entrance of grace then ***why did Christ die to remove Torah and apply grace?*** My friend, you say that removal of Torah was irrelevant to salvation, so, ***why did Christ have to die on the cross and take away Torah, for grace to triumph over Torah?*** Furthermore...

Kurt incredibly says: "the idea that the law had to be removed is totally foreign to Paul's soteriology (theology of salvation)." This is patently false.

Torah was the ministration of death (2 Corinthians 3:6f). Did the deliverance from the ministration of death, to the ministration of life have *nothing* to do with Paul's soteriology?

Paul said Torah could not deliver from the law of sin and death (Romans 8:1-3). He said Christ does deliver from that law! Did the deliverance from the law of sin and death have nothing to with forgiveness?

Torah could not give life or righteousness (Galatians 3:20-21). Did deliverance from that law, to the covenant that gives life and righteousness have nothing to do with salvation?

Paul said those under Torah were under "the curse" (Galatians 2-3). Did deliverance from that curse had nothing to do with redemption?

There was no forgiveness under Torah. There would be forgiveness *when Torah ended at the time of reformation*. **Is forgiveness related to soteriology?**

There was no entrance into the MHP under Torah; there would be entrance into the MHP at the end of Torah, the time of reformation. *Is entrance into the MHP related to salvation?*

Hebrews 9 is Covenant Eschatology, anyway you want to look at it! Torah had to end in order for forgiveness, entrance into the MHP and life to become realities! End of Torah = Covenant Eschatology; End of Torah = Salvation! My affirmative is fully established. **Undeniably, deliverance from Torah had *everything* to do with salvation.** Now to Daniel 12.

At the close of my last, I posed the following: "What was "the ***power*** of the holy people" mentioned in Daniel 12:7? Please, do not ignore this. Clearly define Israel's ***power***." In spite of my appeal, Kurt refused to answer. Why? It is because this single argument establishes *Covenant Eschatology*. So...

What was the ***power*** of the holy people? **Answer**: *It was their covenant with God.* There is no other answer! Israel's power was not their military, their temple, priesthood or sacrifices. All of those were symbols of their "power." So, follow my argument:

> **The power of the holy people (i.e. Old Covenant Israel), was her covenant with God, i.e. Torah. This is indisputable.**
> **The power of the holy people (Israel's covenant with God) would be shattered at the time of the resurrection (Daniel 12:7). This is irrefutable.**
> **The resurrection occurred in AD 70 (Kurt Simmons).**
> **Therefore, Israel's covenant with God, i.e. Torah remained until the resurrection in AD 70.**

Israel's *only power* was her covenant with God. That power of the holy people would endure until it was shattered. The power of the holy people was shattered *in AD 70*, (*not the cross*) when, as Kurt affirms, the resurrection occurred.

This argument proves irrefutably that Torah remained valid until AD 70. This is why Kurt refused to address it.

Kurt cites Delitzsch: "The temple service, though to continue it may be a few years longer in **outward** splendour, is only a bed of state, on which a **lifeless corpse** is lying."

So, Kurt says from the Cross until AD 70, the Torah was a "lifeless corpse." But, how could a *lifeless corpse* have any "*power*" to prevent entrance into the MHP? Paul said in Hebrews 9 that the negative power of Torah was such (in its failure to provide forgiveness) that as long as it stood, no one could enter the MHP! Kurt agrees that the saints could not enter the MHP until AD 70.

By the way, Hebrews 8:13 does not say, or imply that it was the *outward form* of the covenant that was ready to pass. Rather it says, "In that he says 'a new covenant,' He has made the first (the first *covenant*, DKP) obsolete. Now what is growing old (the first covenant, DKP) is ready to pass away." *Hasn't a dead corpse already "passed away?"* The contrast is not between *external forms* of the covenant versus the covenant. It was the Old Covenant that was growing old, it was *the Old Covenant* that was nigh unto passing. (Note that Kurt ignored my argument on Galatians 4). And remember that this has been, until very recently at least, Kurt's position. Commenting on Revelation 18:4 and the impending judgment of Jerusalem, he says– "The old and tattered mantel of Moses could not be patched with material from the garment of Christ; the Mosaic law was grown old; God would fold it up and it would be changed (future tense, dkp) (Hebrews 1:10-12; 8:13; 12:26-28)" (*Consummation*, p. 344).

Okay, so, if Torah no longer had any negative power to prevent entrance into the MHP, since it was *a dead corpse*, Kurt, but if, as you say, the saints could not actually enter the MHP until AD 70, **why** could the saints not enter the MHP? **Paul said** it was Torah that prevented entrance. You say Torah was *now powerless* to prevent entrance. Yet, you say that the saints could still not enter the MHP! We need to know why! What "negative power" still prevented the saints from entering the MHP until AD 70? Will you answer? Here is my argument, again, that Kurt has– and undoubtedly will again– ignored.

As long as Torah–the power of the holy people-- stood binding, there could be no access to the MHP (Hebrews 9:6f).

There was no access to the MHP until AD 70– Kurt Simmons. Therefore, Torah–the power of the holy people-- stood binding until AD 70.

So, Daniel 12 is definitive proof that Torah remained valid until AD 70, the time of the resurrection. The time of the resurrection is when the saints could enter the MHP.

HEBREWS 9, TORAH, REMISSION OF SIN, HADES AND THE MOST HOLY PLACE

"And for this reason He is the Mediator of the new covenant, by means of death, for the redemption of the transgressions under the first covenant, that those who are called may receive the promise of the eternal inheritance." (Hebrews 9:15).

I offered the following based on Hebrews 9– but of course, **Kurt ignored it:** Christ died for the remission (redemption) of sins committed under Torah. *I affirm this!* The Cross was *for* redemption! It does not, however, say that redemption occurred _**at**_ the Cross. Follow closely:

Those under the first covenant were dead Old Covenant saints that Jesus died to give forgiveness.
But, **remember that Kurt wanted to affirm _in this debate_ that the resurrection was *exclusively* the entrance of the souls in Hades into the MHP, i.e. *the dead Old Covenant saints!***
But, if the dead OT saints could not enter the MHP until AD 70, then it is undeniably true that they did not yet have the benefits of Christ's atonement applied to them. And Kurt himself has told us that this is the reason they could not enter the MHP. _**Is this true or false, Kurt?**_ You have refused to answer this, but, you really, *really* need to answer it.

If, as my friend affirms, the atonement was perfected at the cross, then those dead OT saints _**should have**_ entered the MHP at the moment of the Cross, or perhaps Christ's ascension when he "led captivity captive." But remember that Kurt wanted to affirm *in this debate* –that the dead saints could not enter the MHP until AD 70, **and this because the saints did not have the benefits of Christ's atoning blood until the resurrection– in AD 70.** And, he says this is still his view.
But, if the saints were objectively forgiven prior to AD 70, then the benefits of Christ's atonement were applied, and there was no reason to wait for the destruction of Jerusalem– _an event totally unrelated to their forgiveness or the atonement_ in order to enter the MHP! Kurt has not

breathed on this issue! Furthermore, I predict that he won't.

Kurt, do you now affirm that the dead saints received the full benefits of the atonement prior to the resurrection? Yes or No? Please, I ask that you honor the rules that you signed, to answer my questions directly, without evasion or obfuscation.

By still affirming that the saints could not enter the MHP prior to AD 70, Kurt is reaffirming that the saints did not have the benefits of Christ's atoning blood until the resurrection– *in AD 70! Thus, per Kurt's own admission, the "perfection" of the dead saints and by logical extension the living saints, as expressed in Hebrews 12, was proleptic (stated as a past fact, although still future).*

Hebrews 11:40 relates to this issue. According to Paul, the OT saints could not enter into the "better resurrection" (Hebrews 11:35f) without the NT saints, and, the NT saints could not enter before the dead saints (1 Thessalonians 4:15f)! *In other words, OT and NT saints would enter into the MHP at the same time!* So, the proposition that Kurt wanted to affirm in this debate, that the dead saints would enter the MHP in AD 70, proves my proposition, and destroys Kurt's! **Of course, Kurt ignored this argument**.

Kurt says that AD 70 had no redemptive significance and the saints were forgiven from the cross onward. Yet, he says that the saints could enter the MHP until AD 70. But **he refuses to tell us why those "perfected" saints could not enter until the totally irrelevant AD 70 event**. Of course, Hebrews 9 answers the question-- Jesus was coming (in AD 70) to bring salvation. *He was coming to bring man into the MHP!* He was coming- Kurt now agreeing– to perfect the time of reformation.

THE TIME OF REFORMATION
My friend ignored the fact that he was in violation of the "Law of the Excluded Middle" in his flawed syllogism on the passing of Torah and the time of reformation. He amended that syllogism, but it still contained the same **anachronistic** fallacy. Let me restate the case.
As long as Torah remained valid, there could be no entrance into the MHP.
There was no entrance into the MHP until AD 70. Kurt agrees.
Therefore, Torah remained valid until AD 70.
Stated another way, if there was no access to the MHP, then Torah was still binding. Kurt agrees that there was no access to the MHP until AD 70. Therefore, Torah remained binding until AD 70.

84

Torah would remain valid until "the time of reformation" **when man could enter the MHP**.

Kurt argues– **and I agree**– that the time of reformation was **initiated at the cross, but perfected at the parousia.** He says: "When the gifts of the Spirit ceased, *the time of reformation was complete and not before.*" (My emp, dkp) Thank you, my friend, **that is precisely my point!** But this admission nullifies Kurt's claim that I "gave away the debate" when I said that *in and through the cross*, "grace triumphed over law." My argument was, and is, that Christ initiated the work of grace at the cross, and consummated it at the parousia. This is precisely what Kurt's argument demands!

If the time of reformation fully arrived at the cross then man should have been able to enter the MHP from the cross onward. Kurt argues that Torah was removed and grace fully applied there. Yet, Kurt admits that no one could enter the MHP until AD 70. And now he admits that the time of reformation was not completed until the charismata ended– in AD 70! This means that Christ had *initiated* the work of reformation, (grace!) the Spirit *continued* that work, and Christ *perfected* it at the parousia (Acts 3:23f- "The restoration of all things")! Just as I have taught consistently, entrance into the MHP– **at the end of Torah**– was at the time of reformation: "When the gifts of the Spirit ceased, the time of reformation was complete and not before."

Please, Catch the power of this: *Kurt admits that there was no entrance into the MHP at the initiation of the reformation, i.e. at the cross. Entrance came only when the time of reformation– the work of grace– was complete, at the parousia.* This is my view. This is Covenant Eschatology. And folks, this is not just "good argumentation," although it is *that!* This is logically inescapable, irrefutable fact.

So, man could only enter the MHP in AD 70 (KS), But, man could not enter the MHP while Torah remained valid. **Torah would remain valid until man could enter the MHP at the time of reformation**. Thus, Torah ended when the time of reformation was completed, and man could enter the MHP, in AD 70.

Kurt has surrendered his objection to the initiation of grace, salvation and covenant transition. He has unwittingly affirmed Covenant Eschatology. So, *once again*:

> **There could be no access to the MHP as long as Torah remained binding (Hebrews 9).**
> **But, man could not enter the MHP until AD 70 (Kurt Simmons).**
> **Therefore, Torah remained binding until AD 70.**

I ask that the readers of this debate focus on this singular argument. Kurt cannot ignore it. Nor can he effectively negate it. My affirmative is established on this one argument, especially in conjunction with the argument above on Daniel 9 and the power of the holy people. **This is Covenant Eschatology confirmed**.

MY TRANSFIGURATION ARGUMENT

Kurt says my argument on the Transfiguration is my weakest argument. But, he denies the inspired text.

Kurt denies that the Transfiguration was a vision of Christ's second coming. What was his evidence? ***He did not give us a word of exegesis*** of 2 Peter 1, to justify his rejection of the Transfiguration as a vision of the parousia! *Not one word.* Perhaps its because he feels that proper exegesis of 2 Peter 1 is "a distraction at best"?

I must take note of this: In his vain attempt to negate my arguments on Isaiah 27 Kurt said repeatedly (even presenting me with another box!), that not one commentator applied Isaiah 27 to AD 70. Kurt should re-think this!

From the very beginning of Christian commentary, **the Transfiguration has been viewed as a vision of the parousia, *based on 2 Peter 1*! It is all but impossible to find an exception!**

I have been researching the Transfiguration for years now, and I can say with total confidence that this is unequivocally true. **So, my friend, "all the commentators" refute your claim that the Transfiguration was not a vision of the second coming**. The fact that Jesus, Moses and Elijah discussed Jesus' death does not negate this. You cannot use their discussion to deny Peter's words. My argument stands:

The Transfiguration was a vision of the Second Coming of Christ (2 Peter 1:16f).

But, the Transfiguration was a vision of the end of the Mosaic Covenant and the establishment of the New Covenant of Christ.

Therefore, the end of the Mosaic Covenant was at the Second Coming of Christ.

This argument alone is a total refutation of Kurt's position, for it posits the passing of Torah, not at the Cross, but at the parousia. He cannot dismiss it by refusing to properly exegete 2 Peter 1, or by simply calling it a weak argument.

ISAIAH 27

Some of my friend's statements are simply *staggering*. He says that this debate is "not about the proper exegesis of Isaiah 25-27. Issues of Isaiah 27:7-11 are a distraction at best."

So... In Romans 11 Paul discusses the taking away of Israel' sin at the coming of the Lord. In justification for his doctrine, he cites Isaiah 27:9f and Isaiah 59 as the source of his expectation. Yet, my friend says that "proper exegesis of Isaiah 27 (and Isaiah 59), "are a distraction at best."

So, according to Kurt, we need not be concerned with the proper exegesis of the verses that gave rise to Paul's doctrine of the salvation of Israel! If we do not need to be concerned with the proper exegesis of Isaiah 27 / 59, then we most assuredly don't need to be concerned with the proper exegesis of Romans 11:25-27. Kurt, it is your responsibility to **prove** that a proper exegesis of Isaiah is irrelevant and a distraction. Your claim is null and void without some **proof**, which you have utterly failed to produce.

Kurt's Objections to Isaiah 27

Kurt is probably hoping the reader will have forgotten what I had written about Isaiah 27 and 59 in my first affirmative, but, I have not forgotten. Kurt's objection to Isaiah 27 takes three forms:

1.) **Just because he says so**, Isaiah 27 is irrelevant to any discussion of Romans 11. This is specious.

2.) Isaiah 27 has no Messianic application, *whatsoever*! He says it refers *exclusively* to the Assyrian invasion of the 8th Century BC.

3.) Isaiah 27 cannot even be typological in meaning: Kurt asked: "What about typological significance? Could there be a double meaning so that the "purging of Jacob's iniquity" looks ahead typologically to AD 70 and redemptive salvation from sin? NOT A CHANCE!" (His emp.)

Of course, **just last year**, in his *Sword and Plow*, when objecting to my position on Romans 11 / Isaiah 27, Kurt said: "We do not disallow the possibility that there is a *plenior sensus (fuller meaning, DKP)*, to Isaiah 26:21 that may look beyond its historical setting to Christ's second coming." Realizing the *fatal nature of this admission*, Kurt has now completely reversed himself.

So, **just last year** Kurt said that Isaiah 27 could apply to both the Cross and AD 70. But now, he denies that it speaks of either one! It is exclusively the Assyrian invasion! That is three, radically different positions on the same text, within a matter of months! No wonder my friend speaks disparagingly of logic and proper exegesis!

And now, Kurt desperately claims that I have not: "established ANY CONNECTION between Rom. 11:25-27 and Isa. 26. NONE! The same is true of Isaiah 59." This is *astounding*. **Just last September, (2009)** in the Sword and Plow, **Kurt wrote**: "In Romans 11:26, 27, Paul blends two passages from Isaiah together into one. He quotes Isa. 59: 20, 21, then follows up with Isa. 27:9."

87

Kurt, do you remember that? Of course, that admission is fatal to your new theology so you now claim there is no connection between Romans 11 and Isaiah 27 / 59. *But, what is your proof, my friend?* You have given none, because you can give none.

Also, Kurt just appealed to "all the commentators." But, Kurt, *"all the commentators" agree* that Paul cites Isaiah 27/59–**just as you admitted**! You have **no support** for rejecting the connection. *The only "evidence" you have is your preconceived, new theology that violates the text.*

Isaiah 59

Kurt says Isaiah 59 is not relevant to our study. What is his proof? **He offered none!**

I offered the following argument on Isaiah 59:

The coming of the Lord for the salvation of Israel in Romans 11:26-27 is the coming of the Lord predicted in Isaiah 59. Remember, last September, Kurt agreed that Paul quoted Isaiah 59.

But, the coming of the Lord predicted in Isaiah 59 is the coming of the Lord in judgment of Israel for shedding innocent blood. This is irrefutable.

Therefore, the coming of the Lord in Romans 11:26-27 is the coming of the Lord in judgment of Israel for shedding innocent blood. This is inescapable.

Isaiah 59 presents the identical hermeneutical challenge as Isaiah 26-27. Kurt must explain why Paul cites– **as Kurt admitted**-- two OT prophecies of the coming of Christ in judgment of Israel for shedding innocent blood, when in fact, according to Kurt, those prophecies had no Messianic application whatsoever, and, Paul was not discussing *in any way* Christ's judgment coming. Kurt has not touched this problem, top, side or bottom. *And, I predict he won't*. Kurt's theological position has no explanation for Paul's use of Isaiah 27 and 59. And his denial of a connection is completely untenable.

THE POWER OF AN ABROGATED COVENANT

I feel confident that the readers of this exchange were stunned to discover from Kurt that provisions of a covenant are still binding after a covenant has been abrogated! Kurt's answer was nothing but smoke and obfuscation. Furthermore, Kurt knows full well that his claims would not stand up in a true court of law for even one moment!

Kurt, here is a challenge for you: Find some law on the books of American jurisprudence from, let's say, the early 60s, that provided prison time or severe financial penalties for violation.

Make sure, for the experiment sake, that the **courts have struck down and abrogated that law.**

Now, my friend, what we want you to do is find some one in violation of that nullified law, and have them arrested, tried, convicted and imprisoned for violation of that abrogated law! Then show us where that imprisonment stood up in appeals court.

My friend, you are a lawyer. Tell us what would happen if you or anyone else, did this? We will very eagerly await your answer, but, of course, you will not answer this candidly. You can't, for to answer this forthrightly, without obfuscation, is to surrender your new theology.

Kurt claimed: "Don, provisions of wrath recited in Leviticus are not proof the covenant is still valid when wrath is poured out." I had noted the following: "In his comments on Revelation 15:8, Kurt says: "The angels emerge from the tabernacle of the testimony with *the covenantal curses and plagues*" (*Consummation*, 292, my emphasis). As he comments on the judgment of Babylon he says: "The threefold judgments of death (pestilence) mourning, and famine were foretold by Moses: And I will bring a sword upon you, *that shall avenge the quarrel of my covenant*: and when ye are gathered within your cities, I will send the pestilence among you...(Leviticus 26:25, 26, 29-32)."

Now watch. *Leviticus says* that the punishments– the punishments described in Revelation that were about to come on Jerusalem in AD 70– would be God's "covenant quarrel" with Israel. The judgment actions would be "covenantal curses" (KS). Yet, according to Kurt, *none of this means Torah was still binding!* In other words, God was going to dredge up dead curses from the dead covenant (forty years dead!), and apply those dead covenant curses on Jerusalem!

Incredibly, Kurt argues: "If the latter (a king under covenant with another king, dkp) breaks the terms of the covenant, the former is certainly entitled to come and lay siege to the other kingdom. His making war in no way depends upon the continuing validity of the covenant. Just the opposite, it is because it is broken that the latter is entitled to make war!"

This is obfuscation and Kurt well knows it. The trouble is, he claims that I agree with his argument. He quotes me, but, he has badly misused my statements. Here is what he quoted: "Here is the principle that that any destruction of Israel was proof that she was out of covenant relationship with Jehovah" (*Like Father, Like Son*, p. 175).

Kurt wants to make me out to say that any violation of the covenant meant that the covenant was abrogated. I have never taught this. To the contrary, it meant that Israel, being judged, was being brought "under the bond of the covenant" (Ezekiel 20:37). The application of the covenant curses meant that

Israel had broken the covenant, (thus, she lost the ***covenant blessings***). **But, she was still under the covenant and subject to its curses!** My friend's attempt to manipulate my words demonstrates his desperation to find some semblance of support for his failed argument.

JESUS' TWO-FOLD ENTRANCE INTO THE MHP
Kurt made a historically unprecedented argument about Christ entering the MHP twice. You must catch that! Kurt, where are the commentators that agree with you assessment of Christ entering the MHP twice, *legally piercing the veil*, and then at the ascension? Where are they my friend?

Kurt claims that I misrepresented him by saying that this means Jesus must have entered at his death. So, Kurt says: "We believe that the typology of sprinkling the blood before the Mercy Seat was fulfilled when Jesus died." And he says Jesus "legally pierced the veil." He wound up saying what I said he did! You can't say he pierced the veil and sprinkled his blood on the mercy seat without saying he entered the MHP! This is semantic sophistry. **Where was the mercy seat, Kurt?** If Jesus offered his blood on (or before) the mercy seat, where did he have to be? **Not outside the MHP!** And your claim about piercing the *legal veil* falls in light of Hebrews 6:20– Christ *actually*, not just in some vague legal sense, *Christ actually entered.*
Kurt has Jesus somehow offering his blood before the mercy-seat, **while he was on the cross**, but then, he has Jesus actually entering the MHP (*where the mercy seat was!*) at his ascension.

Kurt's attempt to deflect my argument by saying that Jesus died "a sinner's death," and thus had to enter the MHP twice (but of course the first time he did not actually enter!) is specious. As I noted, ***the only reason*** the High Priest had to enter the MHP twice was **because he had to offer two sacrifices, one for his own sins, the other for the sins of the people.** Thus, if Jesus entered the MHP twice– **either legally or actually– he had to offer two sacrifices, and he had to offer a sacrifice for his own sin!** However, Hebrews 9:12 proves that Christ entered the MHP *once*. Kurt says twice. Jesus made one sacrifice, not two, and his entrance into the MHP – and his return– was essential for the fulfilling of the typological actions of the atonement. Kurt's **unprecedented argument** is simply wrong.

THE SPIRIT AS THE GUARANTEE OF REDEMPTION
I want to repeat an argument from my last. Kurt completely ignored it. This issue is critical and destructive to Kurt's position.
The promise of the Spirit was made to Israel *to raise her from the dead* (Ezekiel 37:10-14).

This "death" from which Israel was to be raised was not physical death, but *covenantal death* (Isaiah 24:4f; Hosea 5-6; 13:1-2). Living people were called *dead*, but they continued to "sin more and more" (Hosea 13:1-2). Biologically dead people cannot do this!

This is *spiritual death*- alienation from God as a result of sin (Isaiah 59:1-2-- The sin that needed to be removed at the coming of the Lord, Isaiah 59:20f-- Romans 11!). Sin brought death. Thus, forgiveness would bring resurrection (cf. Acts 26:17-18)!

This resurrection, *guaranteed by the Spirit*, would be Israel's salvation (Isaiah 25:8-9). This is the resurrection promise of 1 Corinthians 15 when sin, *the sting of death*, would be overcome (1 Corinthians 15:54-56– *Romans 11:26-27)*. In other words:

1 Corinthians 15 foretold the resurrection (when sin would be put away, v. 55-56), predicted by Isaiah 25.
The resurrection of Isaiah 25 is the resurrection of Isaiah 26-27 (and thus, Romans 11:26-27), which would occur at the coming of the Lord in judgment of Israel for shedding innocent blood. (Kurt, should we be concerned with the proper exegesis of Isaiah 25, since it is the source of Paul's resurrection doctrine)?
But, the coming of the Lord -- at the resurrection to put away sin-- of Isaiah 25-27 / 1 Corinthians 15-- would be the coming of the Lord in judgment of Israel for shedding innocent blood.
Therefore, the coming of the Lord of Romans 11 to take away Israel's sin-- to bring her salvation-- is the coming of the Lord at the time of the resurrection, in judgment of Israel for shedding innocent blood, i.e. AD 70.

I want to ask the reader to focus on this argument, and ask yourself why Kurt would ignore it. He ignored it *because he cannot answer it,* and because it *completely nullifies his entire (new) theology.*

The resurrection of 1 Corinthians 15 is the resurrection foretold in Isaiah 25-27.
The resurrection of Isaiah 25-27 is the coming of the Lord *for the salvation of Israel* in Romans 11.
Therefore, the coming of the Lord for the salvation of Israel in Romans 11 is the time of the coming of the Lord for the resurrection (the salvation of Israel), in 1 Corinthians 15–which Kurt posits in AD 70!

Let me offer more:
The resurrection is when sin, the sting of death was to be overcome, (1 Corinthians 15:54-56).

The miraculous gifts of the Spirit were the guarantee of that resurrection (2 Corinthians 5:5; Ephesians 1:13).
Therefore, the miraculous gifts of the Spirit *were the guarantee of the final victory over sin!*

Let me offer another related affirmative as follow up:
The last enemy to be destroyed was death (Kurt agrees).
But, sin produced death (Romans 6:23; "the Law of sin and death).
The last enemy would be destroyed at the resurrection in AD 70 (Kurt agrees).
Thus, sin, which produced death, would be destroyed (for those "in Christ," and the power of his resurrection) at the resurrection in AD 70.

So, again, since the charismata was the guarantee of the resurrection, and since the resurrection is when sin, the sting of death would, of necessity, be overcome, it therefore follows that the charismata were the guarantee of the final victory over sin!

Kurt ignored all of this, but it proves, *prima facie* that while the cross was the power for the putting away of sin, that the work of the cross was not completed until the resurrection in AD 70. It proves that AD 70 was redemptively *critical*.

Since the Spirit was the guarantee of the resurrection, (in AD 70 per KS!), the time when sin, the sting of death would be overcome, it therefore follows that the coming of the Lord to put away sin in Romans 11:26f was the time of the resurrection in AD 70.

Kurt appeals to the fact that Christ would appear the second time "apart from sin" for salvation, and claims that this proves that the atonement was already completed before the parousia. It proves no such thing.

"Apart from sin" means that he would not make *any further sacrifice for sin. That part* of the atonement process was finished. He had already offered himself as sacrifice, now, he would return *to consummate the atonement process*. This is what Hebrews 9:28-10:1f affirms (which, again, **Kurt ignored**). The author said Christ had to appear the second time "*for* the Law, having a shadow of good things to come." I have repeatedly asked Kurt to honor the present tenses, and the fact that Christ's second coming would be the fulfillment of the High Priestly actions of offering the sacrifice, entering the MHP, and then coming out, to bring salvation. Kurt has totally ignored. Instead, he has the atonement completed while Christ was on the cross– in clear violation of the typological atonement praxis.

92

And speaking of the resurrection, let me repeat my argument on Isaiah 27: The coming of the Lord in Romans is the coming of the Lord of Isaiah 26-27, which is the coming of the Lord at the *resurrection* (Isaiah 25-27). Kurt says the resurrection was in AD 70. Therefore, the coming of the Lord in Romans 11 was in AD 70. (Kurt ignored this). I made other arguments on Isaiah 27, but Kurt ignored them also.

My friend tries desperately to tell us that Isaiah 25-27– in spite of the fact that Paul appeals to these chapters– had nothing whatsoever to do with Biblical eschatology! So, again, why would Paul in his eschatological predictions, use these prophecies when per Kurt, they had *nothing to do with what Paul was predicting*!

BTW, Kurt claims that the sounding of the Trump in Matthew 24:31 had nothing to do with Isaiah 27. Well, Kurt, *virtually all commentators* who take note of the OT background of NT prophecies, tell us that Isaiah *is* the source of Matthew 24:31! Greg Beale, in his heralded, *Commentary on the New Testament Use of the Old Testament* (Grand Rapids, Baker Academic, 2007)87, says Matthew 24:31 "echoes Isaiah 27:13 with its trumpet sounding on the day of deliverance, an allusion to the ingathering of Israel." I could list *volumes* of scholars in support. And, did you notice that Kurt did not challenge me to put "even one commentary" in a box in support of this? He knows full well that the scholarly consensus is that the sounding of the Trumpet in Matthew 24:31 is taken directly from Isaiah 27:13. So, my argument stands.

SUMMARY AND CONCLUSION

Kurt lays out four points that he claims I must prove to carry my proposition on Romans 11:

- The coming referred to is the second, not first, advent of Christ. **Proven!**
- The judgment and sentence associated with sin hung over the saints until AD 70; *viz.*, the cross did not cancel sin's debt. **Proven!** I have consistently proven that *the cross is the power of forgiveness*, and **gladly accept Kurt's argument that the benefits of Christ's atonement were not applied until the resurrection in AD 70.**
- AD 70 represented the *legal* climax and termination of the Mosaic Covenant age; *viz.*, the law, including circumcision, animal sacrifices, the priesthood, dietary restrictions, etc, was valid and binding until AD 70. **Proven! Hebrews 9**– for those outside of Christ, (All blessings are "in Christ") **these stood valid until the time of reformation in AD 70. With Kurt now agreeing that the time of reformation did not fully arrive**

until AD 70, which is Covenant Eschatology!

- The judgment and sentence associated with sin were set aside in AD 70 by annulment of the law. **Proven!** I gladly accept Kurt's statement: "Christ tied the judgment to the end of the Mosaic age and the destruction of Jerusalem." (*Consummation*, 229).

I have fully proven each point.

In closing, let me urge the readers to go back and list all of my questions, and logical arguments that Kurt refused to even mention. This is revealing! If he could answer my questions and refute the arguments, he would do so with gusto! I assure you that when I am in the negative, I will not avoid Kurt's questions and arguments as he has done mine.

As I close, let me re-ask just a fraction of the questions I have asked Kurt, and all but begged him to answer. **He has ignored every one of them**. Unfortunately, I predict he will continue to do so. But of course, you the reader will be fully aware that he has done so.

If the removal of Torah was unnecessary for salvation, then *__why did Christ die to remove Torah and apply grace?__*

Is the forgiveness of sins and entrance into the MHP, *which would only come at the end of Torah*, necessary to salvation?

What was "the *__power__* of the holy people" mentioned in Daniel 12:7, that would not be broken until the resurrection in AD 70?

If Torah died at the cross, and no longer had any negative power to prevent entrance into the MHP, yet the saints did not actually enter the MHP until AD 70, *why could the saints could not enter the MHP until AD 70?*

My friend calls on me to recant Covenant Eschatology. Yet, he rejects proper exegesis, disparages logic, refuses to answer my arguments, ignores my questions. Furthermore, his own arguments and admissions affirm Covenant Eschatology! He has not given me **one good reason to reject the truth of Covenant Eschatology.**

I have, in every way, with explicit statements of scripture, with proper exegesis and hermeneutic, with valid logic, demonstrated, confirmed and proven my proposition. I now stand ready to negate Kurt's affirmative proposition.

94

A Vindication of Christ's Cross Against the
Errors of Covenant Eschatology

Simmons' Third Negative

"Be not carried about with diverse and strange doctrines." Heb. 13:9

Truth of Preterism, Falsity of Covenant Eschatology

In opening my third negative, let me state that, despite my disagreement with
Don about "Covenant Eschatology," I remain fully convinced of the truth of
Preterism. Preterism can be demonstrated by an abundance of proofs from
both the scriptures and early church fathers. Origen (AD 185–254), the most
learned and illustrious of the early fathers said:

> *We do not deny, then, that the purificatory fire and the
> destruction of the world took place in order that evil might
> be swept away, and all things be renewed; for we assert that
> we have learned these things from the sacred books of the
> prophets...And anyone who likes may convict this statement
> of falsehood, if it be not the case that the whole Jewish
> nation was overthrown within one single generation after
> Jesus had undergone these sufferings at their hands. For
> forty and two years, I think after the date of the crucifixion
> of Jesus, did the destruction of Jerusalem take place."
> Origen, Contra Celsum, IV, xxi-xxii; Ante-Nicene Fathers,
> Vol. IV, p. 505, 506.*

Origen was almost certainly a Preterist; he could not make this statement
otherwise. Another early Christian writer who was a Preterist is Eusebius of
Caesarea (AD 263–339), whose works are widely known and cited both in
and out of Preterist circles. The Preterism of these and other early Christian
writers establish Preterism as an interpretative method entitled to its place
among respected scholarship. However, Covenant Eschatology is another
thing entirely. Preterism traces its roots to the earliest history of the church
and has been present in every age since, but Covenant Eschatology is new,
whipped up by the imagination of Max King less than 40 years ago. The
Mormons started in the 1830's. The Seventh Day Adventists date from about
1840's. The Jehovah's Witnesses date from about 1887-1912. Covenant

Eschatology dates from the 1970's. The very newness of the doctrine is its own repudiation. Can Covenant Eschatology truly claim a rightful place in the "faith once delivered to the saints" when it is so totally new and unprecedented in its basic doctrines? Where was it ever heard in all of Christendom and its 2,000 years that the saints were under the law until AD 70? Where was it ever heard or taught that justification from sin was postponed until the asserted removal of the law AD 70? We find Preterism present from the very start, but Covenant Eschatology? Never! This should raise for us a warning flag, for *what is new in things Christian is invariably false.*

It is a general rule that the *one thing that makes any particular sect unique in Christendom is often the one thing that is wrong.* Seventh Day Adventists claim E.G. White was a latter day prophet and that Sabbath and dietary restrictions of the law are still binding. These are what make Adventists unique within Christendom, and it is these very things that are patently false. Jehovah's Witnesses deny the divinity of Christ, claim it is unlawful to receive blood transfusions, to celebrate birthdays or to vote. These things make them unique, and each of these is manifestly false. Covenant Eschatology claims the law was still valid after the cross, that the saints continued under bondage to sin, and were not justified until the law was allegedly removed until AD 70. These are the things that make Covenant Eschatology unique and these are the very things that make it false.

As proof of the very real danger the error of Covenant Eschatology presents, we need only look to its author, Max King. It is no secret or coincidence that King is now the teacher of a false gospel; King's "Presence Ministries" preaches Universalism by which all men are allegedly saved without *faith,* without *repentance,* without *confession,* without *baptism*, and without the *cross.* The seeds of King's error appeared early on. Jim McGuiggan commented upon King's tendency to Universalism in their debate in the early 1970's (p. 111). Consider this comment from King's debate with McGuiggan (emphasis in original):

> "The sting of death was **SIN**. But **WHAT** was the **STRENGTH** of sin? Paul said **"the Law."** The victory is obtained through God's making…a **new creation…** where sin has strength no longer. Hence, the sting of death is removed forever." (McGuiggan/King Debate, p. 98).

Notice, that at the very point where King should have said, the victory was obtained through the cross; instead the victory is attributed to removal of the law! The cross is displaced by AD 70! As King said in his later work, "*"The defeat of sin is tied to the annulment of the old aeon of law...death is abolished when the state of sin and the law are abolished*." (Max R. King, *The Cross and the Parousia of Christ*, p. 644, emphasis added). Sin is defeated by removal of the law? What?!!! What happened to the cross?!!! Notice also the latent seeds of Universalism inherent in this thought, where the asserted removal of the law disarmed the power of sin and death. *If the law condemned all men, and if the law was removed for all men, then all men are freed from condemnation of sin by the law.* Voila! Universalism! Compare King's statement with the words of Tim King, Max's son, 30 years later:

"Simply stated, man is changed because his world changed. Man is reconciled to God because he no longer lives under the rule of sin and death as determined by the Mosaic world. Through the gift of Christ he dwells in a world of righteousness and life. The issue is cosmic and corporate, not individual and limited" (Tim King, *Comprehensive Grace,* 2005).

Notice that King says *reconciliation is not individual, but cosmic and corporate, viz.,* universal. All men are under grace and "dwell in a world of righteousness and life." Notice also that the cross is totally away from King's "Comprehensive Grace" (as he calls it). Man is not saved because the cross of Christ brought grace. He does not say, "Man is reconciled because of the death, burial, and resurrection of Christ." No! Man is saved because the Mosaic law was taken away! Reconciliation did not happen at Calvary when Christ carried the debt of sin to the cross. No! Reconciliation happened when the law was supposedly removed by the destruction of Jerusalem! King's 2009 conference was entitled "One Inclusive God." A visit to his site will convince anyone that they have left Christianity and arrived at some form of new age religion and philosophy of man. I say with full sincerity that I believe Jehovah's Witnesses and Mormons are more Biblically grounded than anything you will find in King's ministry these days.

Yet, notwithstanding the obvious danger "Covenant Eschatology" presents and its *established record* of leading men into serious error and *eternal peril*, Don has clung tenaciously to it. Don once wrote, *"You cannot teach a doctrine without implications. And if the implications are dangerous, then the doctrine is dangerous."* (Elements, p. 244). Somewhat ironically, when he said this Don was writing against Universalism among Preterists! Covenant Eschatology is the very fount and source of Universalism among Preterists! How can Don possibly defend it?

Don, the Cross, and Torah's Mysterious "Negative Power"

We have repeatedly charged that Covenant Eschatology overthrows the cross of Christ. We have repeatedly stated that the cross has dropped out of Don's system of soteriology. We stated

"If the cross did not <u>triumph</u> over the law at Calvary, if man had to wait until the law was <u>removed</u> to be justified from sin, then <u>nothing</u> happened at the cross. This is the long and short of Don's teaching: nothing happened at the cross."

There could be no more serious charge leveled at the gospel preacher than to accuse him of overthrowing the cross. If there was any topic in this debate Don should have been zealous to vindicate and explain it is the accusation that Covenant Eschatology overthrows the Savior's cross. Let the reader take note that despite repeated invitations, Don has absolutely refused to give us an explanation of what happened at the cross. Why? How difficult could it be? I could do it; the reader could do it; any Christian could do it. Why won't Don? Clearly, it is because the cross and Covenant Eschatology are *mutually exclusive* systems, and to affirm the one is to deny the other. I know Don loves and honors the cross in his heart. But when the two systems are laid side by side, they cannot be reconciled. All that Christianity and the scripture normally associate with the cross, Covenant Eschatology attributes to AD 70.

Covenant Eschatology spiritualizes the resurrection and makes it equal with justification. Therefore, it cannot acknowledge that the debt of sin was extinguished ("blotted out" – Col. 2:14) at the cross, for that would not allow for a spiritualized resurrection in AD 70. Preterism simply states that the souls in Hades were received into heaven in AD 70, and therefore offers no violence to the cross. But the spiritualized resurrection of Max King and Don, which keeps man under the debt of sin until AD 70, must *relocate* justification and atonement, and to do so they must *take from the cross*. This is why Don has studiously sought to avoid discussion of the cross in this debate; he cannot credit *anything* to the cross without first taking *something* away from Covenant Eschatology. Consider the chart below: all that appears in the column under Covenant Eschatology, Christianity and scripture historically ascribe to the cross. Covenant Eschatology leaves the column below the cross completely empty. If this charge is false, then let Don place beneath the cross any item on the list. I think we will find that that there is nothing on the list Don is willing to say *arrived* or *happened* at the cross.

Cross	Covenant Eschatology
?	Atonement - AD70
?	Justification – AD 70
?	Reconciliation – AD 70
?	Forgiveness of sins – AD 70
?	Legal admittance into presence of God with the veil – AD 70
?	Time of Reformation – AD 70
?	Spirits of just men made perfect – AD 70
?	Old Testament fulfilled and legally annulled – AD 70
?	Grace triumphant over law – AD 70

Don answered our question scripturally in his second affirmative, saying the cross triumphed over the law. But he takes it back in his third affirmative when he argues that the law was valid and imposed until AD 70 and had to be *independently removed* before grace could enter! (Don never did explain to us how the cross could triumph over the law, and not triumph over it at the same time. If the law still held man under the debt of sin after the cross, there obviously was no triumph!) Don states "***removal of Torah was essential for man's justification after all!***" (emphasis in original). Don states, "Torah had to end in order for forgiveness, entrance into the MHP and life to become realities!" Dear reader, *we deny this totally and emphatically*. The law was taken away, not so grace could enter in, but because it was a *mere schoolmaster* to bring us to Christ; it was a system of types and shadows *pointing* to Jesus. Once Jesus was come, there was no further utility in the Mosaic system; it had served its provisional need and purpose and so was *annulled*. Nothing more or less.

That the law had to be removed for grace to enter is very serious error. Don states "Torah...prevented man from entering the MHP due to its inability to forgive." According to Don, "the negative power of Torah was such (in its failure to provide forgiveness) that as long as it stood, no one could enter the MHP!" Read that again. Why does Don insist that Torah had to be removed before grace could enter? BECAUSE TORAH COULD NOT FORGIVE! According to Don, it possessed some mysterious "negative power" that forestalled grace and the cross of Christ! *Don, how does the inability of Torah to forgive prevent the addition of grace?* Explain that for us, please! What is the mysterious "negative power" you mention? We deserve your explanation on this. I will gladly ignore that you have produced even a single verse showing the Old Testament was valid after the cross, and give you a *fourth affirmative* to explain for us what this mysterious "negative power" is. So, by all means, please provide us with this information. Moreover, please explain how the animal sacrifices, dietary restrictions, and other items of the law could forestall the atoning power of Christ's blood? What is there in the continuing temple ritual that allegedly over-powered Jesus' sacrifice and prevented it from providing forgiveness of sins until it was taken away?

Dear reader, this is the whole debate right here. If Don cannot provide some lucid, rational explanation from scripture about this mysterious "negative power" in Torah that prevented the power of Christ's cross from bringing grace until Torah was allegedly removed in AD 70, then you must know his proposition is lost. Don MUST explain this. He said it; so he obviously has something in mind, and we are giving him a whole fourth affirmative for our edification and instruction. Preterism must settle this issue of Max Kingism once and for all so it free itself of these errors and move on. Will Don accept? Dare he refuse?

Dear reader, obviously, there is *nothing* in the temple ritual or *anywhere* in the law that can forestall God's grace in Jesus Christ. NOTHING. Law doesn't prevent grace, it invites it! *The inability of Torah to forgive in no way implies it also possessed a negative power to prevent or forestall forgiveness of sin!* What is Don's proof of this "mysterious "negative power?" He has none! The whole concept is just one more bare assertion by Don without one "book, chapter, and verse" to back it up. To the contrary, grace triumphed over law. It is the *addition of grace that saves us, not removal of the law.* Proof of this is seen in the moral law and the law of sin and death ("the wages of sin is death" Rom. 6:23). The moral law and law of sin and death have *never been removed.* Sin is as much condemned by God's moral law today as it ever was! Fornication, adultery, theft, and murder are as unlawful, sinful, and condemned by God today as under the law of Moses. This has never changed and never will! Don, is it unlawful and sinful today to murder, rape or commit incest? Of course it is! Were these laws codified and part of the law of Moses? Yes, of course they were. Did these laws exist before Moses. Yes. Do they exist now; did removal of the law of Moses remove these laws? No, of course not. Does God's law condemning immorality and sin prevent men from finding grace in Christ today? God forbid, may it never be! The very fact that the moral law (much of which was codified by Moses) continues to condemn today, but men can find forgiveness *proves* – irrefutably – that removal of law is in no way necessary for God's addition of grace!

Don's argument that the law had to be removed before grace could enter or obtain is *serious, serious error*; it overthrows the power and efficacy of Christ's cross. It changes the very mechanism of salvation from the triumph of grace over law, to grace accomplished removal of law, fundamentally changing and perverting the gospel of Christ.

Don's Proposition and Burden of Proof

Don is in the affirmative and has the burden of proof. To carry his case he must prove each and every element of his affirmative. At a minimum, Don must prove

- The coming referred to in Rom. 11:25-27 is the second, not first, advent of Christ.
- The judgment and sentence associated with sin hung over the saints until AD 70; *viz*., the cross did not cancel sin's debt.
- AD 70 represented the *legal* climax and termination of the Mosaic Covenant age; *viz.,* the law, including circumcision, animal sacrifices, the priesthood, dietary restrictions, etc, was valid and binding until AD 70.
- The judgment and sentence associated with sin were set aside in AD 70 by annulment of the law.

We are in the negative and need only negate ONE of the essential elements of Don's proposition to prevail. In order to carry his case and establish his affirmative, we challenged Don if he could produce even ONE VERSE showing the saints continued under the debt of sin from and after the cross (#2 above). We put a box on the page and predicted that at the end of the debate it would still be empty. Don has now concluded his affirmative. He has written almost 50 pages of argument, but has failed to produce even ONE VERSE that expressly states or teaches that the saints continued under the debt of sin after the cross. I believe it is axiomatic that if Don cannot produce a verse to substantiate an essential tenant of his doctrine, that he has not and cannot carry his case. His failure on this one point has therefore negated his

101

proposition.

In our second negative, we added a box for Don and challenged him to produce even ONE VERSE that stated or taught the saints required to observe the law, and that it was valid and binding (imposed) and until AD 70 (# 3 above). Here again Don failed. He could not produce even ONE VERSE, not one. We also asked Don if he could produce even ONE COMMENTATOR who agreed with his interpretation of Isa. 27:7-11 (#1 above). Again he failed. He could not cite one commentator who applied Isa. 27:7-11 to the fall of Jerusalem. His whole case turns upon his ability to prove Isa. 27:7-11 refers to the AD 70 coming of Christ, but not one commentator agrees with him. Don says all commentators agree that Paul quotes Isa. 27:7-11 in Rom. 11:25-27, but that does not mean they apply it to AD 70. If Don cannot provide some commentator that agrees it applies to AD 70, then we maintain he cannot prove his case.

Finally, we concluded our second negative saying Don could not produce a verse that taught justification occurred in AD 70 (#4 above). Again, Don could not produce even ONE VERSE. Thus, for each of the *four essential elements* of Don's proposition he cannot produce even one verse or commentator who agrees with him. Remarkable is it not? A doctrine that has deceived so many for the better part of 30 years, and when put to the test not even ONE VERSE can be produced to sustain its most basic suppositions!

So much for what Don could not produce or prove, what about the verses we brought forward to negative Don's case? Don has consistently ignored all verses that show the law was fulfilled and taken away, and that justification was full and free from and after the cross. He grandstands a lot about my exercising my right to pass over his arguments without comment, but he has ignored every verse we produce that shows grace was full and free from and after the cross. Here are *some* of the verses we have marshaled:

We noted that the gospels and Acts state **twenty-nine** times that Jesus fulfilled the law, providing these verses: Matt. 1:22; 2:15, 17, 23; 4:14; 8:17; 12:17; 13:35; 21:4; 26:54, 56; 27:9, 35; Mk. 14:49; 15:28; Lk. 4:21; 24:44; Jn. 12:38; 13:18; 15:25; 17:12; 19:24, 28, 36, 37; Acts 1:16; 3:18; 13:27, 29. Don ignored them.

We noted that the law of blood sacrifice foreshadowed the work of Christ upon the cross and was fulfilled in Jesus' substitutionary death and atoning sacrifice. We brought forward verses which state "by one offering Christ hath perfected forever them that are sanctified" (Heb. 10:4). HATH

PERFECTED FOREVER. This is perfect tense, showing completed action in the past. Don made no attempt to controvert this, he just ignored it.

We brought forward Rom. 7:1-4, which states "YE ARE BECOME ARE DEAD TO THE LAW BY THE BODY OF CHRIST" Don says the law was still valid, binding and obligatory until AD 70. Paul says, it was dead. Who will you believe? Don ignored the verse. We brought forward Rom. 8:2, which states, "For the law of the Spirit of life in Christ Jesus hath made me free from the law of sin and death." HATH MADE ME FREE FROM THE LAW OF SIN AND DEATH. What part of "hath made free" would Don deny? We'll never know because he just ignores these verses and refuses to interact with them. Another verse we brought forward is Rom. 6:14: "For sin shall not have dominion over you: for ye are not under the law, but under grace." NOT UNDER THE LAW, BUT UNDER GRACE. This verse seems important to the subject, but did Don not address it? Of course not, how could he?

We cited Col. 2:14, which says Jesus nailed the debt of sin to his cross and took out of the way the handwriting of ordinances that was against us. Don denies this, too, totally ignoring this verse. He would not so much as interact with it. In Ephesians, Paul says Jesus had "abolished in his flesh the enmity, even the law of commandments contained in ordinances" (Eph. 2:14, 15). HATH ABOLISHED IN HIS FLESH...THE LAW OF COMMANDMENTS CONTAINED IN ORDINANCES. Don says the law was still valid and binding; all was valid until none was valid, right Don? Paul says it was abolished in Jesus' flesh. Don ignores all this and pushes blindly ahead.

The writer of Hebrews states that Christians had come to "God the Judge of all and the spirits of just men made perfect" (Heb. 12:23). THE SPIRITS OF JUST MEN MADE PERFECT! Made perfect how? By the blood of Christ. Don denies this and says the saints continued under bondage to sin until AD 70, otherwise they would have been resurrected at the cross! In this case he did at least acknowledge the verse, claiming it was merely "proleptic" and looked forward to the perfection that would only really come at AD 70. His authority? Bare assertion, nothing more. He has to "re-write" the passage to fit his doctrine and upon his own authority does so. The Hebrew writer also says believers had come to the "church of the firstborn" and to "Jesus the mediator of the new covenant, and to the blood of sprinkling that speaketh better things than that of Abel" (Heb. 12:23,24). Don, are these proleptic? Will you now tell us that the church was not established until AD 70, that the New Testament, ratified by Jesus' blood, did not come until AD 70? If one part is "proleptic" why are not they all? I think the reader can see that Don's creative re-writing of the text to fit his doctrine is without merit and that the blood of Christ had made the spirits in Hades perfect just as it had "perfected forever" (Heb. 10:14) the saints on this side of eternity.

Continuing on, touching this last point, we cited Col. 2:10 "and ye are complete in him." "Complete" here has the meaning of being soteriologically perfected, lacking nothing necessary to our salvation. Did Don interact with this verse to show us why this was not true, why it would only become true in AD 70? No, he just ignored it. We showed that Paul said, "For if when we were enemies, we **were reconciled** to God by the death of his Son, much more, **being reconciled**, we shall be saved by his life. And not only so, but we also joy in God through our Lord Jesus Christ, by whom we have **now received the atonement**" (Rom. 5:10, 11). WERE RECONCILED. HAVE NOW RECEIVED THE ATONEMENT. Notice the verb tense. Perfect tense, showing completed action in the past. Don denies the atonement was received or even complete until AD 70. Needless to say, he simply ignores these verses and will not even so much as acknowledge they exist. Perhaps he felt that since he cannot even produce one verse in his own support, he needed to ignore our verses to help "even things up."

But ignoring these verses doesn't make them go away; it only demonstrates the weakness of his case. If we produced only ONE VERSE, (and those above are but a sample of the many we cited), we would have produced 100% more verses than Don! If we cited ten verses, it would be 1,000% more than Don. But we produced dozens and dozens of verses, all which Don just ignores. Don has NO VERSES, we have MANY VERSES. If we had only ONE VERSE it would be sufficient to negate Don's proposition, because he has NONE. Clearly, Don's case is lost and it is a perfect absurdity for him to pretend otherwise.

Max King's Contradictions

Since the topic of the continuing validity of the law has come up, it is worth our while to point out that Max King contradicts himself on this very topic. McGuiggan caught him in this during their debate. It is essential to King's position that Christians continued under bondage of sin by the law until AD. This is Don's position in this debate. Obviously, this is a very tenuous position to take; Don cannot produce a single verse to support it. Is it any wonder then that King was forced to contradict himself on this critical issue? First, let us notice King's position that places Christians under the law:

"The natural body that was sown (verse 44) answers to the fleshly or carnal system of Judaism...Though the saints were in the kingdom that was

104

conceived on Pentecost, they were not yet delivered from the world or natural body (Judaism) wherein this conception took place." (*Spirit of Prophecy*, p. 200, 201)

So the "natural body" equals Judaism, and the saints were part of the natural body (Judaism), and NOT YET DELIVERED, right? Now, let us ask, Where did death reign? King's answer:

> "But how was death swallowed up in victory? The answer is quite obvious, Where was death resident? Did it not reign in the mortal or natural body of Judaism?...But when that died, and from it arose a spiritual body clothed with incorruption and immortality, death was defeated. It lost its hold over the subjects of the natural body because they were raised through Christ into the spiritual body of life and immortality. Death was in the 'natural body' because of sin, and sin received its strength from the law." (Ibid, p. 202).

"Death" for King is not physical death, but spiritual death or "sin-death" as his also calls it. Thus, spiritual death and sin reigned in the mortal body of Judaism by the law, of which Christians were part, but were delivered only when Judaism died in AD 70. Death lost its hold when the natural body died and a spiritual body allegedly arose in AD 70, right? (Dear reader, have you ever read any passages anywhere at any time about the resurrection of "Judaism" into a new body in AD 70? I haven't, but this is what Don asks us to believe. Note, also that according to King and Don, Gentiles were under Judaism waiting "resurrection" too!) Now, hear King contradict himself and say the church was NOT under the law:

> "No one contends that Gal. 1:4 speaks of their deliverance from the Law (Jewish system) but rather from the Jewish age, the vicious persecution and distresses heaped upon the saints." (McGuiggan/King debate, p. 93).

Deliverance from the mere persecutions of the Jewish age? Not under the Law? Hear him again:

"And to speak of the 'shackles of Judaism' is not to say that those saints were under the Law."

Here King attempts to deny his teaching that the saints were under the law! But McGuiggan would have none of it and caught him cold in his contradictions! (pp. 107, 108) But King's contradictions are not confined to his debate. His book "Spirit of Prophecy" also expressly denies the saints were under the law!

> "Second, the law did not end at the cross, nor was it completely fulfilled then as seen in Matt. 5:17, 18. It was, however, taken out of the way for *those who accepted Christ.* Through Christ they died to the law and received deliverance from it. All of the New Testament scriptures that speak of the law's being 'nailed to the cross,' or 'taken out of the way' are in reference to the saints that came by way of the cross. 'In Christ' was the state wherein the law was abolished or done away, but aside from Christ not one jot or title passed from the law till all was fulfilled. The law did not end in death or destruction but in fulfillment!"

This is clearly contradictory of everything King (and Don) teaches elsewhere about the saints being in the natural body of Judaism under bondage of "sin-death" and looking for deliverance at the second coming. He now says in this passage that **"the law was abolished or done away"** for Christians! But if the law is done away for Christians, then they clearly are not in the "natural body" of Judaism looking for deliverance (justification) in AD 70! Hopeless contradiction! And why is King forced into this position? Because it is impossible to make all the verses Don has ignored in this debate go away, so King tries to reconcile them, still clinging to his abstract notions about a spiritualized resurrection. But all he ends up doing is contradicting himself. The lesson for us is that Covenant Eschatology is a sojourn in "cloud land," an imaginary world of double-speak and self-contradiction invented by Max King that has no existence in the real world or scriptures.

Two Concurrent, Conflicting Covenants?
One of the more obvious problems of Covenant Eschatology is its insistence that the ceremonial and other ordinances of the Old Testament were valid and imposed until AD 70 even though the New Testament was in place. King and Don must postpone justification and grace until AD 70 in order for their idea of a spiritualized resurrection to occur at that time, and therefore must keep the dead ordinances of the law alive, even though the gospel of Jesus Christ was already in force and effect. Thus, if we are to believe them, there were two, conflicting, mutually exclusive covenants in force at the same time! If there was ever a system of belief rife with self-contradiction,

106

this would have to be it! On the one hand we have the shadow system of ceremonial law that can never forgive sins and therefore styled by a "ministration of death", and on the other hand we have the gospel of life and grace ordained to replace the Old system, both theoretically valid and binding at the same time! Imagine, if you will, a State legislature amending its penal code, replacing the corpus of criminal statutes with new, conflicting ones, then having both valid at the same time! Which laws are men charged to obey? They cannot obey both, for one contradicts the duties and obligations of the other. Both cannot be valid for one set of statutes makes illegal what the other expressly commands! The very notion of two covenants in force at one time is so totally at odds with scripture and all human experience that it is hardly necessary to refute it. Let us look at few scriptures that show the Old Testament was annulled at the cross. We looked at some of these before, but Don ignored them.

Heb. 9:17 states **"a testament is of force after men are dead."** Thus, the New Testament and gospel of Jesus Christ came into force and effect AT HIS DEATH UPON THE CROSS. No one can have two valid wills; one must always amend or replace the other! Ask any lawyer, or anyone who has ever made a will. When a man changes his will, he always recites that the amended will revokes all previous wills. The only exception would be a codicil, in which case one merely amends his existing will, rather than replacing it. It is abundantly clear that the New Testament did not merely amend the Old; it is not a codicil of the Old Testament, it altogether replaces it. "When he said, Sacrifice and offering and burnt offerings and offering for sin thou wouldest not, neither hadst pleasure therein; which are offered by the law; then said he, Lo, I come to do thy will, O God. He taketh away the first that he may establish the second" (Heb. 10:8, 9). TAKETH AWAY THE FIRST THAT HE MAY ESTABLISH THE SECOND. When was the second, the New Testament established? At Jesus' death! A testament is of force after men are dead! Don must deny the legal efficacy of the New Testament in order to keep the dead ordinances of the Old Testament alive, or admit that the latter gave way to the former at the cross.

Rom. 7:1-4 teaches us that the law of the first husband (Old Testament) was nullified by the death of Christ, so that we could enter a new marital covenant with a new husband (the risen Savior) under a new law (the gospel). These four verses show not only that the saints were **"dead to the law"** by the body of Christ and therefore loosed from the debt of sin, but also that the old law was nullified *in toto*. The law of marriage terminates upon the death of the husband. "The woman which hath a husband is bound by the law to her husband so long as he liveth; but if the husband be dead, she is loosed

107

from the law of her husband" (Rom. 7:2). The law of the first husband was the Old Testament. "Wherefore, my brethren, ye also are become dead to the law by the body of Christ" (v. 4). DEAD TO THE LAW BY THE BODY OF CHRIST. This is Christianity 101, folks! To buy into Covenant Eschatology you have to forget the ABC's of salvation. The Old law died with the body of Christ at the cross. Don, what part of "dead to the law" would you deny?

Gal. 5:1 – "Stand fast therefore in the liberty wherewith Christ hath made us free, and be not entangled again in the yoke of bondage." This verse, indeed, the *whole book* of Galatians, stands for the proposition that the saints were *not under the law* but under liberty and grace, and were not to submit to Judaizing teachers who insisted the law was "valid, binding, and obligatory" (like Don). The ceremonies of the law could not bring remission of sins. To obtain salvation, one had to stand fast in Christ. To revert to the system of law was to deny Christ and to fall from grace (v. 2, 4). "For I through the law am dead to the law, that I might live unto God" (Gal. 2:19). "Through the law" (through Christ's fulfillment of the law by his substitutionary death and atoning sacrifice) "I am dead to the law" (I am loosed from the sentence of sin and death by the sacrifice of Christ) "that I might live unto God" (turn from sin and reliance upon my own merits, trusting instead upon the merits of Christ's blood). Given that this whole book is devoted to the topic of showing that Christians were not under the law, and, indeed, specifically charged not to submit to it, how can Don honestly ask us to believe that both systems were equally valid, or that there was any validity in the continuing ritual of the law?

The Time of Reformation

For Don, the time of reformation equals the Christian era and gospel system, which he says arrived in AD 70. "The time of reformation did not arrive until the second coming AD 70," Don says. Since two Testaments cannot be in force simultaneously, apparently Don wants us to believe that the gospel did not attain legal efficacy until AD 70. This would be the logical implication of his view that the cross did not triumph over the law, but that it had to be separately removed by the destruction of Jerusalem. Thus, the Romans took away what Jesus' cross could not! Good grief! We believe, however, the better view is that the *time of reformation* answers to the *time of transition* during which the ordinances of the law were annulled and those of the gospel laid down. The time of reformation was marked by the gifts of the Holy Ghost, which served to guide the apostles into all truth. It began at the cross and ended when "that which is perfect is come" (I Cor. 13:), or no later than AD 70 when the charismata ceased. In our view, "that which is perfect" answers to the "restitution of all things" (Acts. 3:21). Peter said that heaven would receive Jesus *until* the restitution/restoration of all things (that is, when all things were put aright), then the Lord would return. This of course is what we see in Heb. 9, where the time of reformation *precedes (not follows)* the return of the Lord (v. 28). Thus, reformation brought us to the point where all things were "put aright," then Christ returned, all by AD 70. However, where Don wants the time of reformation to **arrive** in AD 70, instead we find that is when it ended!

Dear reader, had the reformation arrived when Martin Luther began his work of reform or not? Of course it had. What kind of nonsense would it be to talk about the Reformation arriving at the *end* of Luther and the reformers' work?! "The Reformation arrived when Luther was done." No, the Reformation describes the period when the work *began* until it was *complete,* then it passed away and the *restored church* assumed its place. This is why we always speak of the Protestant Reformation in the past tense. The church is now "reformed" and hopefully "restored" to its apostolic purity (more or less!). Catholic "Canon Law" was imposed UNTIL the Reformation began. It was not valid during the Reformation, not at least to the Reformers. In the same way, the law of Moses was imposed UNTIL the time of reformation was initiated at the cross, but was not valid during the reformation. Jesus said "the law and the prophets were UNTIL John: since that time the kingdom of God is preached" (Lk. 16:16). That is, the message of Moses and the prophets was exhausted and had run its course; beginning with John a new message was preached. The time of reformation served as a transitional phase during which the outmoded and obsolete rituals of the law were *taken out of the way* and replaced by the ordinances of the gospel.

As we have seen over and over again, the Jews' continued adherence to the law marked them as enemies of Christ. Like Don, they claimed the law was still valid and binding and sought to impose it upon the church in Palestine, Asia and the world. For this, Paul said they were preaching "another Jesus" and "another gospel" and pronounced a curse upon them. Covenant Eschatology is identical to 1st century Judaism in claiming the law was obligatory and binding after the cross. Can't you hear the Judaizers? "The law is binding and valid notwithstanding the cross." And what does Don say? "The law was binding and valid notwithstanding the cross." Unless the Judaizers were right and Paul wrong, I would suggest the law was annulled at the cross. Isaiah said that the rituals of the law before the destruction of Jerusalem were abominated by God (Isa. 66:3). Don agrees and says that it was the Jews' *keeping the law* that marked them as objects of divine wrath. ***"The old city had not only served its purpose, it had also become the enemy***

109

of God, by holding onto the Old Covenant" (Ibid, p. 193). So, Don tells us on one hand the law is binding and divinely imposed, but that it made those who obeyed into enemies of God! Don, how can what God abominated and marked the Jews for wrath have been valid, binding and obligatory? Tell us please.

Atonement Ritual and Resurrection of Christ

Max King invented the notion that atonement for sins was delayed until AD 70 to accommodate his view of a collective, spiritualized resurrection in AD 70. This is *not* the figurative resurrection of believers as they *one-by-one* obey the gospel and are baptized (Rom. 6:3-6; Eph. 2:1, 6). Rather, King's view is that the whole (collective) body of believers was somehow mysteriously raised up out of the purported grave of Judaism in AD 70 into a new resurrection body in Christ. Of course, Paul speaks of the body of Christ (the church) already existing long before AD 70, so where this resurrection body purportedly came from, how it died merely because Jerusalem was destroyed, and was then raised again in yet another body is a total mystery upon which the scriptures are absolutely silent. Max King is a great fiction writer and supplies the details in his books, and anyone who is interested in the genre of fantasy may pursue the topic at their own leisure and peril.

In order to postpone justification until AD 70, King came up with the idea that the atonement ritual began at Christ's ascension and was not complete until he came a second time. Support for this notion was found in Heb. 9, particularly verse 28 where Christ appears a "second time without sin unto salvation." This "salvation" is assumed to be salvation from sin, but we believe the better view is that the salvation in mind is the putting all enemies beneath Christ's feet (Heb. 2:8; 10:13) and the deliverance of the church from her persecutors by the outpouring of wrath upon the Jews and Romans. If there was anything to the idea that the saints continued under the debt of sin from and after the cross, or that they were only justified in AD 70 by removal of the law, Don should have been able to put one or two verses in the boxes we gave him. But since after 50 pages of argument Don could not find a single verse to put in any of the boxes (he could not even suggest a verse for us to argue over, he left the boxes completely empty), we can safely dismiss King's notion for the frivolous and unscriptural piece of fiction it is.

When then was the blood accepted by God within the veil and the atonement deemed legally complete? We believe this occurred at the cross, at the time of our Savior's death. Evidence for this fact is seen in the veil being "rent in twain" when Jesus died, showing the debt of sin was paid and the way into the presence of God within the Holy of Holies was now open. Don denies this, but when we asked him to explain the theological significance of the veil being rent in two, he fell suddenly silent and declined comment. His silence must therefore be taken as an admission that he has no alternative explanation to offer. Other evidence corroborating our view is the writer of Hebrews, who urged Jewish Christians not to shrink back under the Old Testament ritual typified by the first sanctuary, but to draw nigh unto God, and "boldly enter" his presence within veil (the Holy of Holies) by virtue of Jesus' sacrifice.

Obviously, this does not contemplate actual and spatial entrance into God's presence, for that cannot occur until man puts off the body in death. Therefore, the entrance contemplated by the writer was legal and covenantal. Just as they "had come" unto the "heavenly Jerusalem, to God the judge of all, to the innumerable company of angels, to the general assembly and church of the firstborn, to the spirits of just men made perfect, to Jesus the mediator of the New Testament, and to the blood of sprinkling" (Heb. 12:22-24), just as they had done all these legally and covenantally, they could and should enter boldly within the veil, legally and covenantally, where they could find grace and help in time of need (Heb. 4:16). **The Holy of Holies was a figure for the New Testament** (Heb.9:9), and if the New Testament was valid, then the way into the Holy of Holies *ipso facto* was open and valid. But as entrance into God's presence was closed until the atonement was complete, it is axiomatic that ratification of the New Testament, atonement, and entrance within the veil were concurrent events, and that all happened at the "death of the testator" (Heb. 9:17). And we have Paul's word for it, saying, "we have now received the atonement" (Rom.). Reduced to a syllogism, it might look like this:

No man could enter the Holy of Holies until the atonement was complete.
But the Holy of Holies was a figure for the New Testament and gospel.
The New Testament was of force from and after the cross. Therefore,
The atonement was complete and man could enter (legally and covenantally) the Holy of Holies from and after the cross.

We hasten to add that Jesus' resurrection was God's objective proof that the atonement was complete. Having died a sinner's death under imputation of sin, Jesus could not rise from the dead and enter heaven unless and until that imputation was removed. Therefore, Paul says, "he was delivered for our offenses, and was raised for our justification" (Rom. 4:25). It is the fact that Jesus was raised justified that also justifies us. This is why Peter says we are born again by the resurrection of Jesus Christ from the dead (I Pet. 1:3; *cf.*

3:21). The acquittal of Jesus from the imputation of sin at his resurrection is the basis for our acquittal from sin. And this is reflected in Christian baptism. Baptism is a symbolic and sacramental participation in the death, burial, and resurrection of the Lord. Each time someone is baptized, the death, burial and resurrection of Christ is re-enacted, and Christ's justification by receipt of his blood within the veil *at his death* is shown anew. In baptism, the subject is "buried with Christ by baptism into death," and "raised in newness of life" (Rom. 6:3-6). If we are raised from baptism justified from sin, then Christ was necessarily raised from the dead justified from sin, for it is his death, burial, and resurrection we are united with in baptism. Will Don deny Jesus died under imputation of sin? Will he deny he was raised justified, free from imputation of sin (Rom. 6:7, 10)? But if Christ was justified from the imputation of sin at his resurrection, it is clear that his blood was received by God within the veil *before* his ascension, and that can only mean it was received by God *at his death*. Hence, the notion that mankind had to wait for the second coming for the atonement to be complete and grace to enter is totally at odds with the most elementary instruction of the church and scripture as embodied in the ordinance of baptism and the resurrection of our Lord. Covenant Eschatology yet *again* is show to be a dangerous doctrine contradicting the most basic teachings of the Christian faith.

Miscellaneous Arguments of Don

Argument from the Transfiguration - Don argues that the Transfiguration of Christ is a before-the-fact vision of his second coming. Naturally, there is nothing in the Transfiguration taken alone that would suggest this. However, because Peter used the word "parousia," saying they had not believed cleverly devised fables when they made known the "power and coming" of the Lord, but were eye witnesses of his majesty on the Mount of Transfiguration, men have supposed that the second coming is referred to. Personally, I have never been persuaded of that fact. I have always taken II Pet. 1:16 in reference to the *first advent* of our Lord. I have always felt that it was the miracles and works of wonders that he is assuring the reader are not mere fables, and that Peter evokes the events he witnessed during the Transfiguration as proof of the verity of what had been reported. Dear reader, do you see *anything* in the transfiguration normally associated with the second coming? I don't. I don't see any of the imagery that occurs in Revelation or Matthew 24. I don't see visions of Hades delivering up its dead. I see nothing that would suggest the second coming is in view. The only way you can get the second coming out of the Transfiguration is to go to II Peter, and then only by his use of the word "parousia" which word is used of Titus, Timothy, and others and has no inherent reference to the second advent of the Lord. To my mind, if the transfiguration is a vision of anything, it is a revelation of Jesus' divinity and Sonship, nothing less or more.

But whether the transfiguration is a vision of the second coming or not is really moot. We can grant Don his "major premise" and it will not help him, for his "minor premise" is totally suppositional and without support. Don's syllogism reads like this:

The Transfiguration was a vision of the Second Coming of Christ (2 Peter 1:16f).
But, the Transfiguration was a vision of the end of the Mosaic Covenant and the establishment of the New Covenant of Christ.
Therefore, the end of the Mosaic Covenant was at the Second Coming of Christ.

Can you spot the error in Don's minor premise? That's right, he assumes the point to be proved! He asserts without proof that the transfiguration was a vision of the end of the Old Testament and the establishment of the New Covenant (he avoids use of the word "Testament" because this ties the event to Jesus' death and, naturally, he can have none of that!). What proof does Don have that the transfiguration is a vision of the end of the Mosaic Covenant? Moses and Elijah appeared on the mount speaking with the Lord about his coming death upon a cross in Jerusalem! (Lk. 9:31). Call me crazy, but if the transfiguration is about the end of the Old Testament as Don asserts, and if Moses and Elijah are speaking with the Lord about his coming death upon a Roman cross, I would tie the end of the Old Testament to the cross, not second coming! Let us be candid. The appearance of Moses and Elijah upon the mount of transfiguration is ambiguous taken alone. The only information we can draw from the event is from what they discussed, and this was not AD 70, but Calvary. Don's attempt to get to AD 70 through II Pet. 1:16 is tenuous at best. Argument is no substitute for verses. If Don could put some verses in the boxes we provided him, he would not have to rely upon "ify" argumentation to fill in the blanks.

Argument from Isa. 27 - Let's revisit Don's argument from Isa. 27:7-11 a bit. In his second affirmative, Don made the following argument: "The coming of the Lord to take away Israel's sin in Romans 11:26f is the coming of the Lord at his coming in judgment of Israel foretold by Isaiah 26-27, when He would call the dead–those scattered to the four winds-- to Him (i.e. the *resurrection*) *by the sounding of the Great Trumpet (Isaiah 27:13)."*
I pointed out that Don has assumed the very fact to be proved; that he had

113

NOT established the connection between Isa. 27:7-11 and Rom. 11:25-27. Don retorts in his third affirmative that I admit the connection between Isa. 27 and Rom. 11 when I made the following statement. "In Romans 11:26, 27, Paul blends two passages from Isaiah together into one. He quotes Isa. 59: 20, 21, then follows up with Isa. 27:9." That is what most, but not all commentators say, and in making that statement I reported the majority opinion. But Don misses the point. Don equates the coming in Rom. 11 with the coming in Isa. 27, right? But the coming in Rom. 11 is taken, *not from Isa. 27*, but Isa. 59! That's right! "The Redeemer shall come to Zion" is from Isa. 59:20, 21. Isa. 27 is not quoted in Rom. 11 in connection with a "coming" at all. Or should I say, "if" at all, for it is more probable that Paul actually quotes Jer. 31:31-34 and not Isa. 27, for the forgiveness of sin connected with the "covenant" (Isa. 59:21) attaches to the New Testament, not the Assyrian invasion (or fall of Jerusalem), right? And this is the position of *James, Brown and Faucett's Commentary:*

"**This is my covenant with them** literally, "this is the covenant from me unto them." **when I shall take away their sins** This, we believe, is rather a brief summary of Jer. 31:31-34."

When we first began our discussion with Don about Rom. 11:25-27 last August or so, we repeated what most commentators say, that Paul quotes Isa. 27:9 in this place, but further study has led us to conclude this is unlikely and that that better view is that Jer. 31:31-34 is in view, as the commentator above states. For what does the forgiveness of sins have to do with the Assyrian invasion? But to return, Don wants to borrow the coming in Rom. 11 quoted from Isa. 59 and apply it to Isa. 27. Good grief! Talk about exegetical summersaults! Dear reader, Isa. 27:7-11 is about the Assyrio-Babylonian invasions and virtually all commentators agree upon this fact. Don could not produce a single commentator who applies it to AD 70 like he does. Clearly, the connection is NOT made and Don's attempt to "borrow" the coming from Isa. 59 quoted in Rom. 11, apply it to Isa. 27, then claim that "the coming of the Lord to take away Israel's sin in Romans 11:26f is the coming foretold by Isaiah 27," is simply untenable. And while we are on this passage, let me point out that Don totally manufactures a quote I never made. Don states:

And now, Kurt desperately claims that I have not: "established ANY CONNECTION between Rom. 11:25-27 and Isa. 26. NONE! The same is true of Isaiah 59."

I hate to be a stickler, but the last seven words of the quote Don attributes to me I never said. Don has somehow made them up! The reader should copy and paste those seven words into his computer's search function and search my second negative to see if I ever made that statement. It gives me no pleasure to point this out, but Don has done this sort of thing so many times in this debate that I feel compelled to speak out. If he is continuously willing to misrepresent me and attribute statements to me that I have not made (four times in his second affirmative alone[1]), how can we have any confidence in his handling of the word of God? If he handles God's word with the same cavalier manner in which he deals with my words, is it any wonder he asserts so much, yet can prove so little, and has no verses to sustain his case?

Unsound Methodology - A point came up in Don's first affirmative that I never bothered responding to, but since he has brought it up again, and because it sheds light on a problem with his overall methodology which may be helpful to both him and the community in general, we'll take it up now. Here is a quote from Don:

> "Of course, **just last year**, in his *Sword and Plow*, when objecting to my position on Romans 11 / Isaiah 27, Kurt said: 'We do not disallow the possibility that there is a *plenior sensus (fuller meaning, DKP)*, to Isaiah 26:21 that may look beyond its historical setting to Christ's second coming.' Realizing the *fatal nature of this admission*, Kurt has now completely reversed himself. So, **just last year** Kurt said that Isaiah 27 could apply to both the Cross and AD 70. But now, he denies that it speaks of either one! It is exclusively the Assyrian invasion!"

Did you notice what Don did? I said it is possible Isa. 26:21 may have a *plenior sensus* that looks beyond its historical setting to the second coming, and Don ran with that and applied it to Isa. 27, saying I made an admission about *that* text! This sort of broad-brush approach is all through Don's material and betrays a fundamental error in his methodology in dealing with scripture, particularly Isaiah (to say nothing about misrepresenting me). More than any other prophet, Isaiah changes topics 3-4-5 times in a single chapter, now speaking of Israel's sin, now of the coming captivity, now about the sins of the nations around Israel, now about the return of the captivity, now about the Messiah, all within the span of often less than 30 verses! In

---

[1] However innocent his mistake, the fact remains I never "claimed Rom.11:26f *predicts* the salvation of individual Jews throughout the entirety of the endless Christian age." The text predicts nothing about ethnic Jews after AD 70, and I certainly never suggested it did. Given the nation was destroyed in AD 70 and God now sees all men alike without regard to ethnicity, it is not the sort of thing I would be apt to say.

115

chapter 27 (which is only 13 verses long), Isaiah changes topics *three* different times. He begins by talking about the defeat of Leviathan (world, heathen civil power), changes to wrath upon the Jews by the Assyrian invasion, and ends talking about the re-gathering of Israel from the Assyrian captivity. Thus, defeat of the world civil power (Assyria/Leviathan) precedes the invasion of Israel, where we would expect instead it to precede the re-turn of the captivity!

This rapid change of subject matter and the random chronological order of events portrayed is what makes Isaiah so difficult to interpret, and anyone who has read the book is aware of this fact. Overlooking this, Don sees something that may apply to the second advent, and automatically assumes that neighboring verses must apply to that event also, when in fact nothing could be further from the truth. He does this in the case at hand. Isa. 26:21 may have a *plenior sensus* that looks to the second coming. But does that mean Isa. 27:7-11 also applies to the second coming? In this case, Don could not find one commentator who agreed with him, so I feel it is safe to say, No, it does not. Don made the same mistake with the "trumpet" of verse 13, where, merely because it was similar sounding to Matt. 24:31, he assumed both referred to the identical event. Yet, Isa. 27:13 is clearly about the return of the captivity from Assyria and Egypt, not the general resurrection as supposed by Don. Yes, they are similar in sound and borrow from a common source and theme (the Jubilee), but that hardly means the same events are in view. This sort of sloppy argumentation from scripture is all through Don's syllogisms and is why syllogisms are so *dangerous* to build doctrine upon, particularly where you have no express statements in scripture to back your conclusions up (like Don's empty boxes)! Syllogisms should be built upon plain statement of scripture, not deductions. Don builds his arguments upon deductions rather than scripture and that is why he errs so great and so often.

Entering the Most Holy

Much of this debate and most of Don's last affirmative turned upon the argument that if the saints were soteriologically complete at the cross, they should then and there have entered the Holy of Holies (heaven). Apparently this is Don's best argument since he makes it so many times (a dozen times it seemed in the last affirmative alone!). Yet, does Don cite any verses? Does he have a verse that says "the dead would enter heaven the *moment* they were cleansed from sin"? No! Don has no verses, but argues totally from deductions! Don, God doesn't have to do things the way you suppose he ought or should; God does things when and as it pleases him. Hebrews describes the righteous dead in Hades, saying they were the "spirits of just men made perfect" (Heb. 12:23). If Don is unwilling to accept this simple

116

statement of scripture, there is nothing I or anyone else can do. That they were still in Hades, though perfected by Christ's blood, is Don's problem, not God's. God said that death would be the *last enemy* put beneath Jesus' feet (I Cor. 15:26). It is the last enemy, because it was the *ultimate enemy*, and it pleased God that the resurrection follow defeat of the Romans and Jews who were opposing the gospel and persecuting the church. There is nothing to Don's argument that they had to enter heaven as soon as they were justified, and it is certainly a poor argument to prove the law was valid until AD 70, for until Don's proves the existence of his mysterious "negative power" in the law, its continuing validity cannot prevent the entrance of grace in any event.

Power of the Holy People

Again, Don argues from deduction without verses. He asserts that the "power of the holy people" was the Old Testament. Really? What was the "power" of the Roman people? What was the "power" of the Assyrian Empire? God said he would "overthrow the throne of kingdoms and destroy the *strength of the kingdoms* of the heathen" at Christ's coming to shake the heavens and earth (Haggai 2:22). This occurred at the *same time* the power of the holy people was destroyed (Dan. 12:7; *cf.* Heb. 12:26, 27). Why should the *strength* of the kingdoms differ from the *power* of the Jews? Clearly, they do not, and Don errs again.

Conclusion

I began to notice the contradictions I had picked up from King about three years ago, and it has taken until only recently for the scales to fall completely from my eyes. This debate has helped a lot, and for that I am indebted to Don. It took me several years to "unlearn" my mistakes, so I do not expect Don to change overnight. Even so, and however much I want to be charitable toward my brother, his persistence in insisting that the law was valid despite so great a cloud of evidence to the contrary worries and disturbs me. It is my belief, indeed, my hope and prayer that after this public debate, privately, Don will quietly distance himself from Covenant Eschatology and that a few years from now we will find that he is no longer advocating this dangerous doctrine. And let me add that most reading this debate would agree that Max King and the people at "Presence Ministries" are at risk of eternal peril for their corruption of the gospel and teaching Universalism. However, that story need not end in tragedy. We encourage Max to renounce Covenant Eschatology and to return to the fold and gospel of Christ while life and hope remain, before it is too late.

117

Preston-Simmons Debate

When was Sin Defeated? AD 70 or the Cross?

Simmons' First Affirmative

It is my turn to be in the affirmative. Here is the proposition I will affirm:

Resolved: The Bible teaches that the coming of Christ for salvation in Romans 11:25-27 occurred at the Cross at the climax and termination of the Mosaic Covenant Age.

Here are the definitions I will employ: "Coming" refers to the *first advent* of Christ, from his nativity to his ascension. "Cross" includes *the death, burial, and resurrection* of our Lord. "Salvation" signifies the work of atonement accomplished in Jesus' substitutionary death. "Climax and termination of the Mosaic Covenant Age" refers to the legal end and annulment of the covenant enjoined by Moses in the wilderness.

Don and I are both agreed that "salvation" in the passage refers to salvation *from sin.* In my negatives, I have already proved that the debt of sin was paid and expunged, and that grace was full and free from and after the cross. But if *salvation* from sin occurred at the cross, it then follows that the *coming* contemplated by the passage also refers to the cross. Thus, proof of one is proof of the other. Moreover, proof that the bondage of sin was broken and men were fully justified in the death, burial, and resurrection of Christ also proves that the Old Testament was annulled. As long as the Old Covenant was in force, men were under bondage to sin. But beginning with the gospel, forgiveness of sins in the death of Christ was announced. It thus follows that the Old Testament was not in force or effect from and after Jesus' cross. Reduced to a syllogism, the argument might be expressed thus:

> The way into the Holiest was not open while the first tabernacle (the Old Testament) had legal standing (Heb. 9:8).

> But the Holiest was a figure for the New Testament (Heb. 9:9).

> The New Testament became of force at Jesus' death (Heb. 9:17). Therefore,

> The way into the Holiest was opened and the Old Testament (first

tabernacle) lost legal standing in Jesus' death.

Moreover, we have shown that it is *impossible* for there to be two concurrent, conflicting covenants in force at the same time. Therefore, proof that the New Testament was of force, *ipso facto* proves that the Old Testament was annulled. To the many verses we have already produced demonstrating this fact, we would add that Dan. 9:27 states that the "sacrifice and oblation" would cease in the midst of the final prophetic week, and that this is traditionally held to signify the legal cessation of the temple ritual by the death of Christ at the conclusion of his three and half year ministry:

"On the ordinary Christian interpretation, this applies to the crucifixion of our Lord, which took place, according to the received calculation, during the fourth year after his baptism by John, and the consequent opening of his ministry."[1]

Thus, proof that the power of sin was broken and men were justified after the death, burial and resurrection of Christ, also proves every other element of my proposition, all of which we have already abundantly demonstrated in the course of our negatives. Therefore, we need not say or produce one proof more. Our proposition stands confirmed:

The coming of Christ for salvation from sin was accomplished in the cross at the termination of the Mosaic covenant.

However, since we promised that we could produce pages of verses showing that grace and full and free, and that the Old Testament was therefore legally annulled and taken out of the way at the cross, we will produce some of those now and then lay down our pen. The following are by no means exhaustive; many more could be produced. Don ignored all the verses we produced before. Perhaps he would grace us with his attention to them now. If not, we will consider Don to have surrendered his position and this debate concluded in favor of Christ's cross.

Romans

1:5 – *"By whom we have received grace."* Note the verb tense "have received."

---

[1] J. E. H. Thomson, *Daniel – The Pulpit Commentary* (Hendrickson, Peabody, MA), p. 275.

1:7 – *"Grace to you and peace from God our Father, and the Lord Jesus Christ."* The gospel of Christ's cross places man in a state of grace and peace with God. AD 70 is nowhere in sight.

1:1, 15 – *"I am ready to preach the gospel (glad tidings)"* The tidings are gladsome because they carry the present assurance of grace. Proof that the gospel was valid *ipso facto* proves the Old Testament was invalid.

1:16 – The gospel *"is the power of God unto salvation."* The gospel is the offer of reconciliation.
Since the gospel was in force, the power of salvation and reconciliation were also in force. Not once verse can be produced showing the saints had to wait until AD 70 to be justified.

1:17 – In the gospel *"is the righteousness of God revealed."* The gospel is the revelation of God's *justification of man* in the atoning sacrifice of Christ.

3:21 – *"But now the righteousness of God without the law is manifested."* The Greek for "righteousness" is *dikaiosune* or "justification." The gospel is God's justification of sinners. Paul says the justification was "now" manifested. This "now" manifestation of justification was also the manifestation of the way into the Holy of Holies (Heb. 9:8), for the one assumes the other.

3:24 – *"Being justified freely by his grace through the redemption that is in Christ Jesus."* The verb tense shows that the saints were in a present state of justification and redemption.

3:26 – *"To declare, I say, at this time his righteousness: that he might be just, and the justifier of him which believeth in Jesus."* Paul here specifically states that God's justification of man was available *"at this time"* (e.g., it was not postponed to AD 70).

4:24 – *"But for us also, to whom it [righteousness/justification] shall be imputed, if we believe on him that raised up Jesus our Lord from the dead."* Paul here states that justification is imputed to all who believe. Again, no postponement until AD 70.

4:25 – *"Who was delivered for our offences, and was raised again for our justification [Gk. dikaiosin]."* Christ's resurrection is proof that Jesus was acquitted from the imputation of sin he bore upon the cross. But if Jesus died under imputation of sin, and was raised justified, then the blood of his

120

sacrifice was received within the Holy of Holies before his ascension, which can only mean that God received it at Jesus' death. The veil of separation was therefore "rent in twain" when Jesus died, showing the way into God's presence was now open.

5:1 – *"Therefore, being justified by faith, we have peace with God through our Lord Jesus Christ."*

5:2 – *"By whom we also have access by faith into this grace wherein we now stand."* Here Paul affirms that the saints "now stand" in a state of grace through the cross of Christ.

5:9 – *"Much more then, being now justified by his blood, we shall be saved from wrath through him."* Notice the verb tense, "being now justified." What part of "now justified" would Don deny?

5:10 – *"For if, when we were enemies, we were reconciled to God by the death of his Son, we shall be saved by his life."* Note the verb tense, "were reconciled." By what, the removal of the law as asserted by Don? No! By the death of Christ.

5:11 – *"And not only so, but we also joy in God through our Lord Jesus Christ, by whom we have now received the atonement"* HAVE NOW RECEIVED THE ATONEMENT. Don, which part of "now received" would you deny?

5:14 – Adam was a *"figure of him that was to come."* Here, Paul shows that it was in Christ's *first* coming that humanity began anew (for those that believe), not his second coming.

5:15 – *"But not as the offence, so also is the free gift. For if through the offence of one many be dead, much more the grace of God, and the gift by grace, which is by one man, Jesus Christ, hath abounded unto many."* Paul states "grace hath abounded," perfect tense, showing completed action in the past.

5:17 – *"They which receive abundance of grace and of the gift of righteousness shall reign in life."* Paul joins "abundance of grace" with the "gift of justification" and makes both the present possession of the church.

5:20 – *"But where sin abounded, grace did much more abound."* The Greek here actually reads "grace super-abounded" over sin and the law. This verse

121

completely overthrows "Covenant Eschatology," by showing that grace triumphed over the law and did not need to be separately removed.

6:7 – *"He that has died is freed from sin."* The Christian "dies" with Christ in baptism; he is made a participant in Jesus' death, and is thus "freed from sin."

6:14 - *"Ye are not under law, but under grace."* What part of "not under law" would Don deny?

6:15 – *"We are not under the law, but under grace."* NOT UNDER THE LAW, BUT UNDER GRACE.

6:18 – *"Being then made free from sin."* Don, what part of "free from sin" would you deny?

6:22 – *"Being made free from sin."*

6:23 – *"For the wages of sin is death; but the gift of God is eternal life through Jesus Christ our Lord."* In Rom. 5:15, 17, Paul says the saints had received the "gift" of justification and life in Christ. Here he says that eternal life was also the present gift of God by acquittal from the debt of sin under the law.

7:1-4 – *"Wherefore, my brethren, ye also are become dead to the law by the body of Christ."* Don ignored these verses before. They teach that the law of the first husband (Old Testament) terminated with the death of Christ, so that we might enter a new covenant (the gospel). These verses teach the same lesson as those in Heb. 9 regarding the way into the Holiest by the sacrifice of Christ. The one covenant ends where the other begins.

7:6 – *"But now we are delivered from the law, that being dead wherein we were held."* Note the verb tense: NOW DELIVERED FROM THE LAW.

7:25 – *"I thank God through Jesus Christ our Lord"* [for deliverance from bondage to sin and death.]

8:1 – *"There is now no condemnation to them which are in Christ Jesus."* NOW NO CONDEMNATION. What part of "now" would Don deny?

8:2 – "For the law of the Spirit of life in Christ Jesus hath made me free from the law of sin and death." HATH MADE ME FREE FROM THE LAW.

Perfect tense, completed action in the past.

8:3, 4 – *"God condemned sin in the flesh [of Christ] that the righteousness of the law might be fulfilled in us."* By Jesus' death, the law of sin and death was satisfied that God might acquit us.

8:30 – *"Whom he called, them he also justified."*

10:4 – *"Christ is the end of the law for righteousness for every that believeth."* END OF THE LAW.

Hebrews

1:3 – *"When he had by himself purged our sins, sat down on the right hand of the Majesty on high."* Note the verb tense "had purged our sins." Perfect tense, showing completed action in the past. Christ "sat down" also shows the work of redemption was complete.

2:11 – *"For both he that sanctified and they who are sanctified are all of one."* ARE SANCTIFIED.

2:14, 15 – *"Through death he might deliver them."* It was in Jesus' death that man was saved, not his second coming.

2:17 – *"Wherefore in all things it behooved him to be made like unto his brethren...to make reconciliation for the sins of the people."* Reconciliation was made in Jesus' death, not removal of the law.

4:16 – *"Let us therefore come boldly unto the throne of grace, that we may obtain mercy, and find grace to help in time of need."* This verse compliments Heb. 9:8; 10:19 which invite believers into the presence of God within the veil, showing they have been justified from sin.

6:19 – *"Which hope we have as an anchor of the soul, both sure and stedfast, and which entereth into that within the veil."* Entering the veil is predicated upon prior remission of sins.

7:12 – *"For the priesthood being changed, there is made of necessity a change also of the law."* Here the fact of Christ's priesthood is offered as proof that the law had been changed, for it is impossible to have two conflicting priesthoods both legally valid at the same time.

123

7:18 – *"For there is verily a disannulling of the commandment going before for the weakness and unprofitableness thereof."* Here the commandment (Old Testament) is expressly stated to have been annulled.

7:19 – "For the law made nothing perfect, but the bringing in of a better hope did, by which we drawn nigh unto God." MADE PERFECT, BY WHICH WE DRAW NIGH TO GOD. What part of "made perfect" would Don deny?

8:6 – *"But now he hath obtained a more excellent ministry, by how much more he is the mediator of a more excellent covenant."* A MORE EXCELLENT COVENANT. The New Testament supplanted the Old; the two could not be valid simultaneously. Christ's priesthood replaced the Levitical priesthood, and his Testament replaced the Old.

8:12 – *"I will be merciful to their unrighteousness, and their sins and their iniquities will I remember no more."* This is the promise of the New Testament. The testament became of force at Jesus' death (Heb. 9:17), therefore forgiveness of sins became of force at his death as well.

9:8 – *"The Holy Ghost this signifying, that the way into the holiest was not yet made manifest, while as yet the first tabernacle was yet standing."*

No man could enter the Holy of Holies until the atonement was complete.

But the Holy of Holies was a figure for the New Testament and gospel.

The New Testament was of force from and after the cross. Therefore,

The atonement was complete and man could enter (legally and covenantally) the Holy of Holies from and after the cross.

9:12 – *"Having obtained eternal redemption for us."* Perfect tense, showing completed action in the past.

9:15 – *"He is the mediator of the new testament, that by means of death, for the redemption of the transgressions under the first testament, they which are called might receive the promise of eternal inheritance."* This verse plainly shows that the New Testament was then in force and provided redemption that could not obtain as long as the Old Testament was valid.

124

9:17 – *"For a testament is of force after men are dead: otherwise it is of no strength at all."* The New Testament supplants the Old; both cannot be valid at the same time.

9:26 – *"But now once in the end of the world hath he appeared to put away sin by the sacrifice of himself."* Christ's *first appearance* dealt fully and completely with the problem of sin by Christ's sacrifice. Thus, the coming in Rom. 11:25-27 being to save from sin, was clearly Christ's first coming.

10:9 – *"When he said, Lo, I come to do they will, O God. He taketh away the first, that he may establish the second."* Here we see that the first covenant was taken away at Christ's first coming, not second. The first had to be taken away that the second (New Testament) could be established. Why? Because it is impossible both be valid at the same time.

10:10 – *"By the which will we are sanctified through the offering of the body of Jesus Christ once for all."* The "will" here is the New Testament, by which are sanctified through the offering of Christ. The passage is in the present tense, showing present sanctification.

10:12 – *"But this man, after he had offered one sacrifice for sins for ever, sat sown on the right had of God."* That Christ "sat down" shows his work of atonement was complete.

10:14 – *"For by one offering he hath perfected forever them that are sanctified."* Note the verb tense, HATH PERFECTED FOREVER.

10:17 – *"Their sins and iniquities will I remember no more."*

10:18- *"Now where remission of these is, there is no more offering for sin."* The writer's point here is to show that Jesus' sacrifice totally supplanted the temple ceremony, so that there was no other offering for sin.

10:19 – *"Having, therefore, brethren, boldness to enter into the holiest by the blood of Jesus."* The whole point of this verse is to show that because they had been perfected by Christ's sacrifice, the saints can now enter the presence of God legally and covenantally through Christ.

10:22 – *"Let us draw near in full assurance of faith, having our hearts sprinkled from an evil conscience."* "Sprinkling" the conscience here signifies the removal of guilt, by which we are emboldened to enter the presence of God.

10:29- *"The blood of the covenant, wherewith he was sanctified...the Spirit of grace."* The verb tense here shows that the saints were already sanctified by Jesus' blood and the Spirit of grace.

12:7, 8 – *"God dealeth with you as with sons."* Sonship is predicated upon reconciliation and atonement. Under the Old Testament men were deemed servants (Gal. 4:7; Rom. 8:15); but under the New Testament we received the adoption of sonship. This shows that the atonement has been made and that the Old Testament of servitude was annulled.

12:15 – *"Looking diligently lest any man fail of the grace of God."* Grace is the very essence of the New Testament and is predicated upon Jesus' atoning sacrifice. Grace was already arrived when the gospel began to be preached on Pentecost after Christ's ascension.

12:18 – *"For ye are not come unto the mount that might be touched, etc."* Here the writer explicitly states that believers had left the Old Testament economy typified by Sinai and were come to the New Testament economy typified by Zion.

12:22 – *"But ye are come unto mount Sion, and unto the city of the living God, the heavenly Jerusalem."* This verse is offered to prove that the time of our estrangement and banishment from God was over and the saints were now admitted (legally and covenantally) into the presence of God in the heavenly Zion.

12:23 – *"To the general assembly and church of the firstborn, which are written in heaven, and to God the Judge of all, and to the spirits of just men made perfect."* SPIRITS OF JUST MEN MADE PERFECT. Notice that God "the Judge of all" is joined by the writer to the justification of spirits in Hades. Thus, God had acquitted them based upon reception of Christ's blood. The saints on earth were numbered in the assembly of those justified.

12:24 – *"And to Jesus the mediator of the new covenant, and to the blood of sprinkling, that speaketh better things than that of Abel."* Abel was the first martyr, but his blood could not extinguish the debt of sin. Jesus was also a martyr, but his blood brought atonement. The passage shows that the sprinkling and thus the atonement were present realities.

13:10 – *"We have an altar, whereof they have no right to eat which serve the tabernacle."* The "altar" is Christ's sacrifice. We "eat" from that altar probably the sacrament of the Lord's Supper, which Paul teaches is a participation ("communion") in the body and blood (sacrifice) of Christ. Christians had an altar that unbelievers had no right to approach. The validity of the one altar implies the invalidity of the other.

13:20, 21 – *"Now the God of peace, that brought again from the dead our Lord Jesus, that great shepherd of the sheep, through the blood of the everlasting covenant, make you perfect in ever good work."* The resurrection of Christ assumes his justification from the imputation of sin he bore upon the cross. We participate in Jesus' death through baptism (Rom. 6:3-6). Therefore, we are justified in Jesus' death, burial, and resurrection. The blood of the everlasting covenant makes perfect all who are in covenant relationship with God.

I Peter

1:2 – *"Elect according to the foreknowledge of God the Father, through sanctification of the Spirit, unto obedience and sprinkling of the blood of Jesus Christ: Grace unto you, and peace, be multiplied."* Peter here assures the Gentile believers in Cappadocia and the area of the Black Sea of their sanctification by the sprinkling of Jesus' blood, and the grace attending their adoption of sonship by God.

1:3 – *"Blessed be the God and Father of our Lord Jesus Christ, which according to his abundant mercy hath begotten us again unto a lively hope by the resurrection of Jesus Christ from the dead."* The verb tense here is perfect, showing completed action in the past. "Hath begotten us again." The new birth is predicated upon reconciliation and atonement. The resurrection of Christ is proof that justification was a present fact.

1:18, 19 – Ye were redeemed by *"the precious blood of Christ, as of a lamb without blemish and without spot."* Verb tense shows present possession of redemption. What part of "were redeemed" would Don deny?

1:22 – *"Seeing ye have purified your souls in obeying the truth."* Perfect tense, showing completed action in the past. HAVE PURIFIED by obedience. (So much for "faith alone." Man must obey if he would be purified from sin.)

2:10 – *"Which in time past were not a people, but are now the people of God: which had not obtained mercy, but now have obtained mercy."* HAVE NOW OBTAINED MERCY.

127

2:24 – *"Who his own self bare our sins in his own body on the tree, that ye, being dead to sins, should live unto righteousness: by whose stripes ye were healed."* Perfect tense, completed action in the past.

3:18 – *"For Christ also hath once suffered for sins, the just for the unjust, that he might bring us to God, being put to death in the flesh, but quickened by the Spirit."* This bringing to God implies our entrance within the veil, washed and made pure by the blood of Christ. His resurrection is evoked in token of our justification from sin.

3:21 – *"The like figure whereunto even baptism doth also now save us...by the resurrection of Jesus Christ."* Here, baptism is analogized to the waters of Noah by which the believing were saved. Peter makes Jesus' resurrection the power that gives the sacrament and ordinance of baptism effect; *viz.*, the blood of Christ received within the veil at Jesus' death made the atonement and justified him from the imputation of sin, so that his resurrection stands in power and evidence of the atonement in which believer's share.

II Peter

1:2 – *"Grace and peace by multiplied unto you through the knowledge of God, and of Jesus our Lord."* Grace is the state of present reconciliation.

1:9 – *"And hath forgotten that he was purged from his old sins."* Past tense – was purged from his old sins. When? AD 70? No, AD 33 at the cross.

I John

2:2 – *"He is the propitiation of our sins: and not for ours only, but also for the sins of the whole world."* The word "propitiation" here is actually "mercy-seat" and shows that Jesus' sacrifice enters within the veil, coving the debt of sin by the law.

2:12 - *"Your sins are forgiven you for his name's sake."* AD 70? No, AD 33.

Galatians

Gal. 2:4 – *"Because of false brethren unawares brought in, who came in privily to spy out our liberty which we have in Christ Jesus, that hey might bring us into bondage."* The Judaizers, like Don, claimed that the law was still binding, but Paul told the church not to submit to obey its demands.

Gal. 2:9 – *"For I through the law am dead to the law, that I might live unto God."* By Christ's atoning sacrifice, we are redeemed from the law and become dead to its demands.

2:21 – *"I do not frustrate the grace of God: for if righteousness come by the law, then Christ is dead in vain."* Here Paul shows that grace was the present possession of the church and that submitting to the law (which Don says was still obligatory) would frustrate God's grace.

3:13 – *"Christ hath redeemed us from the curse of the law, being made a curse for us."* Note the verb tense, "hath redeemed."

3:25 – *"But after that faith is come, we are no longer under a schoolmaster."* The law was a schoolmaster to bring us to Christ. Paul says the church was no longer under the law once the gospel arrived.

5:1 – *"Stand fast therefore in the liberty wherewith Christ hath made us free, and be not entangled again with the yoke of bondage."* If the law was valid as Don alleges, then Paul was under serious misapprehension of the facts.

5:18 – *"But if ye be led of the Spirit, ye are not under the law."* NOT UNDER THE LAW. If Christians were already delivered from the law, then the salvation from sin contemplated by Rom. 11:25-27 was clearly tied to the cross.

Colossians

2:9, 10 – *"For in him dwelleth all the fullness of the Godhead bodily. And ye are complete in him, which is the head of all principality and power."* "Complete" here has the sense of soteriological perfection. In Christ the saints were complete, lacking nothing to make them acceptable for salvation. And when were they complete? At AD 70? Of course not. They were complete from and after the cross.

2:13 – *"And you, being dead in your sins and the uncircumcision of you flesh hath he quickened together with him, having forgiven you all trespasses."* HAVING FORGIVEN ALL TRESPASSES. When, AD 70? No! The Cross!

2:14 – *"Blotting out the handwriting of ordinances that was against us, which was contrary to us, and took it out of the way, nailing it to the cross."* The "handwriting of ordinances" here is not the Ten Commandments as is commonly supposed, but a memorandum, like a mortgage, reciting our debt before the law. When a man paid off his debt, it was nailed to the post of his door, providing public evidence that he was freed of his former obligation. So here, Paul says Christ carried the debt of our sin to the cross, nailing it there, showing publicly its cancellation in his death. If Don were permitted to have his way, we would have to rewrite this verse so that the debt was nailed to a Roman catapult in the siege of AD 70!

2:15 – *"And having spoiled principalities and powers, he made a shew of them openly, triumphing over them in it [his cross]."* The principalities and powers Christ triumphed over were the very power and dominion of sin and death themselves. The sting of death was sin and the strength of sin was the law (I Cor. 15:56). Christ triumphed over the law, spoiling the strong man of sin in his substitutionary death and atoning sacrifice. He did not take the law away (the moral law still exists and condemns our sins as much as ever). Rather, he triumphed over it by bringing in his all sufficient grace.

Don's Empty Boxes

The reader will recall that we challenged Don to produce verses showing that the saints were under the debt of sin until AD 70 and gave him a box to put the verses in (Box No.1). Don could not produce even one verse. We then added a box challenging Don to produce even one verse that showed the law was binding until AD 70 (Box. No. 2). Again, Don could not produce even one verse. We then asked him to produce even one commentator that agreed that Isa. 27:7-11 referred to the AD 70 destruction of Jerusalem. Again, nothing. Finally, we challenged him to produce even one verse showing that the saints received justification from sin in AD 70. Still nothing. We on the other hand have now produced about nine pages of verses. Probably nine more could be added.

Don's Box No. 1 Verses?	Don's Box No. 2 Verses?	Don's Box No. 3 Verses?

Don's Box No. 4 Verses?

In school sports, when one team cannot even get on the score board and the other has 7 touch-downs, the referee calls the game as a matter of good sportsmanship. That is what needs to happen here. Since Don has no verses, not even one, we feel there is no point in pursuing this discussion further. Don must directly refute *each verse* we have produced, or we will "call the game" and consider this debate over.

Conclusion

Scripture abundantly testifies to the fact that atonement was complete and justification full and free from and after Jesus' cross. But if salvation from sin arrived at the cross, then the coming of Rom. 11:25-27 was Christ's first coming. And if men could enter a state of grace from and after the cross, then the New Testament became of in force, and the Old Testament annulled in Jesus' death. Covenant Eschatology is a system of error that denies Jesus' cross.

SUBJECT:
THE PERFECTION OF SALVATION
AND PASSING OF THE OLD COVENANT

DON K. PRESTON'S FIRST NEGATIVE

Kurt's first affirmative reminds me of a dispensational debate I witnessed. The Zionist read passage after passage that foretold the kingdom, the wolf laying down with the lamb, turning swords into plowshares, etc.. No exegesis. As he sat down he said, "That is my position!" So it is with Kurt. He lists some 88 verses that speak of justification, grace, salvation, etc, and says "This proves my position!" No exegesis, no exposition, and of course, no proof for his proposition!

KURT AND THE COMMENTATORS
Kurt has made a great deal of his false claim that no commentator has ever applied Isaiah 27 to AD 70. I have not addressed this because I am concerned with *scripture*, not commentators. But, do any commentators apply Isaiah 27 to AD 70? **Matthew Henry** says Jesus referred to it when speaking of the unfruitful vine being burned up, and it was fulfilled, "in a particular manner in the unbelieving Jews." **John Gill** and **Albert Barnes** applied Isaiah 27 to the second coming. **Adam Clarke** says that Matthew 24:31 anticipated the fulfilment of Isaiah 27:13. So, **commentators do apply Isaiah 27 to AD 70 and the second coming**! So much for Kurt's appeal to the commentators!

ISAIAH 27
It just keeps getting more confusing as we read my friend's attempt to explain why Paul cited Isaiah 27. He now claims that when he said that Paul cited Isaiah 27 along with Isaiah 59 that he was relating what most commentators say (*Sword and Plow*, Sept, 2009). *This is not true!* **He said not one word** to indicate that he was relating what the commentators- as opposed to Kurt-- say about Romans 11 and Isaiah 27. He was patently admitting that Paul cited Isaiah 27. But now, when that admission backfires on him, he claims that Paul was not referring to Isaiah 27! (But remember, **virtually** all commentators disagree with him, *and he even admits it*)!

And now, my friend tries a totally new approach– **his *fourth position* on Isaiah 26-27!** He says Isaiah 27:10f is not related to the coming of the Lord of 26:20f, which he now, belatedly, admits *again* applies to AD 70. And this after saying that Isaiah 26 has "nothing" to do with AD 70! So,

132

he said that Isaiah 26:20f *could* apply to AD 70. Then he *denied it. Now*, he admits it!

He says Isaiah 27:9f has nothing to do with 26:10f because Isaiah supposedly changes his subject, over, and over, and over again, all within a few verses. **Not so!** Notice that the destruction of Leviathan (27:1) would be "in that day" *the Day of the Lord when the Lord would avenge the blood of the martyrs (26:20-21).* Kurt says 26:20f can be AD 70, but that 27:1 must be the destruction of Assyria. *No, 27:1 is the Day of 26:20f that he admits is AD 70!* But notice, that "in that day" is likewise the time of Israel's salvation at her judgment and the sounding of the Great Trumpet (27:10-13). The references to "in that day" falsify Kurt's desperate claim that Isaiah constantly changes the subject. Thankfully, Isaiah was not as disorganized as Kurt suggests.

Finally– Isaiah 59!

Do you see what my friend has done? I tried for **three presentations** to get Kurt to address Isaiah 59. He said my only "relevant" argument was on Isaiah 27 (which he _now denies_ has *any* relevance)! *Now* he says that Isaiah 59 is the only relevant text. Yet he ignored Isaiah 59 until his last negative, and makes some **new arguments**.

KS– "The coming in Rom. 11 is taken, *not from Isa. 27*, but Isa. 59! That's right! "The Redeemer shall come to Zion" is from Isa. 59:20, 21. Isa. 27 is not quoted in Rom. 11 in connection with a "coming" at all." Kurt cites Jamieson, Fausett and Brown (JFB) for support, (Note: JFB do not **deny** a connection with Isaiah 27. *They simply do not mention it*). But notice the following about JFB: **1.)** They apply Isaiah 27 (JFB, p. 541) and Romans 11:26 to **the second coming**– contra Kurt. **2.)** They say Isaiah 27 / Romans 11 speaks of a yet future conversion of *ethnic Israel*, and they say that those (like Kurt) who reject this view do "great violence" to the text! **3.)** They apply Isaiah 59 and Jeremiah 31 to the second coming– **contra Kurt**. So, Kurt selectively argues **from what they do not say**, and **rejects what they do say, yet claims they agree with him!** But, let's look closer at Kurt's admission that Paul quotes Isaiah 59. He was silent about the arguments I have made, so, let me refresh the reader's memory.

In Isaiah 59 YHVH accused Israel of shedding innocent blood and violence (v. 1-8). The Lord saw Israel in her sinful condition and, "His own arm brought salvation for Him; and His own righteousness, it sustained Him for He put on righteousness as a breastplate, and a helmet of salvation on His head; He put on the garments of vengeance for His clothing, and was clad with zeal as a cloak. According to their deeds,

133

accordingly He will repay, Fury to His adversaries, Recompense to His enemies." **Isaiah 59 predicted the salvation of Israel at the coming of the Lord in judgment of Israel for her guilt in shedding innocent blood.**

Please catch the power of Kurt's admission that Paul is citing Isaiah 59. Kurt says of Romans 11: **a.)** The coming of the Lord is referent to the cross, not AD 70. **b.)** Israel is not OC Israel, but the church. **c.)** The salvation is referent to the conversion of Jews and Gentiles throughout the Christian age. However...

> **The coming of the Lord for salvation, in Romans 11:26-27, is the coming of the Lord predicted in Isaiah 59–** _**Kurt Simmons now agreeing!**_
> **But, the coming of the Lord of Isaiah 59 is the coming of the Lord in judgment of Israel for shedding innocent blood.** _**(It is not a prediction of the cross, or the salvation of the church throughout time).**_
> **Therefore, the coming of the Lord for salvation in Romans 11:26-27, is the coming of the Lord in judgment of Israel for shedding innocent blood. (Which was in AD 70-Matthew 23).**

Nothing in Isaiah 59 even remotely resembles Kurt's view of Romans 11! _Nothing_! Yet, Isaiah is, _Kurt now agreeing_, the source of Paul's prediction in Romans 11:26. Kurt must explain why Paul cited a prophecy that had nothing whatsoever to do with the subject he was discussing, in order to validate what he was discussing. Kurt has refused to answer this _because he cannot answer this_. Yet, his admission that the coming of Romans 11 is the coming of Isaiah 59 is _100% fatal_ to his new theology. His admission proves that all of the verses in Kurt's first affirmative must speak of a _process begun_, but a process to be _perfected_ at the Second Coming. My affirmative proposition is established by Kurt's fatal admission.

ENTRANCE INTO THE MHP

I asked: What is **the one thing** that prevented man from entering the MHP– He refused to answer.

I asked: If the destruction of Jerusalem was irrelevant to man's spiritual justification, and the saints were perfected prior to that event, **why did the saints have to wait until AD 70 to enter the MHP?** He refused to answer **because he has no answer**.

Kurt threw up a cloud of dust about the time of reformation. His admission that the time of reformation was not completed until AD 70, when the saints could enter the MHP is **fatal** to his rejection of Covenant Eschatology.

Note Kurt's ever shifting position on the time of reformation: He said it began at the cross, (but man could not objectively enter the MHP). He then said that the time of reformation was *completed* in AD 70 with the completion of the Spirit's work. But **now**, he says the time of reformation *ended* (it was not perfected) in AD 70!

Hebrews 9:6-10– If the time of reformation fully arrived at the cross as Kurt originally contended, man should have begun to **actually** enter the MHP, from that point. But, no, Kurt tells us **man could not truly enter the MHP until AD 70!** Kurt admitted, and I agree, "When the gifts of the Spirit ceased, *the time of reformation was complete and not before.*" (My emp., DKP). But, realizing the fatal nature of this admission, Kurt now says: "The time of reformation *ended* in AD 70." (My emp., DKP) Do you see the problem? On the one hand he correctly says the time of reformation was completed in AD 70. But that is self-destructive, so he now says the time of reformation *terminated* in AD 70. This is a blatantly self contradictory.

Hebrews 9 says there could be no entrance into the MHP *until the arrival–not* **termination**- *of the time of reformation.* The time of reformation began at the Cross– and was guaranteed by the Spirit-- but was not perfected until AD 70. And, **there was no true entrance into the MHP until AD 70 (KS).** If the time of reformation *ended* in AD 70, Kurt, **then man could *never* enter the MHP**, and **the time for man to enter the MHP ended without so much as one person ever entering the MHP!** Man could not, per Kurt, enter before AD 70. But, per his *newest* position, the time of reformation (when man could *supposedly* enter) **terminated**, in AD 70! Kurt has hopelessly entangled himself.

I have focused on the time of reformation because it is in some respects, what this debate is about. So, let me reiterate my argument, which Kurt has totally ignored, and which he must ignore:

Kurt admits that there was *no entrance* into the MHP at the *initiation of the reformation,* i.e. at the cross. *Entrance came only when the time of reformation– the work of grace– was completed, at the parousia.* Now watch as we apply this *to the atonement:*

Kurt offered another syllogism. Unfortunately for him, his efforts fail. Here is his self-contradictory argument:

No man could enter the Holy of Holies until the atonement was complete.

But the Holy of Holies was a figure for the New Testament and gospel.

The New Testament was of force from and after the cross. Therefore,

135

The atonement was complete and man could enter (legally and covenantally) the Holy of Holies from and after the cross.

Those who have been paying attention to this debate will see instantly that Kurt has, once again, **changed his position** and destroyed his own argument.

Kurt– **"No man could enter the Holy of Holies until the atonement was complete."** (Amen, brother! This is a *fatal admission*).

Kurt– "I never said the saints entered heaven (The MHP, Revelation 15:8, DKP) before AD 70!"

Therefore, the atonement was not completed until AD 70!

ATTENTION! Did you notice Kurt's shift from the MHP being _heaven_ to being the New Covenant? He has changed theological positions _again_! Watch this.

No man could enter the MHP while Torah remained binding (Hebrews 9:9f)

The MHP represented the New Covenant (Kurt's New Position).

But, no man could enter the MHP until AD 70 (Revelation 15:8-KS supposedly agrees).

Therefore, Torah remained binding and no man could enter the New Covenant until AD 70.

Kurt has re-embraced Covenant Eschatology! Kurt's desperate attempt to radically redefine the MHP from his earlier position backfires on him.

Kurt says: "The atonement was complete and man could enter (legally and covenantally) the Holy of Holies from and after the cross. This is *sophistry*. If man was "covenantally" able to enter the MHP (But, what proof did Kurt offer?) then man should have been able to _objectively_ enter the MHP! It was *covenant* that prevented objective entrance *(Hebrews 9:6f)*. Therefore, if the New Covenant was completed prior to AD 70, then man should have been able– *objectively*– to enter the MHP! This is _irrefutable_. Yet, Kurt admits: "I never said the saints entered heaven before AD 70!" Furthermore, Kurt (ostensibly) understands that the New Covenant, *while established by Jesus' death* (Galatians 3:15) was not fully revealed and confirmed through the Spirit's ministry until AD 70! This is called *covenantal transition*.

So, Kurt adamantly tells us that he has "never" said that man could enter the MHP before AD 70. Now of course, *he has changed horses again*, saying that the MHP was the New Covenant and that man was fully in the New Covenant before AD 70! Yet, he still (?) says man could not *objectively* enter the MHP until AD 70! Confused? You should be.

The truth is that man could not enter the MHP **while Torah remained valid. Torah would remain valid until man _could_ enter the MHP at the time of reformation**. Thus, Torah ended when the time of reformation was completed, and man could enter the MHP, in AD 70. Kurt has surrendered his objection to the _initiation_ of grace, salvation and covenant transition. He has unwittingly affirmed Covenant Eschatology. So, **_once again_**:

> **There could be no access to the MHP as long as Torah remained binding (Hebrews 9).**
> **But, man could not enter the MHP until AD 70 (Kurt Simmons).**
> **Therefore, Torah remained binding until AD 70.**

This is the _correct_ use of logic and the argument is indisputable.

The Triumph of Grace Over Law, and the so-called "Mysterious" Negative Power of Torah

My friend expends a great deal of steam on grace triumphing over law. He simply reiterates his claims, with no exegesis, and then, amazingly, makes the following statements: "Don states '_removal of Torah was essential for man's justification after all!'_" (emphasis in original). Don states, "Torah had to end in order for forgiveness, entrance into the MHP and life to become realities!" Dear reader, _we deny this totally and emphatically_. The law was taken away, not so grace could enter in, but because it was a _mere schoolmaster_ to bring us to Christ; it was a system of types and shadows _pointing_ to Jesus." Then, in some of his more amazing comments, my friend adds this: "There is _nothing_ in the temple ritual or _anywhere_ in the law that can forestall God's grace in Jesus Christ. NOTHING. Law doesn't prevent grace, it invites it! **_The inability of Torah to forgive in no way implies it also possessed a negative power to prevent or forestall forgiveness of sin!_** What is Don's proof of this "mysterious "negative power"? He has none!"

Readers, here is the crux of the matter, and the problem with Kurt's new theology. It is in flagrant denial of the Biblical text and manifest demonstration of my friend's abuse of logic. Follow...

A.) Kurt sets up a false dichotomy. He says that Torah had no negative power, for it was "a mere schoolmaster." So, per Kurt, Torah could not exercise negative power by being the schoolmaster; it was **either** a schoolmaster or a negative power. It could not be both! This is an abuse of logic.

B.) Kurt says removal of Torah was not necessary for grace to enter. But wait, Torah was to bring man to "the faith" and Christ, and would endure until then. So, **Torah was a schoolmaster until the arrival of grace!** Yet, Kurt says no, **it was just a schoolmaster** and not a negative power, although **according to Paul, as a schoolmaster**, it was given to make sin abound, it brought death, it could not deliver from death, and could not provide forgiveness and grace.

C.) Kurt emphatically denies that Torah had negative power. Hebrews says as long as Torah remained, there was no forgiveness. Kurt says this is not a negative power, "forestalling forgiveness and grace." I will stand with scripture on this.

D.) Kurt says Torah had no power to prevent entrance into the MHP. Hebrews 9 says as long as Torah stood, there could be no entrance into the MHP. I will stand with scripture on this.

Has my friend forgotten what Hebrews 9:6-10 says, or is he simply willing to deny what it says?

Why could man not enter the MHP? What does the inspired text *say*, Kurt? As long as Torah stood binding, there was no entrance into the MHP! *Torah had the negative power to prevent entrance to the presence of God! Torah had no power to forgive*, thus, no power to bring man into the presence of God. *That sure sounds like a negative power to me!* What is so "mysterious" about that? It is what the text says. So...

As long as Torah remained binding, there was no forgiveness of sin, no entrance into the MHP (Hebrews 9:6-10).

No entrance into the MHP until AD 70– KS (ostensibly) teaches this truth.

Therefore, Torah remained binding and there was no objective forgiveness until AD 70!

Kurt's new theology however, denies this and sees no relationship between Torah, lack of forgiveness and entrance into the MHP. He claims now that removal of Torah was not even necessary for grace to triumph over law! **Did you catch that?** If removal of Torah was not necessary for grace to triumph over law, **then removal of Torah was not necessary to bring forgiveness, and entrance into the MHP, Kurt!** Let me remind you again of Kurt's *total silence* in the face of these questions.

Kurt claimed that removal of Torah had *nothing* to do with Paul's soteriology, and *now* claims it had no negative power "to prevent or forestall forgiveness." **(Kurt, where are your commentators in support of this new theology?)** I offered the following and urged the readers to watch for Kurt's answer. *We are all still waiting for his response.*

Torah was the ministration of death (2 Corinthians 3:6f). Kurt, did the deliverance from the ministration of death, to the ministration of life have *nothing* to do with soteriology? If Torah was a ministration of death, was death, empowered by Torah, not a *negative power*?

138

Paul said Torah could not deliver from the law of sin and death (Romans 8:1-3). He said Christ does deliver from that law! **Did the deliverance from the law of sin and death have nothing to do with forgiveness?** Was being under the power of the law of sin and death not a negative power, Kurt? Come now, my friend, *please* answer the question.

Paul said Torah killed, "The commandment came, sin revived, I died" "sin, working death in me by that which is good...became exceedingly sinful" (Romans 7:13). Kurt, are these positive, or negative aspects of Torah?

Torah could not give life or righteousness (Galatians 3:20-21). Did deliverance from that law, to the covenant that gives life and righteousness have *nothing* to do with salvation?

Paul said those under Torah were under "the curse" (Galatians 2-3). Did deliverance from that curse had nothing to do with redemption? *Was the curse of Torah a negative power, Kurt?*

There was no forgiveness under Torah. There would be forgiveness *when Torah ended at the time of reformation.* **Is forgiveness related to soteriology?** Is unforgiven sin positive or negative, Kurt?

There was no entrance into the MHP under Torah; there would be entrance into the MHP at the end of Torah, the time of reformation. *Is entrance into the MHP related to salvation, Kurt?*

Hebrews 9 is Covenant Eschatology, anyway you want to look at it. Torah had to end in order for forgiveness, entrance into the MHP and life to become realities! End of Torah = Covenant Eschatology; End of Torah = Salvation! Kurt can ridicule this, but it will not change the indisputable facts as specifically stated by inspiration. Hebrews 9:6f stands as an insurmountable bulwark against Kurt's insistence that Torah was removed at the Cross. Furthermore, his admission that man could not, after all, enter the MHP until AD 70 is an open admission of my position.

DANIEL 12– THE POWER OF THE HOLY PEOPLE

My friend's desperation manifested itself for all to see in his "response" to my question. He *says* that Israel's "power" (Daniel 12:7) was the identical power as the pagan nations. This is *astounding*! YHVH always said that His special covenant relationship with Israel was totally distinctive. *When He gave them Torah* He said, "If you will indeed keep my covenant then you will be a special treasure to me above all the people; for all the earth is mine, and you shall be to me a kingdom of priests and a holy nation (Exodus 19:5-6). In Deuteronomy 26:18-19, at the second giving of the Law, God said, "Today the Lord has proclaimed you to be His special people, just as He promised you, so that you should keep His commands. In Psalms 147:19-20 God said,

"He gave His statutes to Jacob. He has not done so with any nation"! In spite of all of this– and much more could be added– Kurt tells us that Israel's power was not her covenant with YHVH. In fact, *Israel was just like the pagans in regard to her power.* This argument is manifest demonstration of the desperation and falsity of Kurt's position. To deny that Israel's power, *her only power*, was her covenant with God is patently false. And since Daniel posits the destruction of the power of Israel at AD 70, this is irrefutable proof that Torah remained valid until AD 70. ***This is Covenant Eschatology.***

TRANSFIGURATION
Kurt claims that the Transfiguration was a vision of **Jesus' first appearing**, not the second coming. He says the Transfiguration was not about covenant contrast and transition.

Response: **First**, Kurt's argument is virtually unprecedented in the entire history of Christian commentary which agrees that the Transfiguration was a vision of Christ's second coming. **2.)** Peter was not writing against those who denied Jesus' incarnation, but his second coming (2 Peter 3:3). **3.)** Peter wanted to establish three equal tabernacles. God would not allow it. ***This is a covenant contrast.*** **4.)** The Voice said of Jesus "This is my beloved Son, hear him." In the Greek, the "hear him" is literally "*Him, hear!*", and is in the emphatic, meaning that *in contrast to Moses and Elijah*, Jesus is to be heard. **5.)** Moses and Elijah vanish away, at the voice that says of Jesus "Him hear!" Yet, Kurt eschews the text, rejects the virtually unanimous testimony of the commentaries, and says he "feels" that it is not about covenant contrast, or Jesus' second coming. No, the Transfiguration is about *the covenantal transition from Moses to Christ,* and it was a vision of the second coming. The Transfiguration is therefore, all about **Covenant Eschatology.**

Passing of Torah– Subjective and Objective
Kurt makes one of the most illogical "arguments" a person will ever read. He claims that when Paul said, "you become dead to the Law through the body of Christ" that this actually means that ***the Law itself had died!*** This is like saying that when a person gets a divorce that the entire institution of marriage is destroyed! Watch the following illustration.

For decades the Berlin Wall stood as a barrier to freedom. East Berliners longed to escape the oppressive communist law. Now, Kurt, when someone managed to escape from East Berlin into the West (prior to the fall of the

"Wall") *did that mean that East Berlin communism was dead?* Patently not. The *individual* who escaped *had died to communism!* Just like Paul said those coming into Christ through baptism had *died to the Law through the body of Christ!* (Incidentally, Kurt claims I ignored Romans 7:4. Not true. I *appealed* to Romans 7!) Paul did not say Torah had died. Just so, in 2 Corinthians 3:10f, Paul said that *when a person turned to Christ,* the veil of Torah was removed for them. He did not say Torah had passed. Huge difference! This is what Paul affirms in Ephesians 2, Colossians 2, etc... When a person, through faith, entered into the power of the cross, *they died to the Law!* Kurt admits this in his first affirmative! But when a person died to the Law, the Law did not die. The NT speaks of the objective passing of the Law itself, however.

ATTENTION!! Kurt admits that Colossians 2:14f *does not say that Torah was nailed to the Cross*: "What was nailed to the cross? Not the Mosiac (sic) law, but the sentence of the law (the law of sin and death) condemning the transgression of men" (Sept. 09, S-P- And first affirmative). **Folks, this is fatal!** If Colossians 2 does not (and it *doesn't*) say that Torah was nailed to the Cross, then no passage does, and **Kurt has admitted that it doesn't!** Note his contradiction: Torah was *not* nailed to the cross. *His proposition*: Torah ended at the cross! There is no way to reconcile Kurt's self-contradiction. He has totally surrendered his proposition. Do not fail to catch this!

In Hebrews 8:13, Paul says that *the Covenant* –not some already dead outward form of the Law– was "nigh unto passing." In chapter 12:25f– the heaven and earth of the Old Covenant had not yet passed, but was **about to be removed.** Furthermore, Jesus did say that not one jot or one tittle of the law could pass until it was all fulfilled, and *even the ceremonial aspects of Torah had not yet been fulfilled,* since Paul said those ceremonial sacrifices remained, when he wrote Colossians and Hebrews, "shadows of good things about to come" (Colossians 2:17; Hebrews 10:1-4). Torah, **objectively speaking,** had not been done away. *This is why there was still no access to the MHP until AD 70. As long as Torah remained valid, there was no access to the MHP,* and Kurt admits there was no entrance into the MHP until AD 70. **This is Covenant Eschatology validated and proven.**

In Kurt's first affirmative he desperately argues, falsely, that God could not have two systems in force at the same time. **Kurt, did God have two**

systems in place when He gave Torah to Israel, but not to the pagans? Were there two "systems" in place when John preached the baptism of repentance and faith in the coming of Messiah, while the Temple cultus was still in effect? John's baptism was not Torah "baptism!" And consider Galatians 4.22f. Paul, anticipated the yet future casting out of the bondwoman– which he says was **the Old Covenant** and her seed– **for persecuting the Christians.** The allegory has the two sons *dwelling in the same house*, but Ishmael was cast out for persecuting Isaac. And Paul said "as it was then, even so it is now." Paul said the Old Covenant and seed would be cast out **for persecuting Christians.** But, *there were no Christians before the Cross!* It is therefore irrefutably true that **the two sons dwelt together while the seed of the flesh persecuted the Seed of promise and was then cast out.** Torah and Israel were not cast out at the cross. This is **Covenant Eschatology.** Kurt's essential argument that two systems could not temporarily co-exist is false.

Was Jesus' Resurrection the Proof of the Completion of the Atonement?
Kurt says: "Will Don deny Jesus died under imputation of sin? Will he deny he was raised justified, free from imputation of sin (Rom. 6:7, 10)? But if Christ was justified from the imputation of sin at his resurrection, it is clear that his blood was received by God within the veil *before* his ascension, and that can only mean it was received by God *at his death.*"

Response: Kurt is so desperate to prove his position that he continues to *invent* **historically unprecedented arguments.** Kurt, give us some commentary support for your idea that Jesus had to be justified from the sin of others!

1.) Kurt argues as he does because of his *historically unprecedented argument* that Jesus had to enter the MHP twice (He said Christ "legally" pierced the veil, (that is *once*), and then entered the MHP at his ascension. That is *twice)*. In this view, Christ's ascension and entrance into the MHP was *legally unnecessary*, since the work of atonement was finished when he "legally pierced the veil" **while hanging on the cross! Kurt, where are the commentators who agree your unprecedented argument?**

2.) Kurt has consistently ignored Hebrews 9:12– Christ entered the MHP *ONCE!* **Not twice.** Not once *legally* (whatever that means), and then once *actually*. *ONCE!* Kurt says twice, Paul says ONCE! Kurt is wrong.

3.) Kurt said it was appropriate for him to draw the analogy with Jesus and the OT priest who had to enter the MHP twice. But:

A.) The OT high priest had to enter *twice* because ***the first time*** (the cross per Kurt's analogy) the priest had to offer sacrifice ***for his own sins– not for the sins of the people!*** Kurt argues that Jesus died the sinner's death and legally, *but not actually,* pierced the veil, when he bore the sins of the people! **But in scripture,** the priest bore the sins of the people at the *second entrance into the MHP* The **second time, Kurt, *not the first!*** You have no analogy.

B.) The OT priest had to **actually** enter twice. He did not enter in some vague, "legal" sense, and then **actually**, as in Kurt's new paradigm.

C.) Jesus' sinlessness voided any need for him to enter the MHP twice. He entered ***ONCE***, and that for the sins of the people (Hebrews 9:12). ***Do not lose sight of this verse amid Kurt's smoke screens!***

D.) Jesus had to appear the second time *"for (This is the reason why Jesus had to come again!)* the law, *having (present tense,* Kurt) a shadow of good things *about to come"* (Hebrews 10:1f). *Kurt has repeatedly ignored this argument, even though he admits to the Greek present and future tenses in his book.* So, Jesus *had to* come again, to fulfill the typological (ceremonial) aspects of atonement / Torah, which were, when Paul wrote, *still valid and binding shadows.* Kurt himself has said that there could be no entrance into the MHP until the atonement was perfected, and there could be no entrance into the MHP until AD 70! Do not fail to catch this amidst all of Kurt's smoke. It is fatal to every single one of his claims.

Kurt's List and His Unequal Emphasis on the Greek Tenses

We do not have space to examine every one of the verses listed by Kurt, nor need we to. His argument can be summed up under certain headings of: forgiveness, redemption, salvation, atonement, New Covenant, etc.. If it can be demonstrated that these soteriological elements were not completed at the Cross, but was awaiting perfection in AD 70, then my friend's entire affirmative is negated.

In spite of the use of the past tense in the verses cited by Kurt, **each of these elements is also couched in future tense verbs.**

Redemption: Already –> "In whom we have redemption" (Ephesians 1:7). **Future:** "You were sealed with the Holy Spirit of promise *until the day of redemption"* (Ephesians 1:12-13; 4:30)–> If redemption was already perfected, why did they need the charismata *to guarantee its completion*? Why did Paul look forward to the day of redemption? Kurt, why do you ignore these future tenses and the work of the Spirit?

143

Notice: Paul equates redemption with forgiveness: "in whom we have redemption, *even the forgiveness of our sin.*" Yet, again, **the Holy Spirit was the guarantee of the future day of redemption!** So, redemption = forgiveness, and redemption would not fully arrive until Christ's second coming in AD 70. It follows inexorably that forgiveness would objectively arrive in AD 70– precisely as Romans 11:26f says! Kurt, why do you ignore the future tense of the Day of Redemption?

Adoption / Sonship: **Already**–> "We have received the spirit of adoption" (Romans 8:14). **Future**–> "longing for the adoption, to wit, the redemption of the body" (Romans 8:23). Kurt, why do you ignore the future tense?

Atonement: **Already**–> "We have received the atonement" (reconciliation, DKP, Romans 5:10)– **Future**– "We shall be saved by his life" (Romans 5:10). Also, KS– "The soul could not enter the presence of God in heaven without the atoning sacrifice of Christ, so the dead were sequestered in Hades until the general resurrection." So, **even according to Kurt**, the atonement was not completed until AD 70!

Inheritance: **Already**–> Ephesians 1:11: "In Him also we have obtained an inheritance." **Future**–> Ephesians 1:14: "who is the guarantee of our inheritance until the redemption of the purchased possession." Now watch: Kurt appeals to Hebrews 9:15 to prove that the New Covenant was already fully in place and that those from the first covenant now had redemption. If that is true, Kurt, **why could those in the Hadean realm not enter the MHP until AD 70 (Revelation 15:8)?** Oh, wait, you have (*inadvertently*) answered this: "The soul could not enter the presence of God in heaven without the atoning sacrifice of Christ, so the dead were sequestered in Hades until the general resurrection" (S-P, Sept. 09). So, Kurt himself informs us that the inheritance and forgiveness through completed atonement did not arrive until AD 70! If the atonement and forgiveness of sin– *sin being the only thing to keep man from the MHP*– was fully realized at the cross, then those under the first covenant (i.e. in Hades) had already received "the better resurrection," and the eternal inheritance! Kurt has distorted Hebrews 9:15, and contradicted his own writings, *again.*

New Covenant: Already–> I have repeatedly noted the *present tense verbs* that speak of the then passing of Torah (2 Corinthians 3:6f; Hebrews 8:13, etc.), and the **future** passing of the Law (Hebrews 12:25f). I have noted the Greek present tenses that prove that Torah, including the sacrificial system, was still, when Paul wrote, typological of good things *about to come* (future tense). *In his book, Kurt acknowledges these present tenses, but now he denies them!*

144

Furthermore: The Holy Spirit was the guarantee of the New Covenant, and that through the distinctive personal ministry of Paul. Kurt affirms that covenant transition was over and done at the cross. Paul disagreed, and said that the transition from the Old Covenant to the New was ongoing when he wrote 2 Corinthians 3-4: "we are being transformed from Glory to Glory, by the Spirit. wherefore, having this ministry..." Paul uses the *present tenses* several times to speak of the present and impending passing of Torah. *Kurt, why do you reject the present and future tenses?*

Furthermore, if the New Covenant was perfected, why was the ministry of the Spirit necessary, Kurt? Paul said it was the ministry of the Spirit to reveal the New Covenant and to bring about the transition from the Old to the New (2 Corinthians 3). But that work of the Spirit was unnecessary in Kurt's paradigm.

Kurt falsely claims that in Hebrews 7:12f Paul affirmed the past tense of the passing of the Law. *False. Paul uses the present tense!* Kurt says Christ could not serve in a priestly capacity unless Torah had been removed. Again, false. *Jesus was serving as high priest in the true heavenly tabernacle (Hebrews 8:1f),* where he *could serve* because he was no longer subject to the law. Yet, Paul is emphatic, "if he were on earth, he could not serve as priest, seeing there are (present tense) priests who serve (present tense) *according to the Law"* (Hebrews 8:5). Kurt even claims on Hebrews 10:9 that Torah "was taken away." *This is inexcusable.* Paul uses the *present tense*: "He is *taking away* the first that he might establish the second." We have already noted the present tenses in Hebrews 9:6-10:1f *which Kurt acknowledges in his book,* but now wants to deny. Kurt, *why do you ignore these Greek tenses?*

Clearly, *there were two systems in effect at the same time!* Christ was serving as priest in the heavenly tabernacle. The Aaronic priests were serving under Torah. The earthly system was "nigh unto passing" while the heavenly city and tabernacle were "about to come" (Hebrews 13:14).

So, what we have are proleptic (a form of past tense) statements, present tense statements, and future tense references. No proper exegesis of all of this evidence can ignore *two out of three uses of the Greek tenses* and claim to be the whole picture, *yet this is precisely what Kurt has done.* **Kurt, what is your linguistic or grammatical authority for rejecting the present and future tenses?** You have *no authority for this* other than your newly invented theology.

145

Grace: **Already**–> "By grace are you saved through grace" (Ephesians 2:8-9). **Future**: "hope to the end for the grace that shall be brought to you at the coming of the Lord" (1 Peter 1:7-8).

Perfect in him: **Already**–> "And you are perfect in him" (Colossians 2:10). **Future**–> "That we might present every man perfect in Christ" (Colossians 1:27). Notice that the early church had the charismata to "equip the church for the work of the ministry...until we all come to the perfect man" (Ephesians 4:13-16). Kurt, if they were already perfected, *why did they need the gifts to bring them to the perfect man?*

Salvation: **Already**–> "By grace are you saved through grace" (Ephesians 2:8-9). **Future**: "to those who eagerly look for him, he will appear the second time, apart from sin, for salvation, *for*, the law having a shadow of good things about to come" (Hebrews 9:28-10:1); the salvation "ready to be revealed in the last times" at the parousia (1 Peter 1:5-12).

In each verse cited by Kurt, he ignores the transitional period. He sees covenant transition completed at the cross. This is false. He likewise ignores the work of the Spirit as *the guarantee of the completion of what began at the cross*. Furthermore, from Pentecost onward, the church was betrothed –*not married*-- to Christ. Kurt admits this. This is a *process begun*, awaiting consummation! Likewise, the foundation for the New Covenant Temple was laid, but, "construction" was on-going from Pentecost onward. The Temple was not complete at the Cross (Ephesians 2:19f; 1 Peter 2:4f). *Note the present tenses.* Kurt, *do you deny these present tenses?*

Let me reiterate: Paul uses past, present and future tenses to speak of each of the elements Kurt emphasizes. *Proper hermeneutic* cannot emphasize one of the tenses to the exclusion of the others. This is to practice presuppositional theology. This is precisely what Kurt has done. Let me now introduce some critical factors.

DO NOT MISS THIS!! Kurt ignores the **indisputable fact** that each element he lists had to do with **the fulfillment of God's promises to OC Israel**. If salvation was completed at the cross, *then Israel's salvation (resurrection! Isaiah 25:8-9; Romans 9:28) was completed at the cross: "Salvation is of the Jews" (John 4:22), i.e. from the Jews first, then to the nations!* Yet, Kurt admitted (2ⁿᵈ Neg) that Romans 9:28 referred to the salvation of "national Israel" in AD 70! How could Israel have been cut off at the cross, if Israel was not saved until AD 70? How could salvation be completed at the cross if Israel's salvation was in AD 70? This is a fatal contradiction! Let me build on that concept.

146

The resurrection of 1 Corinthians 15 is the resurrection predicted in Isaiah 25:8.

The resurrection of Isaiah 25:8 would be the time of **the salvation of Israel**.

Therefore, the resurrection of 1 Corinthians 15 would be the time of the salvation of Israel.

Kurt says 1 Corinthians 15 is about the death of *individuals* throughout the Christian age. **Paul said** the resurrection he anticipated was *the salvation of Israel!* Whom shall we believe?

Furthermore...

The resurrection of 1 Corinthians 15 is the resurrection predicted in Hosea 13:14.

The resurrection of Hosea 13:14 would be the resurrection, ***of Israel***, from alienation from God through sin (Hosea 13:1-2: "When Israel sinned, he died").– I.e. it would be resurrection through forgiveness and reconciliation.

Therefore, the resurrection of 1 Corinthians 15 would be the resurrection, **of Israel**, from alienation from God through sin (Hosea 13:1-2).– I.e. it would be resurrection through forgiveness and reconciliation.

The resurrection of 1 Corinthians 15 would be the resurrection, **of Israel**, from alienation from God through sin (Hosea 13:1-2).– I.e. it would be resurrection through forgiveness and reconciliation.

But, the resurrection of 1 Corinthians 15 was still future when Paul wrote.

Therefore, the resurrection, **of Israel**, from alienation from God through sin (Hosea 13:1-2).– I.e. resurrection through forgiveness and reconciliation was still future when Paul wrote.

Of course this means that Israel was not cut off at the cross. God's promises to her were "irrevocable" (Romans 11:28), **and until His covenant promises to her were fulfilled she would not enter her salvation (Romans 11:26f) at the resurrection.**

The last enemy to be destroyed was death (Kurt agrees).

But, sin produced death (Romans 6:23; "the law of sin and death").

The last enemy would be destroyed at the resurrection in AD 70 (Kurt agrees *theoretically*, but not truly. See below).

147

Thus, sin, which produced death, would be destroyed (for those "in Christ," and the power of his resurrection, 1 Corinthians 15:22) at the resurrection in AD 70.

The resurrection is when sin, the sting of death was to be overcome, (1 Corinthians 15:54-56).
The miraculous gifts of the Spirit were the guarantee of that resurrection (2 Corinthians 5:5; Ephesians 1:13).

Therefore, the miraculous gifts of the Spirit *were the guarantee of the final victory over sin!*
So, again, since the charismata were the guarantee of the resurrection, and since the resurrection is when sin, the sting of death would be overcome, **it therefore follows that the charismata were the guarantee of the final victory over sin. Kurt says the charismata endured until AD 70. Thus, the final victory of sin was in AD 70.** Kurt has ignored these arguments.

Kurt's False View of Sin, Death and Resurrection

Let me introduce the problem of Kurt's false view of sin-death-forgiveness. Kurt says physical death was the "immediate" result of Adam's sin– thus, physical death is the result of sin today, and, "it is from physical death that the promise of resurrection was given" (KS, Oct. 2009, S/P).
Kurt correctly believes in the *substitutionary death of Jesus*. Substitutionary means "in the place of." Consider what this means.

Jesus died a substitutionary death for man.
Jesus' physical death was the substitutionary death that he died.
Substitutionary means "in the place of."
Therefore, Jesus died physically so that man would not have to die physically.
Please pay particular attention to this. You cannot argue, as Kurt does, that Jesus' ***physical death*** was his substitutionary death, and then say that even those in Christ and ostensibly in the power of his death still have to die physically! What does *substitutionary* mean, after all? If Jesus died so that those in him *do not have to die*, then why do those in him have to die physically? Did Jesus' substitutionary physical death do no good? Or, has no believer has ever entered fully into the benefit of his substitutionary death?

148

It will do no good to say that resurrection delivers man *out of death*, **after man dies**! Death is the penalty of sin: "The wages of sin is death." Thus, the physical death of even the most faithful Christian is proof positive that the Christian was still under "the strength of sin," and has not experienced deliverance from sin, if physical death is "the immediate result of sin"! The bottom line is that if Jesus' physical death was *substitutionary, as Kurt says,* **then people of faith should never die physically.** This is logically inescapable, and reveals just part of the problem with Kurt's theology.

Kurt claims that "sin was defeated in Christ's cross." It was actually "the law of sin and death" (**not Torah itself!**) that was nailed to the cross. He says forgiveness of sin was objectively applied from then. Well, if sin brings physical death, then if sin was defeated and those of faith were (or are) objectively **forgiven of sin**, then why does man have to die physically? *Forgiveness is the removal of that which kills, is it not?* So, if sin brings physical death, but, a person is completely forgiven, **with no sin in their life**, why does that person still experience physical death, Kurt? If, as you say, Christ nailed the law of sin and death to the cross, *then why are Christians still subject to the law of sin and death?*

My friend's view logically demands that the physical death of even the most faithful Christian is a powerful testimony to the lack of forgiveness in their life. Kurt even says that if the Christian sins, "he comes again under the power of sin and death" (S-P, Sept. 09). Thus, *physical death is the indisputable proof that the Christian is under the power of sin!* And, since that physical death is the *final testimony of the power of sin*, this *logically demands* that that person is *lost*, for the final act in their life was *not forgiveness*, but *the imposition of the law of sin and death: i.e. you sin, you die!* The believer's *physical death* proves, *indisputably*, that they were not objectively forgiven, for they died a sinner's death! So, exactly how did Jesus nail the law of sin and death to the cross, Kurt?

Summary and Conclusion
I have demonstrated *prima facie*, that Kurt has mis-applied the Greek past tenses, by ignoring the transitional work of the Holy Spirit as *the guarantee of the finished work of salvation*, and by ignoring the present tenses and the future tenses of the work of salvation. He is guilty of mis-representing the present and future tenses, actually claiming that they are past tense applications.

I have shown indisputably that covenant transition was not complete at the cross. I have even shown **from Kurt's own hand that Torah was not nailed to the cross!** *Do not miss that!*

I have shown that every tenet listed by Kurt is inextricably bound to the hope of Israel and the fulfillment of God's OT promises to her. Those promises were to arrive at the end of her age in AD 70: "These be the days of vengeance in which all things that are written must be fulfilled" (Luke 21:22).

I have demonstrated that the Cross is to the parousia what the foundation is to the finished structure of a house (cf. Ephesians 2:19f again).

I have shown from Isaiah 59 that the coming of the Lord of Romans 11:26f cannot be referent to the cross. Kurt has not breathed on this argument.

I have shown that Kurt's position on sin, death and resurrection is false and logically demands that Christ's death has accomplished nothing at all, **even for Christians**, since all men, just like Adam, suffer the consequences of the law of sin and death.

Do not miss what Kurt said in his last negative: "We must be careful not to let our hermeneutic *drive* our interpretation of scripture." But, if there was ever a case of a presuppositional hermeneutic driving interpretation, it is Kurt. 1.) He denied that we need to be concerned with the "proper exegesis" of Isaiah 27. 2.) He has eschewed the use of logic. 3.) He has made *historically unprecedented arguments*. 4.) He has repeatedly changed his arguments when caught in self-contradiction. 5.) He has abused the Greek tenses– contradicting what he has written in his books. 6.) He has admitted, fatally, that *the Mosaic law was not nailed to the Cross!* 7.) He has ignored the fundamental connection between the fulfillment of Israel's salvation promises- and salvation for Gentiles *flowing from that--* and the parousia.

Kurt says the debate, like a ball game, should be called. The trouble is, that for a game to be called a team has to score some points, and Kurt has not even gotten to first base! He has in fact, struck out.

Preston-Simmons Debate

When was Sin Defeated? AD 70 or the Cross?

Simmons' Second Affirmative

In this debate we attempt to resolve when salvation from sin arrived. For 2,000 years, the church has taught that salvation occurred at the cross. This has never been questioned or doubted. It is an essential tenant of the faith. Then Max King came along and taught that salvation was *postponed* until AD 70. King taught that the debt of sin survived the cross until the law was allegedly taken away in AD 70, and that it was *only* by removal of the law that man is finally saved. (*"The defeat of sin is tied to the annulment of the old aeon of law...death is abolished when the state of sin and the law are abolished."* [2]../Local Settings/Temporary Internet Files/Content.IE5/My Webs/pres-buildingwithstubble.htm - _ftn46# _ftn46) Thus, all that Christianity has historically assigned to the cross, King and Don assign to removal of the law and the fall of Jerusalem in AD 70. This is what makes this debate important and why, although we are both Preterists, this issue must be resolved in a brotherly manner.

Forgiveness: Addition of Grace, or Removal of Law?

The idea that the debt of sin survived the cross until the law was supposedly removed in AD 70 is the most important issue addressed in this debate. It is our position that the debt of sin was canceled ("blotted out" Col. 2:14) at the cross; that man is saved by the addition of grace, and that grace triumphs over law. We maintain that there was *nothing* in the Old Law that could forestall the grace given us at Jesus' cross. Indeed, while the Old Testament was done away, most of the law *still exists* and condemns men of sin just as much as it ever did. If we will take the time to analyze it, we will find that the only law removed by the passing of the Old Testament was the ceremonial law and various incidental laws associated with Israel's nationhood, and that these had *nothing* to do with either condemning or justifying man. Because this is critical to the issues in this debate, let's take a few moments to examine the law.

---

[2] Max R. King, *The Cross and the Parousia of Christ*, p. 644 (emphasis added).

151

Moral Law & the Law of Sin and Death

Sin is the violation of *moral imperatives* arising in the positive commandments of God or man's conscience. When we violate our conscience, we are not acting in obedience to faith, and that is sin ("whatsoever is not of faith is sin" – Rom. 14:23). Every commandment of God carries with it the duty of obedience and its willful violation brings the sentence and penalty of death. God told Adam, "In the day thou eatest thereof thou shalt surely die" (Gen. 2:17). This commandment carried with it the sentence and penalty of eternal (not physical) death. This is the law of "sin and death" ("the wages of sin is death," Rom. 6:23). Because man has a moral duty to obey God, *all commandments of God in the final analysis are moral in nature.* Even ceremonial law has this moral element attached to it; no man can disregard God's ceremonial law without violating his moral duty.

The commandments given by Moses "thou shalt not murder, thou shalt not steal, thou shalt not commit adultery, *etc.* did not create the moral sins of murder, theft, adultery, etc; it merely *codified* them. These sins had always existed and still exist today. Some will ask, *If the law of sin and death existed before the law of Moses, why did Paul call the Old Testament a "ministration of death" (II Cor. 3:7); doesn't this show that there was some especial power in the Mosaic law bringing condemnation and death that did not exist before?* The answer is, No, the Mosaic law contains no condemnation or power that did not already exist. If the Mosaic law never existed, man would still be under bondage to sin absent the cross of Christ. Paul called the Old Testament a "ministration of death" because it *institutionalized* sin and the law. What existed before in unwritten precepts was codified and institutionalized by Moses, enshrined in the nation's law and ritual. Paul said "By the law is the knowledge of sin; I had not know sin but by the law" (Rom. 3:20; 7:7). The *moral* precepts of the law made known to man his sinful condition; the *ceremonial* law stood as a grand object lesson of man's condition and his need of redemption and atonement, pointing forward to Christ. Thus enters the law of substitute and blood sacrifice.

The Law of Substitutes

The "law of substitutes" is the law God set in place that allowed the blood of another to make atonement for man's sin. This law was first set in place in the garden by the offering of a lamb, and was ever after kept in force as a prophetic type and foreshadow of the substitutionary death and atoning

152

sacrifice of Christ. In Exodus, it was formed into a national institution in the Levitical priesthood and temple service. Paul said that the temple ritual and the ceremonial feasts and Sabbaths of the law stood as "a shadow of things to come; but the body is of Christ" (Col. 2:16, 17). A shadow has no substance of its own and stands as a mere silhouette of the body. When Paul says "the body is of Christ," he means that the tangible stuff and substance of our salvation is in Jesus. Don argues that the law was not nailed to the cross and this proves the law did not end there. Don is wrong. *A shadow ends where the body begins.* Thus, the writer of Hebrews states:

"Sacrifice and offering thou wouldest not, but a body hast thou prepared for me...He taketh away the first, that he may establish the second" (Heb. 10:5-9).

Although the debt of our sins that was nailed to the cross and not the law itself, a shadow cannot reach beyond the thing that creates it. Paul says in Romans "Christ is the end of the law" (Rom. 10:4). In Ephesians, he says Chirst"abolished in his flesh the enmity, even the law contained of commandments contained in ordinances" (Eph. 2:15). This verse refers to the wall of separation in the temple, segregating Jew and Gentile, and shows that the temple ritual was done away in Jesus' cross.

Mosaic Law & Economy

Except for certain laws incidental to nationhood (*i.e.,* territorial boundaries) and the ordering of society and commerce, most law is an expression of moral duty. Since there will always be moral *duty*, there will always be moral *law*. The laws given by Moses may be categorized roughly as 1) national/civil, 2) social/moral, and 3) religious/ceremonial. Underlying them all was the moral law and the law of sin and death, which attach to violations of man's moral, social, and religious duties. The merest reflection will show that most of the laws embodied in the Old Testament exist in some form or other today, and where they don't find expression in human laws, they still exist as the unwritten judgment of God to which every man is accountable. Health and Safety laws may take different forms, but the same basic *duty of reasonable care* for our fellow man (a duty enjoined by no less authority than heaven itself) underlies them all. Likewise crimes and punishments may change in form, but the basic moral judgment underlying them has not changed. Only the religious and ceremonial law was totally abrogated.

Old Testament & National Israel

National/Civil	Social/Moral	Religious/Ceremonial
National Boundaries Land & Succession Immigration/Naturalization Health & Safety Crimes & Punishments Torts & Contracts Marriage & Children	**Impurity Deceit Violence Oppression Lust**	**Priesthood/Temple Sacrifices Feasts/Fasts Circumcision/Diet Ceremony/Ritual**

The Old Testament did not have a mechanism to provide forgiveness of sin (the blood of bulls and goats cannot take away sins – Heb. 10:4). But the lack of a mechanism to forgive does not equate with a negative power to forestall the grace of Christ's cross! That is Don's big mistake. He thinks the law was valid until AD 70, and that it trumped the grace that otherwise should have come *at Jesus' death*. What saves us is not the *removal* of the law, but the *addition* of grace by Jesus' death. Judge for yourself: What is there in the Old Testament that does not exist today, save and except the ritual law? Did the temple ritual have power to prevent or forestall the grace of Christ's cross? Of course it couldn't. **It is true that the temple ritual was taken away at the cross, but that is not because it prevented grace, but because it was a shadow pointing to Christ. Once Christ was come, the purpose and utility of the ritual was spent.** "He taketh away the first that he may establish the second" (Heb. 10:9).The moral law still exists today, condemning men of sin, but today men can find salvation because God has *added* grace in Jesus Christ. **Grace triumphs over law.**

Christ's Substitutionary Death Fulfilled the Law of Sin & Death

As the chart below shows, the moral law gives rise to man's duty and accountability to God. This law has always existed and always will.

Violation of this law brings man under the law of sin and death, the source of man's liability and bondage. It is this debt Christ died to satisfy. Moses codified the moral law, adding the ceremonial law as an object lesson and prophetic type pointing to Christ. The prophets expounded upon the law, but did not themselves add anything substantive to it. Then came the day when Christ arrived, bringing salvation. He nailed the debt of sin to his cross, triumphing over the law of sin and death. All who come to Christ in faith share in that triumph and obtain acquittal from the debt of sin.

Moral Law/ Commandments of God (source of man's duty and accountablity	→	Law of sin and Death (source of man's liability and bondage	→	Codified by Moses	→
Expounded on by Moses	→		Satisfied by the Cross of Christ (source of man's salvation		

Don Admits Saints in a State of Grace and Justification Prior to AD 70

Out of 88 verses we produced in our first affirmative, Don graced us with his response to only one, Rom. 7:1-4. He says he did not have space for more, but this is not true. We have given Don 8,000 extra words and additionally offered him a full fourth affirmative in which he could have handled this if he were so inclined. The truth is Don cannot answer the verses, so he pleads lack of space. Sorry, Don, we're not buying!

Don's one response to our 88 verses amounts to a false charge that we say the institution of marriage ceased when the first husband died. Ridiculous! The covenant (not institution) of marriage ended with the deceased spouse, leaving the surviving spouse free to enter a new marriage covenant. The Old Covenant thus died with Christ, so that we could enter the New Covenant as his bride, washed and cleansed by his redeeming blood (Eph. 5:25-27). Although Don's argument comes to nothing, he does say something useful. Don says:

155

"When a person, through faith, entered into the power of the cross, they died to the law."

This is remarkable! The scripture knows only two states for man: He is either under the law and condemnation, or in a state of grace and justification. There is no middle ground between these two. There is no "limbo infantum" between the condemnation of law for sinners and God's justification by grace. Yet, Don now says that the saints could enter the power of the cross *prior to AD 70*, having died to the law! But if they died to the law, then they were under grace and justification. And if they were under grace and justification, the saints were not under the power of the law or condemnation of sin, and there was no spiritualized resurrection in AD 70! Moreover, if they were "dead to the law" as Don states, then the law most certainly was not imposed upon them. Thus, Don is in hopeless contradiction with himself...again! On the one hand, he says the law was imposed until AD 70 and all were under its debt and obligation (he says this, but could not produce a single verse to substantiate it!). Now he says Christians were "dead to the law." Which is it, Don? It cannot be both. Please tell us how Christians were dead to the law, but still under its debt! Reader, look for Don's response.

Do not miss this! Don has overthrown his whole system. He has set the saints in a condition of grace and justification beginning with the cross. If men could enter the power of the cross before AD 70 as Don affirms, then salvation arrived with Christ's *first coming*. And if salvation from sin arrived at the first coming, then my proposition has been sustained. *"The coming of Christ for salvation from sin occurred at the cross, at the climax and termination of the Mosaic covenant age."*

Internally Inconsistent

Throughout this discussion, it has been Don's position that it was *essential* for the law to be removed before man could be justified. According to Don, *"Hebrews says as long as Torah remained, there was no forgiveness. Therefore, Torah remained binding and there was no objective forgiveness until AD 70!"* But wait! At the same time Don claims it was essential that the law be taken away before grace could enter, he also claims that the *atonement was postponed* until AD 70 so that justification could occur at that time! (He also claims Christians were "dead to the law" and could enter the power of Christ's cross prior to AD 70, a curious confluence of contradictions if ever there was one!) King and Don postpone the atonement in order to delay grace. But what is this if not an admission that it is the addition of grace that saves? Why postpone the atonement if grace does not triumph over the law? And if grace triumphs over law, then, removal of the law and AD 70 are *irrelevant* for justification. And if AD 70 is irrelevant to justification, then **the coming of Christ for salvation from sin occurred at the cross,** and my proposition is established.

The Frivolous Results of King's Spiritualizing Method

This debate is about when justification came to the saints, not the resurrection. It is only because Max King spiritualized the resurrection, equating resurrection with justification that the topic comes up at all. Because Don is a follower of King, he defines *resurrection as the time when sin was defeated.* Naturally, this is glaringly wrong. Resurrection is the time when death is defeated; justification is the time when sin is defeated. The one was defeated at the cross, the other when Hades was destroyed and the saints entered into their heavenly reward. The fact that these events are separate in time and event is clear from Corinthians where Paul states that the Corinthians were "washed, sanctified, and justified" (I Cor. 6:11) but were still waiting the resurrection! However, if you accept Don's definition of the resurrection, then you, dear Christian, are already resurrected! Moreover, if you accept Don's definition, you have already received your immortal body, *and* you are already in heaven (surprise!). These are the logical implications of Don's position. If there is only one resurrection as Don claims, and that resurrection has happened, then all the things associated with that resurrection are come, and you are now in heaven and possess your immortal body! And if you think I am making this up or exaggerating, then be assured that many prominent Preterists who are followers of King affirm that we are in "heaven now."

"Again, you wrote, 'The Christian is not ACTUALLY in heaven until he puts off the physical body.' This DESTROYS Preterism...In Revelation 21, the New Jerusalem COMES DOWN to earth. The Glory of the Lord RESIDES in his heavenly temple, which is NOW the Church. Welcome to heaven."

There you have it! A very prominent, visible Preterist and follower of King's theology claiming that Preterism is destroyed unless we are willing to delude ourselves with the belief that we are in heaven now! This same group of

Preterists also affirm that we have our "immortal body now," while still others deny that there is "marriage now" (because there is no marriage in the resurrection – Matt. 22: 30). All these ridiculous, tragic absurdities that discredit Preterism flow from the poison spring of Max King's spiritualizing method and failure to "rightly divide the word of truth." **Dear reader, resurrection is *not* justification and reconciliation. These are different concepts, separate in time and function.** Sin is defeated by the grace of Christ's cross. Justification and reconciliation happen when we enter the power of Christ's cross by faith, repentance, and baptism. Death is defeated by receipt of eternal life in heaven above.

Hebrews 9 and the Two Covenants

Don argues that, if the atonement was complete at the cross, the souls of the saints in Hades should have entered heaven then and there. Don bases this on Heb. 9:8 where the writers says the "way into the Holiest was not manifest while the first tabernacle still had legal standing." However, Heb. 9 does NOT address the resurrection and the soul's entrance into heaven. Don keeps arguing this point, but it is not in this chapter. It does seem to be implied in Rev. 15:8 where it says no man could enter the temple until the wrath of God was complete, but this is because Hadean death was the LAST ENEMY. Not until the Jews and Romans were put beneath Christ's feet was Hades destroyed. This is why the resurrection from Hades occurs at the end of Revelation, after defeat of the dragon, beast, and harlot (Rev. 20:11-15). Entrance into heaven is NOT the point of Heb. 9. The dichotomy in this chapter is between the Old and New Testaments and man's reconciliation to God, not the Old Testament and the soul's entrance into heaven. Don chides us with changing our position on this, but that is not true. The "time of reformation" has been discussed many times throughout this debate and both Don and I agree this refers to the New Testament. The "time of reformation" is set over against the "time then present" in which were offered gifts and sacrifices that could not provide atonement. Thus, the two covenants are at bottom here, not entrance into heaven as Don suggests.

The Tabernacle and the Two Covenants
"We have now received the atonement" - Rom. 5:11

Holy Place– Old Testament		Most Holy Place- New Testament
"Time then Present"		*"Time of Reformation"*
Worldly Sanctuary		*Heavenly Sanctuary / Spiritual Temple*
Way To Holiest Closed		*Holiest Opened by Jesus*
Could Not Perfect (Save)		*Hath Perfected forever (Heb. 10:14)*

During the Old Testament period, the worshipper remained in a condition of legal estrangement, banishment, and exile from God, unable to enter his presence because of sin. The New Testament marked the time when reconciliation was made, the veil of separation was "rent in twain," and man could come into God's presence free from the taint of sin. Thus, the "Holy place" and "Most Holy Place" answer to the two covenants: Jameson, Brown, and Faucett agree:

"The Old Testament economy is represented by the holy place, the New Testament economy by the Holy of Holies. Redemption, by Christ, has opened the Holy of Holies (access to heaven by faith now, Hbr 4:16 7:19, 25 10:19, 22; by sight hereafter)."

And that the temple service ended at the cross, no less authority than Calvin agrees:

"Nor is it any objection that he uses the present tense in saying, gifts are offered; for as he had to do with the Jews, he speaks by way of concession, as though he were one of those who sacrificed... As soon then as Christ came forth with the efficacious influence of his death, all the typical observances must necessarily have ceased."

159

Daniel's 490 Prophetic Weeks and Legal Termination of the Old Testament

The legal termination of the Old Testament at the Cross is corroborated by Daniel's 490 prophetic weeks. Dan. 9:27 states that Messiah would cause the "sacrifice and oblation to cease" in the *midst* of the final prophetic week. Don agrees that the final prophetic week ended with the destruction of Jerusalem. (See Don's booklet, *"Seal Up Vision and Prophecy"*) Therefore, Messiah's causing the "sacrifice and oblation to cease" in the **midst** of the final week MUST refer to a point *earlier* in time than AD 70. Thus, by Don's own admission, Heb. 9 cannot be made to reach unto AD 70, but MUST fall short. Don again is in contradiction with himself. The traditional interpretation of when Messiah caused the "sacrifice and oblation to cease" is the cross. Matthew Henry states concerning Dan. 9:27:

"He must cause the sacrifice and oblation to cease. *By offering himself a sacrifice once for all he shall put an end to all the Levitical sacrifices, shall supersede them and set them aside; when the substance comes the shadows shall be done away. He causes all the peace-offerings to cease when he has made peace by the blood of his cross, and by it confirmed the covenant of peace and reconciliation."*

The very notion that the sacrifices were valid and binding until AD 70 is idle nonsense. The whole book of Galatians stands in complete contradiction of the law's validity. To keep the law was an implicit denial of the sacrifice of Christ and was to fall from grace! "Ye observe days, and months, and time, and years" (Gal. 4:10). Don's teaching is identical with the Judaizers who tried to say the ritual law was still binding. Paul denounced that teaching with a curse! (Gal. 1:8, 9). Clearly, the validity of the temple ritual ended at the cross, and men could enter legally and covenantally into a "face to face" relationship with the Father, reconciled by the blood of Christ.

God the Author of Paganism?

To uphold King's Covenant Eschatology, the Old Testament must be kept legally valid until AD 70 when the saints were allegedly "resurrected" from the grave of Judaism (justified by purported removal of the law). But, as the New Testament became of force at Jesus' death, this would require that there be two conflicting systems in place at the same time, one offering grace, the other not. This, of course, is impossible, but that doesn't stop Don. Don argues that there were two equally valid systems in place when God gave the law to Israel, but left the Gentiles in paganism!

"In Kurt's first affirmative he desperately argues, falsely, that God could not have two systems in force at the same time. Kurt, did God have two systems in place when He gave Torah to Israel, but not to the pagans?"

Can you believe it? Don argues that paganism is equally valid with the Old Covenant! Good grief! According to Don, God is the author of pagan idolatry! But God also left the pagan system in place when he instituted the New Testament, so according to Don paganism continues to be an equally valid system of practice and belief. What are we to conclude from this? Is Don now a Universalist? All systems are equally valid? Don's willingness to argue that paganism was ordained by God evidences the desperation he is in to save Max King's hopelessly bankrupt and self-contradictory system. Preterists who love the truth will swim away from that sinking ship fast!

Greek Verb Tenses

I am glad Don finally got around to the subject of Greek verb tenses, for this has been a longstanding source of error among Preterists. As we have seen, the overwhelming majority of verses all show the Old Testament was abolished in Christ and the saints were in a present state of justification beginning with the cross. A tiny handful of verses, however, seem to couch these things in future tense setting up a contradiction. Can they be reconciled? Let us survey the verses given by Don:

Redemption (present): "In whom we have redemption through his blood, the forgiveness of sins." (Eph. 1:7).
Redemption (future): "Ye were sealed with the holy Spirit of promise, which is the earnest of our inheritance until the redemption of the purchased possession" (Eph. 1:12, 1 3).

It was only a short while ago that I mistook these verses (vv. 12, 13) as teaching that redemption *from sin* was prospective. My reasoning was like Don's: redemption speaks to legal acquittal and justification. If the saints were still waiting for redemption, they were not yet in a condition of justification. But I have since learned better.

During the siege of Jerusalem by the Babylonians, Jeremiah was in prison. God instructed him to purchase (redeem) his uncle's land in token of the fact that God would bring the captivity back again to their land after 70 years. The evidence of the purchase was *sealed* before witnesses (Jer. 32:1-11). Thus, the legal purchase was made and sealed, just as Paul suggests in Ephesians ("sealed until redemption of the purchased possession"). But while the price was *paid* and ownership complete, Jeremiah's ability to take *actual possession* of the land was future. So, with the saints: We were redeemed by Christ, who nailed the debt of sin to his cross (Col. 2:14), but our actual possession of the inheritance (heaven) must wait until we put off the physical body in death. Meanwhile, God has placed the earnest of the Spirit in our hearts in evidence that we belong to him. The earnest is not the miraculous gifts of the Holy Ghost (a view I formerly embraced). Rather, it is the *inward yearning* of the heart by which we cry "Abba, Father" (Rom. 8:15; *cf.* Gal. 4:6). That this is the proper explanation for Paul's otherwise contradictory language is seen in II Cor. 5:4-8 where the earnest of the Spirit, which in Eph. 1:14 is connected with "inheritance" and "redemption," is there connected with receipt of our immortal bodies at death and resurrection.

*"For we that are in this tabernacle **do groan,** being burdened: not for that we would be unclothed, but **clothed upon,** that mortality might be swallowed up of life. Now he that hath wrought us for the selfsame thing is God, who also hath given unto us **the earnest of the Spirit**. Therefore we are always confident, knowing that, whilst we are at home in the body, we are absent from the Lord. (For we walk by faith, not by sight). We are confident, I say, and willing rather to **be absent from the body, and to be present with the Lord.**"*

This is also the meaning of Rom. 8:19-23, where "redemption of our body" points to receipt of our immortal body in heaven. Christ purchased the inheritance for us, but we must wait until heaven to receive it. Thus, Eph. 1:12, 13 in no way indicates that the saints were waiting for redemption from sin, which Paul clearly says dozens of times was already a present possession.

Adoption (present): "We have received the Spirit of adoption" (Rom. 8:15). **Adoption** (future): "We ourselves groan within ourselves, waiting for the adoption, to wit, the redemption of our body" (Rom. 8:23)

These are the verses provided by Don. However, Gal. 4:5-7 would have been more suitable to show the present condition of adoption and sonship.

"To redeem them that were under the law, that we might receive the adoption of sons. And because ye are sons, God hath sent forth the Spirit of his Son into your hearts, crying Abba, Father. Wherefore, thou are no more a servant, but a son; and if a son, then an heir of God through Christ."

Adoption is essentially a legal act or decree by which one who is not our natural child is deemed a child in contemplation of law and made our legal heir. The legal aspect of our adoption occurred when we obeyed the gospel and were baptized. However, the ultimate object of our adoption is the inheritance of eternal life. Our inheritance must wait until we receive our immortal bodies at death. Thus "adoption" = "redemption of our body" = "receipt of our immortal body" (see Rom. 8:23, above). Thus, when Paul speaks of adoption in this passage, he has in view its ultimate object, the receipt of immortality at our individual resurrection, not the legal act of entering a covenant relationship under the gospel, which was already an accomplished fact.

Inheritance (present): "In whom also we have obtained an inheritance" (Eph. 1:11).
Inheritance (future): "Who is the earnest of our inheritance until the redemption of the purchased possession" (Eph. 1:14).

If a man makes a will and bequeaths certain gifts to his children, they have obtained an inheritance. However, possession of the inheritance must wait until distribution of the decedent's estate. Thus**, one can have an inheritance but also be required to wait for its reception.** In the present case, the New Testament became of force at Christ's death (Heb. 9:17), and we obtain an inheritance as adopted children of God when we obey the gospel. However, possession of our inheritance (eternal life in heaven) must wait until death of the physical body. Don's argument that the souls in Hades should have entered heaven immediately at the cross is without merit. Paul is clear that the *last enemy* was death, not sin. Sin was defeated at the cross. The resurrection waited until the Jews and Romans were put beneath Christ's feet. (See Rev. 20:11-15 where the resurrection follows the defeat of the harlot, dragon, and beast, even though the saints were already justified and clothed in white.)

163

Passing of the law (future): Don provides several verses under this head. Let's list them and then discuss what they *really* say:

II Cor. 3:18 - "But we all, with open face beholding as in a glass the glory of the Lord, are changed into the same image from glory to glory, even as by the spirit of the Lord."

This verse says does not say our being "changed" equates with the abolition of the law. Don simply reads that into the passage and imposes it upon the text. The better view is that our change looks to the receipt of eternal life in heaven. The same word occurs in I Cor. 15:52 ("we shall not all sleep, but we shall all be *changed*"). Paul said the same thing in Rom. 8:29: "Whom he did foreknow, them he also did predestinate to be conformed to the image of his Son." Being "changed" and "conformed" to Christ's image looks to our receipt of eternal life above, not annulment of the Old Testament.

II Cor. 3:11 – "For if that which is being annulled was through glory, much rather that which remains is in glory"

This is a chief Preterist proof text that the law was still valid. The present participle in vv. 11, 13, 14 are offered as proof the Old Testament was still valid. But this only betrays a lack of Greek scholarship. The present tense has many uses, and often signifies past events. We do this all the time in every day speech. One law supplants another, negating its force, and we say "the policy and effect of the old law is being annulled by the new." Yet, clearly, the old law was annulled the *instant* the new replaced it. The present participle does not show the old law is still valid, but that the new presently renders it null. Even today in 2010, the condemnation associated with the law is *being annulled* by the New Testament of Christ. PLEASE NOTE: Every major version (KJV, ASV, RSV, NAS, NEB) renders these verbs in the past tense. Can so many Greek scholars be wrong? But if the present participle shows an on-going process as Don alleges, then the glory on Moses face had not yet vanished! The same participle occurs in reference to the shining on Moses' skin: "The children of Israel could not steadfastly behold the face of Moses for the glory of his countenance, which glory is being done away" (II Cor. 3:7). When Moses entered God's presence, his face shone, so he put a veil on his face when he spoke with the Jews. Moses had been dead for 1500 years, yet Paul here uses the present participle to describe what had ceased millennia before! This destroys Don's theory. But there is another point here we should note. Moses entered the Holiest and there beheld the face of God, causing his face to shine. He covered his face with a veil when he spoke to the Jews, but removed it when he entered the Holiest. Paul says we behold "with open face" the glory of the Lord (II Cor. 3:18). Where do we with unveiled face behold God's face? Within the Holy of Holies! In the New Testament, we enter the Holiest and there behold the face of God in Christ, just as the writer of Hebrews states (II Cor. 4:6; Heb. 10:19, 22).

Heb. 8:13 – "In that he saith, A new covenant, he hath made the first old. Now that which decayed and waxeth old is ready to vanish away."

This verse does not say that the old was still valid or binding. To the contrary, the writer states that the "first covenant had also ordinances of divine service, and a worldly sanctuary" (Heb. 9;1). Notice the past tense ***"had also ordinances"*** showing that these were now replaced by the New Testament. Heb. 7:12 is the same: "For the priesthood being changed, there is made of necessity a change also the law." Did Christ have a priesthood when this was written? Of course he did. Therefore the law was changed. **The Jews kept up the ritual of the Old, but this was in rebellion and denial of Christ**. The tree remained even though the root was cut. The truck of the tree was withered and dead, and about to be taken away, but its legal validity ended long before.

Heb. 7:12 – "The priesthood being changed, there is made of necessity a change also of the law."

Don says the present tense is used here. But the same verb form is used in Heb. 11:4 of Abel, "he *being dead* yet speaketh." Was Abel already dead? Of course he was. Was the priesthood already changed? Of course it was! "But Christ *being come* an high priest of good things to come" (Heb. 9:11). Berry's Interlinear Greek renders the passage "For being changed the priesthood, from necessity also of law a change takes place." Don's objection is baseless.

Heb. 8:4 – "For if he were on earth, he should not be a priest, seeing that there are priests that offer gifts according to the law."

165

This verse does not say that the offerings were valid. How could they be? The law was a shadow pointing to Christ, whose sacrifice annulled them! Isaiah expressly states that the Jews' continued observance of the temple ritual marked them out as enemies of God! *"He that sacrificeth a lamb as if he cut off a dog's neck...they have chosen their abominations...a voice of noise from the city, a voice from the temple, a voice of the Lord that rendereth recompense to his enemies" (Isa. 66:3, 6).* Don's attempt to keep the law valid is hopelessly fraught with contradiction and stands in denial of Christ's cross.

Heb. 10:9 – "Then said he, Lo, I come to do thy will, O God. He taketh away the first, that he may establish the second."

Don says this should read "he *is taking away* the first" etc. Berry's Interlinear reads "He takes away the first." Green's Interlinear reads "He takes away the first," etc. In fact, every major version, and all the minors for all I know, read "he takes away the first." Don is quite alone in his rendering! Don, why don't you test your theory and make out two contradictory wills leaving everything to your wife and family in the first, and everything to charity in the second and see which one the court upholds? Everyone knows the second annuls the first. **Quit playing these silly games!**

Grace (present): "By grace are ye saved through faith" (Eph. 2:8)
Grace (future): "Hope to the end for the grace that is to be brought unto you at the revelation of Jesus Christ" (I Peter 1:13).

Don, is there only one "grace" man receives from God? There are many graces, of course. There is grace in redemption from sin, there is grace in the gifts of the Holy Ghost, there is grace which sustains us day by day, and there is grace that delivered the saints out of the persecution of Nero and the Jews. It is this last that Peter refers to, not salvation from sin. **This also applies to I Pet. 1:5 and the "salvation ready to be revealed in the last time."** God would reveal his salvation to the world by redeeming the church out of her persecutions and the overthrow of her enemies (*cf.* Lk. 21:28). Peter is not talking about salvation from sin.

Perfect (present): "And ye are complete in him" (Col. 2:10).
Perfect (future): "That we might present every man perfect in Christ" (Col. 1:28). Don also notes that the church was given the charismata (miraculous

166

gifts of the Holy Spirit) to bring the church to a "perfect man" (Eph. 4:13-16), and asks why, if they were already perfect did they need the gifts to bring them to perfection? May I say without offense, this is very shallow thinking? Children are in a perfect state of grace, innocent and acceptable to God, but they still need instruction to bring them to maturity. In the same way, the church and individual members may be "complete" in Christ in terms of their sins being washed away, but still in need of growing up from babes to mature believers.

Dear reader, we have now surveyed *all* of Don's proof texts offered to show the law was still "valid, obligatory, and binding." We have addressed each verse he used (too bad Don did not so the same for us!), and there is nothing in them. They do not prove the law was "valid."

Isaiah 59

Since we are on the topic of the New Testament bringing remission of sins at the cross, this is as good a time as any to deal with Isa. 59:20-21. Let me say that the proper exegesis of these verses is really a distraction when one considers that Don cannot produce even a single verse to sustain the most basic elements of his position. If he could produce a few New Testament verses that uphold his case he would not need to rely upon arguments wrested from Old Testament prophets.

Diagram of Isaiah 59

Isa. 59:1-15 – Recital of Israel's sin.		Yea, truth faileth; and he that departeth from evil maketh himself a prey: and the LORD saw it, and it displeased him that there was no judgment
Isa. 59:16-18 – The Lord's response: punishment of Israel and the nations (Assyrian/Babylonia invasions).		And he saw that there was no man, and wondered that there was no intercessor: therefore his arm brought salvation unto him; and his righteousness, it sustained him. Isa (v. 17) For he put on righteousness as a breastplate, and an helmet of salvation upon his head; and he put on the garments of vengeance for clothing, and was clad with zeal as a cloke. (v. 18) According to the deeds, accordingly he will repay, fury to his adversaries, recompence to his enemies; to the islands he will repay recompence.
Isa. 59:19 – The nations will see and fear; the Lord's favor will return to Israel (return of the captivity).		So shall they fear the name of the LORD from the west, and his glory from the rising of the sun. When the enemy shall come in like a flood, the Spirit of the LORD shall lift up a standard against him.

Isa. 59:20-21 – The Redeemer will come; God's covenant to preserve a remnant.		And the Redeemer shall come to Zion, and unto them that turn from transgression in Jacob, saith the LORD. (v. 21) As for me, this is my covenant with them, saith the LORD; My spirit that is upon thee, and my words which I have put in thy mouth, shall not depart out of thy mouth, nor out of the mouth of thy seed, nor out of the mouth of thy seed's seed, saith the LORD, from henceforth and for ever.

As the chart above shows, Isa. 59 treats of God's judgment upon Israel *and* the nations for their sins. The instrument of his wrath, when he put on a breastplate of righteousness, etc., was almost certainly the Assyrian and Babylonian invasions. That is the historical context Isaiah spoke to and we may anticipate it throughout his writings. The return of God's favor to Israel by defending it (v. 19) points to the return of the captivity. Redeemer will come to Zion, clearly contemplates the birth of the Messiah, not his second coming, for it was at the cross that Christ's work of redemption was done ("in whom we have redemption through his blood" – Eph. 1:7). The word in the mouth of the Redeemer's seed points to the gospel and the teaching church. Note that the Lord's coming and his covenant to preserve a remnant *follows* his wrath upon Israel and the nations. This pattern is repeated many times in the prophets. The three great themes of the prophets were the 1) coming captivity, 2) the return of the captivity, and 3) the coming of the Messiah. That pattern is clearly seen here. However, by Don's interpretation, the wrath in vv. 16-19 is the destruction of Jerusalem. Thus, he has AD 70 *precede* the coming of the Messiah in vv. 20-21! Don completely reverses the order of the whole chapter, placing the destruction of Jerusalem before the Messiah ever arrives on the scene! This will not do. Paul shows what the context of the chapter is by what he substitutes. Where Isaiah says

"This is my covenant with them, saith the LORD; My spirit that is upon thee, and my words which I have put in thy mouth, shall not depart out of thy mouth, nor out of the mouth of thy seed, nor out of the mouth of thy seed's seed, saith the LORD, from henceforth and for ever."

Paul substitutes

*"This is my **covenant**, when I shall **take away their sins**" (Rom. 11:27).*

God put his Spirit upon the Redeemer, and the Spirit gave him the word of the gospel, the New Covenant. This covenant brings remission of sins for all that believe and obey. Thus, the *"word"* (gospel) in the mouth of the Redeemer and his seed in Isaiah becomes the *vehicle* for remission of sins in Rom. 11:27. It is the New Testament that brings remission of sins, not the destruction of Jerusalem! Romans 11 is about God's election of a remnant by obedience to the gospel, the breaking off of unbelieving Jews, and grafting in their place believing Gentiles, so it makes perfect sense that the "covenant" and "word" have reference to the New Testament and gospel. By Don's approach, however, the "covenant" and "word" in the mouth of the Redeemer are substituted with the destruction of Jerusalem! Obviously, this makes no sense at all. Here is Homer Hailey's explanation of the passage, which is typical of the vast majority of commentators:

"The Servant-Messiah came unto Zion as King and Savior (Zech. 9:9-10). Jehovah set Him up as King on the Holy hill of Zion (Ps. 2:6). From there Jehovah sent forth the rod of His strength (Ps. 110:2); from there went forth the law and word of Jehovah (Isa. 2:3). This explains the Redeemer's coming 'to Zion.' From Zion He also went forth in the gospel, conquering and to conquer. As Paul said, Christ 'came and preached peace to you that were afar off [Gentiles], and peace to them that were nigh' [Jews] (Eph. 2:17). In this sense, the Redeemer came forth 'out of Zion.'"

Isaiah 27

The pattern in Isaiah 27 is 1) sin, 2) wrath (Assyrian invasion), 3) return of the captivity. The fundamental error of Don's approach is that he makes the wrath portion of the text the point where salvation occurs! He equates the wrath of the Assyrian invasion with the destruction of Jerusalem by Rome and says that is the point where salvation from sin occurred. But salvation in Isa. 27:1,2, 13 comes with the return of the captivity *100 years later*, not at the time of the invasion itself. Israel was carried into captivity because of its sins and idolatry. The invasion and captivity would bring the nation to repentance; then God would return a remnant to the land, saving them. Don makes the salvation occur *by and through* the invasion/destruction! Moreover, where Isaiah has Israel repent and so come to salvation, in AD 70 Israel was forever destroyed. The analogy between these historical events therefore breaks down and Don's theory comes to nothing. Here is Matthew Henry's treatment of the passage which we think settles that it is the Assyrio-Babylonian invasions that are in view, not AD 70:

"Though Jerusalem shall be desolate and forsaken for a time, yet there will come a day when its scattered friends shall resort to it again out of all the countries whither they were dispersed (v. 12, 13)... By what means they shall be gathered together: The great trumpet shall be blown, and then they shall come. Cyrus's proclamation of liberty to the captives is this great trumpet, which awakened the Jews that were asleep in their thraldom to bestir themselves; it was like the sounding of the jubilee-trumpet, which published the year of release." Matthew Henry, Isa. 27:12, 13

Summary & Conclusion

We have reviewed the Mosaic law. We have seen that if it never existed, man would *still* be under the debt and bondage to sin absent Christ's cross. We have seen that King and Don attempt to postpone the atonement until AD 70, and that this is a tacit admission that it is the addition of grace that saves, not the removal of law. There is nothing in the law that can forestall grace; the inability to forgive does translate into a positive power to prevent grace. King's whole system is therefore internally inconsistent and contradictory. We have surveyed all the verses Don produced to show the law was valid and that grace was postponed, and we have seen there is nothing to them. Nine pages of verses showing the saints were in a present state of justification and grace cannot be undone by the obscurities of a few present participles, which all translations render in the past and perfect tense. Paul is emphatic that we "have now received the atonement" (Rom. 5:11), and that the law was "abolished in Christ's flesh" (Eph. 2:15). Even Don admits that the saints were "dead to the law" and could "enter the power of the cross" prior to AD 70. In light of all this, can there be any doubt that Covenant Eschatology is a serious system of error? We urge all Preterists to get away as fast as possible from this dangerous teaching.

171

Preston - V - Simmons Debate

Passing of Torah and the Completion of Salvation

Preston's Second Negative

My friend's desperation mounts. Notice his opening argument:

The church has taught for 2000 years that salvation occurred at the cross.

Preston denies this.

Therefore, Preston must be wrong.

(*Actually*, the church has taught that the *salvation* of Hebrews 9:28 *comes at the end of the Christian age, and* has **never** taken Kurt's view that the salvation was deliverance from persecution!)

Let's turn Kurt's logic (?) around:

The church has taught for 2000 years that Christ's coming occurs at the end of the Christian age.

Kurt denies this.

Therefore, Kurt is wrong.

Do you see how inconsistent Kurt's use of "logic" is?

Isaiah 27– AGAIN

After staking his claim that if I could not produce "even one commentator" in support of the truth that Isaiah 27 applied to AD 70, did you notice that **Kurt ignored the fact that I produced such a commentator**? Kurt's logic (?) was: If Preston cannot produce one commentator to support his view, then he is wrong. Well, conversely, that means that since I did produce one (more), that I am right! Instead of conceding that I fulfilled his challenge, he ignored his defeat.

In spite of Kurt's protestations, the facts are undeniable:

Isaiah *explicitly* says that Israel would be saved through judgment, when the altar would be destroyed.

Virtually all scholars– to use Kurt's appeal to the scholars-- agree that Paul is citing Isaiah 27.

While Kurt denies the Messianic application of Isaiah 27, *the context is united and predicted the resurrection* (Isaiah 26:19-27:1).

Kurt turns Isaiah into a disjointed prophecy full of huge chronological gaps. Israel's salvation was under *Messiah* (Hosea 1:10– *1 Peter 2:9*). The consummation was at the sounding of the Great Trumpet– *in AD 70*– just as Jesus –*citing Isaiah 27:13*-- said (Matthew 24:30-31, 34).

KURT ON ISAIAH 59

My friend's desperation is lamentable. On the one hand he says that a proper exegesis of Isaiah 59 is "a distraction." He then proceeds to try (vainly) to exegete Isaiah 59! *Since when is proper exegesis ever a distraction?*

Kurt's "exegesis" of Isaiah 59 is some of the most confused (and false) bits of commentary you will read. Kurt argues: "The Redeemer will come to Zion, clearly contemplates the birth of the Messiah, not his second coming, for it was at the cross that Christ's work of redemption was done." **This is eisegesis**. He says the coming of the Lord in Isaiah 59:16-19 is different from that in verse 20f. He offers no *proof*. He just imposes it on the text, ***although the context is judgment!***

Here is what Kurt does:
He says v. 16-19 is judgment, but v. 20 is incarnation. But there is *no 600 year gap between verses 16-19 and verses 20f.* Kurt is guilty of doing what my dispensational friends do: inserting huge gaps of time into scripture when they cannot accept the proper exegesis of the text.
The context of Isaiah 59 is undeniably *judgment*, not the *incarnation*: "He put on the garments of vengeance...according to their deeds he will repay...the Redeemer shall come to Zion." There is no huge chronological gap. And this means: The coming of Romans 11:26 is the coming of Isaiah 59. The coming of Isaiah 59 is the coming of the Lord in judgment of Israel for shedding innocent blood. Therefore, the coming of Romans 11 is the coming of the Lord in judgment of Israel for shedding innocent blood, i.e. AD 70. Kurt cannot negate this.

DANIEL 9

Kurt distorts Daniel 9. He says v. 27 refers to the "legal termination" of the sacrifices, not the objective cessation. ***It says no such thing.*** Messiah would "cause the sacrifice to cease" (in the middle of the week). Kurt agrees that the 70th week ended in AD 70. But, if the seventieth week ended in AD 70, then three and one half years prior to that- *the middle of the week demanded by Daniel 9:27,* was ***AD 66. And,*** Josephus said this is when the daily sacrifice ended (Wars, 6:2:1– (Whiston, p. 731). See Whiston's remarks in Josephus, in. loc. Daniel 9 says not one word about a "legal termination."

173

Further, *it was Messiah*, acting sovereignly, that caused the sacrifices to end, in AD 66! *Neither the Jews nor Titus were acting independently of Messiah when the sacrifices ceased!!*

This falsifies Kurt's claim that Torah– and sacrifice-- ended at the cross. (In the P-S, Oct. 2009, Kurt said the prophecy of Daniel 12 and the taking away of the daily sacrifice *occurred in 66 AD.* Daniel 12 is the reiteration of Daniel 9. Thus, *Kurt has falsified his own position, again*! The daily sacrifice was not removed at the cross!

Further:

Daniel 9:24 foretold the coming of *everlasting righteousness.*

Paul and Peter were was still anticipating the arrival of the prophesied everlasting righteousness (Galatians 5:5; 2 Peter 3:13).

Therefore, unless Paul and Peter were anticipating a prophesied world of righteousness *different from Daniel*, then Daniel 9 was not fulfilled at the cross.

Also, Daniel 9 says Messiah would "confirm the covenant" (not *make a new one*!) for one week. That week is the final 70th week. *The covenant being confirmed is Torah* (Matthew 5:17 / Romans 15:8). That final week ended in AD 70. Thus, *Torah ended in AD 70!*

ISRAEL AND SALVATION– THE *CRUX INTERPRETUM*!

Let me reiterate a **critical argument** that Kurt has *repeatedly* ignored. This one argument falsifies Kurt's paradigm.

Salvation was to the Jew *first*, *then the Greek (the nations)*.

Israel's salvation (resurrection) was perfected in AD 70 (KS, Isaiah 25:8-9). Therefore, salvation for the Greek (the nations) was perfected in AD 70.

However, Kurt's theology *demands* that *Gentiles received full salvation before Israel's salvation was perfected!* Kurt, has created another salvation *distinct from Israel*. **Kurt, how did the Gentiles receive salvation before Israel received her salvation? Please answer!!!!**

If salvation was completed at the cross, **then Israel's salvation (Resurrection! Isaiah 25:8-9; Romans 9:28) was completed at the cross.** Yet, Kurt admitted that Romans 9:28 referred to the salvation of "national Israel" in AD 70!

This is critical! How could salvation be completed at the cross if Israel's salvation was in AD 70? How could Israel have been cut off at the cross, if

Israel was not saved until AD 70? Or, how could "the saints" have fully received their salvation– as Kurt claims– before the resurrection, the time of Israel's salvation?

You must not miss this: Every argument Kurt made about atonement, redemption, etc., appealing to the past tense verbs, claiming that those things were completed at the cross, ignores the indisputable fact that those things were *promises made to Israel*– not the church or individuals– separate from Israel! **Kurt admits that Israel's salvation came in AD 70!** Thus, as I have argued repeatedly, **we must honor the present and the future tenses of salvation!**

Israel– and thus Torah-- was *not* cut off at the cross. Her salvation promises were not fulfilled until the resurrection in AD 70. If Israel did not enter her salvation until AD 70– **which Kurt admits–** *then no one else fully entered into salvation*, for salvation was "to the Jew first."
What did Kurt say in response? *Not one syllable!*

KURT'S FALSE VIEW OF RESURRECTION
Kurt says that resurrection was exclusively the release of the dead from Hades.

This is false. Look again at my argument on Hosea 13– which Kurt ignored, (Empty box here!):

The resurrection of 1 Corinthians 15 is the resurrection predicted in Hosea 13:14.

The resurrection of Hosea 13:14 would be the resurrection, *of Israel*, from alienation from God through sin (Hosea 13:1-2: "When Israel sinned, he died"). It would be resurrection through forgiveness.

Therefore, the resurrection of 1 Corinthians 15 would be the resurrection, **of Israel**, from alienation from God through sin (Hosea 13:1-2). It would be resurrection through forgiveness.

Likewise:

The resurrection of 1 Corinthians 15 would be the resurrection, **of Israel**, from alienation from God through sin (Hosea 13:1-2) It would be resurrection through forgiveness.

But, the resurrection of 1 Corinthians 15 was still future when Paul wrote.

Therefore, the resurrection, **of Israel**, from alienation from God through sin (Hosea 13:1-2- i.e. resurrection through forgiveness was still future when Paul wrote.

175

Clearly, while the resurrection of 1 Corinthians included resurrection from Hades, that is not *all* it included.

Kurt argued: "Because Don is a follower of King, he defines *resurrection as the time when sin was defeated*. Naturally, this is glaringly wrong. Resurrection is the time when death is defeated; justification is the time when sin is defeated."

First, I am not a "follower of Max King," although with exceptions, I have great respect for his work. I was 99% a preterist *before I even heard of Max King!*

Second, Paul is emphatic that it is at the resurrection that sin was finally dealt with: "*When* this corruptible shall have put on incorruption, and this mortal shall have put on immortality, *then* shall be brought to pass the saying that is written, Death is swallowed up in victory. O death, where is thy sting? O grave, where is thy victory? The sting of death is sin; and the strength of sin is the law" (1 Corinthians 15:54-56). Notice:

The resurrection is the victory over death.

Sin **gave death its victory;** that which gave sin *its strength* was "the law." (Note: when Paul uses the term "the law" without a qualifier, as here, it is *invariably Torah*!)

Therefore, *the resurrection-- AD 70– is when sin– which gave death its victory– was overcome*. Thus, resurrection was not, as Kurt falsely claims, simply the overcoming of Hades. It was the overcoming of Hades *through the application of Christ's atonement, forgiveness*, as Kurt himself says!

Third, Kurt denies a *relationship between sin and death*! What then is the "law of sin and death"? And why was physical death "the immediately doom" of sin, as Kurt claims? And note: Kurt even appeals to Colossians 2:12 to speak of *resurrection, through forgiveness!*

There is a ***direct relationship*** between sin-death-justification- resurrection! Kurt posits a *direct relationship* between *sin and death*, but *no connection* between *forgiveness and life*. This is false. If sin brings death, then *forgiveness brings deliverance from death!*

KURT ON SIN AND DEATH

Kurt has changed positions, ***again***, on the issue of sin and death. *This is critical!* He says physical death was the "immediate doom brought in by sin." He says, "it is from physical death that the promise of resurrection was given." *Now he tells us, however,* that when God threatened Adam with death, that **it was not, after all, physical death**! Kurt's view of resurrection is convoluted. If physical death was not the threat for sin, then why was physical death the "immediate doom brought in by sin"?

He says Jesus died *a substitutionary death*. And, yet Jesus' physical death on the cross has not kept one single person in history from dying physically! **Kurt, why is this?** If Jesus died (physically) in my place and your's, why do believers die physically? Will you now renounce your oft stated position that Jesus died physically as a substitutionary death?

You say that physical death was "the immediate doom brought in by sin." Why then is *physical immortality* (*no physical death*) not the "immediate result" of forgiveness?

Let me reiterate another argument – which Kurt ignored, because it falsifies his theology.

Kurt claims "sin was defeated in Christ's cross." He said "the law of sin and death" was nailed to the cross. He says forgiveness of sin was objectively applied from then. Well, if sin brings physical death, then, if sin was defeated, if the law of sin and death was nailed to the cross, and those of faith were (or are) objectively **forgiven of sin**, then *why do Christians have to die physically?* **Forgiveness is the removal of that which kills, is it not?** So, if sin brings physical death, but, a person is forgiven, **ostensibly freed from the law of sin and death**, why are they still subject to the law of sin and death?

My friend's view logically demands that the physical death of even the most faithful Christian is a powerful testimony to the lack of forgiveness in their life. Kurt even says that if the Christian sins, "he comes again under the power of sin and death" (S-P, Sept. 09). Thus, *__physical death is the indisputable proof that the Christian is under the power of sin!__* And, since that physical death is the *final testimony of the power of sin*, this *logically demands* that that person is *lost*, for the final act in their life was *not forgiveness*, but *the imposition of the law of sin and death: i.e. you sin, you die!* The believer's *physical death* proves, **indisputably**, that they were not objectively forgiven, for they died a sinner's death! So, exactly how did Jesus nail the law of sin and death to the cross, Kurt?

So, Kurt tells us that physical death was the curse of the Garden, then he tells us it wasn't. He tells us Christ destroyed the law of sin and death, but then he tells us that Christians are subject to the law of sin and death. He tells us forgiveness was objectively applied from the cross, but then he tells us that the dead saints could not enter the MHP, because they did not have the benefits (i.e. forgiveness!) of Christ's atonement– until AD 70. His self contradictions are fatal.

And, don't forget that Kurt's problem is divorcing this entire discussion from the fulfillment of God's promises to Israel.

KURT'S INDIVIDUALIZATION OF ESCHATOLOGY

I hope the readers have caught what Kurt has done. He takes passages (1 Corinthians 15; 2 Corinthians 4-5; 1 Thessalonians 4, etc.) that speak of Christ's coming at the end of the age, and the bestowal of eternal life at that time, and turns them into promises *having nothing to do with Israel*, but, *the coming of Christ for individuals at the time of their death, throughout time!* While Kurt has challenged me to produce supportive commentators, *which I have done*, note that I challenged him to cite even one commentator that supports his idea that these resurrection texts do not speak of the second coming of Christ, but of Christ's coming for the individual at the time of their death. ***He has ignored the challenge. This is an empty box!***

KURT'S REFUSAL TO DEAL WITH HEBREWS 10:40

The reader must catch, once again, how Kurt has ignored Hebrews 11:40. Remember that Kurt adamantly claims that the living saints had fully received the atonement and forgiveness, etc. prior to AD 70. However, he says **the souls in Hades could not enter heaven (The MHP– Revelation 15!) until they received the benefits of Christ's atoning blood (S-P-October, 2009). (Do you catch that?)**

So, Kurt has the living saints in full possession of redemption and atonement. After all, he has confidently pointed to all those past tense verbs, *right*? However, he has the dead saints sequestered in Hades *because they had not received atonement*, and they would not receive that until AD 70! But, as *repeatedly noted*– but ignored by Kurt -- there is a fatal flaw in Kurt's position.

According to Paul, the OT saints could not enter the "better resurrection" (Hebrews 11:35-40) *without the NT saints*, and, the NT saints could not enter before the dead saints (1 Thessalonians 4:15f)! *In other words, OT and NT saints would enter the MHP at the same time!* So...
The dead saints and the living saints would receive their salvation ***at the same time*** (Hebrews 11:40).

178

But, the dead saints would not receive their salvation until AD 70 (Kurt Simmons).

Therefore, the living saints would not receive their salvation until AD 70.

So, the proposition that Kurt wanted to affirm in this debate, that the dead saints would enter the MHP in AD 70, proves my proposition, and destroys Kurt's! **Of course, Kurt ignored this argument**. Little wonder. And consider Kurt's *new definition* of the MHP.

The MHP is the New Covenant-- *not heaven*-- per Kurt's new definition. Kurt says the living saints had the full benefit of the New Covenant from the cross onward..

According to Revelation 15, *the dead saints (*actually, *no one!!)* could not enter the MHP-- the New Covenant, per Kurt-- until AD 70.

However, if the MHP is not heaven that means that in AD 70, the dead saints entered *the New Covenant,* but they could not enter *heaven because the MHP is not heaven, according to Kurt*!

See where Kurt's desperation has led him?

Note: If the MHP is the New Covenant (not the presence of God), then since the dead saints and the living saints would enter the MHP *at the same time,* and since the dead saints could not enter until AD 70, *this means that the living saints did not fully enter the New Covenant until AD 70!* Kurt has, *once again,* falsified his own theology.

Kurt says he has not changed his definition of the MHP-- *Yes, he has*! In his *second negative,* Kurt positively identified the MHP as *heaven*. Yet, he now says it is the New Covenant. *He has changed*, but his change does not help! We call this "debate conversion," when a person cannot sustain their normal position, they change their argument in mid-debate. Kurt has done this *repeatedly* in this exchange.

He now says, amazingly, that Revelation 15:8 only slightly "implies" that there was no entrance into the MHP until AD 70. No, there is no simple "implication." There is *explicit statement*: "***No one*** was able to enter until the wrath of God was fulfilled." Kurt, how is that mere "implication?" Kurt is so desperate to escape the force of the text that he turns *explicit statements* into mere *implications*. (Note also, it says **"no one"** could enter. Kurt insists that the living saints *could enter before the dead! Kurt is wrong*).

179

Now, Hebrews 9 says there would be no entrance into the MHP *while the Mosaic Law remained imposed*. Revelation 15 says there would be no access to the MHP until Jerusalem was judged. Of logical necessity, *the Mosaic Law remained imposed until the judgment of Jerusalem in AD 70*. Kurt has not touched this.

Kurt says AD 70 had no redemptive significance and the saints were forgiven from the cross onward. Yet, he says that the saints could not enter the MHP until AD 70.

But **he refuses to tell us why those "perfected" saints could not enter until the "irrelevant" AD 70 event**. Of course, Hebrews 9 answers the question-- Jesus was coming (in AD 70) to bring salvation. *He was coming to bring man into the MHP!*

Kurt continues to ignore the transfiguration as a vision of the passing of Torah and Christ's parousia. Kurt gave us *no proof* for rejecting this. Yet, this one argument falsifies his proposition. As one scholar noted: "It is perverse to apply the transfiguration to Jesus' incarnation"– as Kurt does.

THE *EARNEST* OF THE SPIRIT

Amazingly, my friend has now abandoned the truth that the earnest of the Spirit– the guarantee of the resurrection and salvation, was the charismata. He now says that the earnest is some gentle voice inside us. This is patently false– but it is necessary for Kurt to maintain any support for his newly created doctrine.

When Paul wrote to the Ephesians he said that when they first believed, they received the earnest of the Spirit. In Acts 19, the account of their conversion, what does the record say they received? They *spoke in tongues and prophesied!* Not one word about some "*inward yearning* of the heart." That is reading something into the text that is not there.

Kurt cannot explain how some "*inward yearning* of the heart" objectively guaranteed (s) salvation. That is pure *subjectivity*! God gave the charismata to *objectively guarantee*– openly confirm His work. The earnest of the Spirit was the *confirmatory work* of the Spirit– and Kurt believes that the work of confirmation was the *charismata*. Well, in 1 Corinthians 1:4-8, Paul said the charismata had **confirmed the Corinthian church**, (not just the _Word_, but the **church**!) and would continue to confirm *them*– until the Day of the Lord.

And, Kurt has, *in this debate*, affirmed that the charismata continued until AD 70. Thus, the charismata was indeed the guarantee (confirmation) of the coming salvation. Kurt is wrong, *again*. Notice...

The charismata served to confirm **both the church and the word** until AD 70 (1 Corinthians 1:4-8).

The charismata was the guarantee (the confirmation) *of the resurrection* (2 Corinthians 5:5; Ephesians 1:7; 4:30).

Therefore, unless there is no relationship between the confirmatory work of the Spirit and the earnest work of the Spirit, then the charismata was the guarantee of the resurrection until AD 70.

Kurt takes the promise of the Spirit as the earnest of the resurrection, and *divorces it from its OT roots*. Kurt says the resurrection in 2 Corinthians 5 is the resurrection of individuals at physical death throughout time. *No, it is the resurrection promised to Israel in Ezekiel 37 / Joel 2,* of which the Holy Spirit was the guarantee (Ezekiel 37:10f; 2 Corinthians 5:5). Kurt has, with no proof whatsoever, created a doctrine of the Spirit *distinct from God's promises to Israel.*

REDEMPTION AND EPHESIANS 1:7
Kurt argues that the redemption of Ephesians 1:7; 4:30, has nothing to do with justification from sin. He appeals to Jeremiah's day and the redemption of land, claiming that Jeremiah fully owned the land, but he had to wait for the end of the captivity to take possession. The trouble is that this is not the thematic context of Ephesians 1. It is the *Exodus / Passover / Redemption* that lies in the background, as virtually all scholars agree. Kurt, will you reject this virtually unanimous scholarly view? Note the redemptive work of that event.

The Passover lamb was slain. But, Israel *was still in Egypt!* Did the lamb "deliver" them? It was certainly the *ground* of their deliverance. But, they were not yet free, and not yet in the promised land.

For the Israelites to be "redeemed" *the enslaving power was then destroyed!* From the perspective of the OT, Israel was not completely redeemed even then! It was not until she entered the promised land that "the reproach of Egypt" was rolled off of them (Joshua 5:2f).

So, Israel's redemption was a process that was *initiated* when the Passover was slain. It progressed as the Egyptians were destroyed. As the Israelites wandered toward the promised land, their salvation was nearer than when they left captivity. But, their redemption was completed when they entered the promised land, and the reproach of Egypt was removed. This is *redemption as a process*, exactly as Ephesians 1-4 presents it. This falsifies Kurt's argument.

KURT AND THE GREEK TENSES

Kurt listed– with not a word of exegesis– (of course, he says solid exegesis is *irrelevant*)– 88 verses that use the past tense for salvation, justification, atonement, etc.. Kurt falsely states: "Out of 88 verses we produced in our first affirmative, Don graced us with his response to only one, Rom. 7:1-4." It is amazing what a person will say when they are desperate.

Fact: I summarized those 88 verses under broad classifications for brevity sake, and provided verses that posit those tenets in the future tense.

If I commented only on Romans 7, how is it that Kurt (vainly) attempts to respond to my comments on those other verses? Here is an example: The issue of adoption. *I offered Romans 8:14-23 as an illustration of the already but not yet of adoption.* Kurt says, *"these are the verses offered by Don."* Okay, so he claims I only commented on Romans 7, but then admits that I commented on Romans 8! He likewise *responded to my arguments* about the inheritance and redemption. So, how is it that I did not say a word about those other verses, *if Kurt responded to what I said?*

Let me say a further word about adoption.

The Roman practice that lies behind Romans 8:14f, was *a two-step practice*. There was an initial *declaration of adoption,* and then *a period of waiting to allow for objections*. After a period of waiting, there was the *official declaration of adoption.* I can personally relate to this, since my wife and I adopted our son. We had a judge's order, and we took the boy home with us. Yet, there was a waiting period– a time of some concern, I can tell you– until the day of what the judge actually called "the final judgment." *It was on that day that the boy became officially our son*! This was an already not yet process, an initiation and a consummation.

Paul said that the declaration of adoption had been made. They had been given the Spirit– the charismata, not some inner soft voice-- as *the objective guarantee of that adoption*. They were awaiting the finalization of the adoption, at the resurrection!

Don't forget, this would be at the time of *the fulfillment of God's promises to Israel!* Paul said the redemption of the body was *the hope of Israel*, to be

182

fulfilled at the resurrection (Romans 8:23–9:4). Kurt turns that into the individual's resurrection when they die. Kurt is wrong.

A CLOSER LOOK AT ROMANS 7
Kurt says: "Don's one response to our 88 verses amounts to a false charge that we say the institution of marriage ceased when the first husband died. Ridiculous! The covenant (not institution) of marriage ended with the deceased spouse, leaving the surviving spouse free to enter a new marriage covenant."

No, I did **not** misrepresent my friend. Here is what he said of Romans 7:1-4: "They teach that the law of the first husband (Old Testament) terminated with the death of Christ." You see, Kurt did argue that *the Old Law itself* died– *not just the relationship between two parties*. However, the text clearly says: *"you died to the law*, through the body of Christ." The law remained binding, but, *by entering the death of Christ*, they had *died to the law*! And, *the Jews did not believe that Torah itself died when a person died!*

TWO SYSTEMS AT ONE TIME
Kurt can only ridicule; he cannot refute the fact that God had two systems in place at the same time. He says: "Don argues that paganism is equally valid with the Old Covenant!" This is *grandstanding*. **It does not answer the argument**.

Kurt, were pagans under Torah, yes or no?

I stand with Paul that the Gentiles *who did not have Torah* were, "without God, having no hope in this world" (Ephesians 2:12f), but that they could, through conscientious living, be justified (Romans 2:14f). That means, *prima facie*, that there were two systems in place at the same time.

And did you notice (*Here is an empty box!*)– that Kurt has totally ignored my *repeated argument* on Galatians 4? Ishmael and Isaac dwelt *together* in the same house? Hagar and Ishmael represented the Old Covenant and the Old Covenant people who persecuted Isaac (the spiritual seed). As a result, Paul said, "cast out the bondwoman and her son." This proves, irrefutably, that the two laws existed side by side until **the casting out of Israel for persecuting the church!** Kurt has not breathed on this and he dare not, for it falsifies his new theology. His emotional appeal to "paganism" does not falsify the argument. His claim that I have surrendered my argument via Romans 7 is a smoke screen. Romans 7 proves my point! I have *consistently argued* that those coming into Christ *died to the Law,* while the Law remained valid until AD 70. Remember my illustration of the Berlin Wall- **that Kurt ignored?** Romans 7 thus proves my point on the Greek tenses.

In his books, Kurt correctly takes note of the present and future tenses in Hebrews 9-10. I have called on him to give us lexical, grammatical justification for now ignoring those present and future tenses. He has ignored this challenge.

Kurt is correct that there are several nuances to the Greek present tenses. However, his appeal to what is known as the "historical present" is misguided.

He claims that in 2 Corinthians 3 Paul refers to the already abolished Torah. (Although remember that Kurt says **it was not actually Torah that was nailed to the Cross!**)
Read my comments on 2 Corinthians 3 again. Kurt has ignored several points I made.
Paul, speaking of the passing of Torah says: "Seeing then that we *have– present tense–* such *hope.* **Paul does not say,** "seeing then that we had hope of the passing of Torah that has now been fulfilled." *He says it was their hope, when he wrote.* Kurt is wrong.
Paul says: "*To this day,* in the reading of the Moses, the veil is still present, but when one turns to the Lord the veil is taken away." As I noted– **and Kurt ignored**– Paul speaks here of a person *dying to Torah,* (as in Romans 7) not Torah being already dead! Kurt turns the text on its head. And note Paul's emphatic "to this day." You cannot turn that into a past tense verb without doing violence to the text. Kurt is wrong. Now watch:

The Spirit was the earnest and agent of the transformation from the glory of Moses to the glory of Christ (2 Corinthians 3:18): "We are being transformed, from glory to glory, through the Spirit."
The transformation was from *the ministration of death, to the ministration of life.* Thus, **the transition from covenantal death to covenantal life!** According to Kurt, that transformation was completed at the cross. He is wrong. The Spirit, through Paul's personal ministry (2 Corinthians 4:1f) was the then present earnest and agent of that transformation. That *transfiguration* (*metamorphosis* as used at the transfiguration in Matthew 17 to speak of the change *from Moses to Christ!*) was being accomplished

184

through the Spirit in Paul's ministry.

If that work of the Spirit was not the miraculous, but the earnest of the Spirit as an inner voice that is still with us, per Kurt, *then covenantal transformation is not completed; the ministration of death– Torah– remains valid.*

If that work of the Spirit was the miraculous– as it clearly was– then the work of covenant transformation was not perfected at the cross, and would not be perfected until the parousia, in AD 70.

Note also that the transformation was from the glory of the ministration of death **written on the tablets of stone**. That was *not the "ceremonial law"* distinct from the "moral law"! The transformation was from *the entire old world– not just some parts of it-- represented by the Law <u>written on the Tablets</u>*, to the greater glory of Christ. Kurt has *the ministration of death, <u>the Law on the tablets, remaining– but without the Sabbath!</u>*; Paul said that glory was being done away. Kurt is wrong.

No matter how you identify the work of the Spirit in 2 Corinthians 3, covenantal transformation was the work of the Spirit, *and that work was not completed when Paul wrote.* This proves that the cross *initiated* covenant transformation. The Spirit *empowered* it. The parousia *consummated* it! This is *Covenant Eschatology.*

Finally, 2 Corinthians 3-6 is Paul's commentary on Ezekiel 37. YHVH promised the Spirit to raise Israel from the dead (vs. 10-14), give the New Covenant and the Messianic Temple (vs. 25-27). Kurt's application of the work of the Spirit *divorces it from Israel*, and says the New Covenant was completed *before the Spirit was even given!* Paul said, however, that the promised covenantal transformation was taking place *through his Spirit empowered ministry.* Undeniably, the Old had not yet passed. The transformation from "glory to glory" was not yet completed.

Now, notice more on Kurt's abuse of the Greek. He says all the typological, ceremonial laws were fulfilled at the cross, and Torah was removed at the cross. (Yet-- *remember*!--he says Torah was <u>not</u> actually nailed to the cross!) However, notice:

In Colossians 2:14f, Paul says the *New Moons, Feast Days and Sabbaths*, "are shadows of good things about to come." Notice that Paul uses the present tense "<u>are</u> a shadow." Then he uses "*mello*" which Kurt admits means "to be on the point of." So, we have a present tense and a future tense. Yet, Kurt claims that we must *deny* the present and the future tenses and impose a past tense on the text! His authority? He gave none.

Likewise, in Hebrews 9:6-10:1, the apostle said the high priests stand daily (present tense) offering (present tense) sacrifices that can never make the worshipper perfect. He said those sacrifices "are symbolic for the present time" (not the past). He then predicted Christ's coming for salvation– the salvation tied to the atonement process (*not deliverance from physical persecution*), and says Christ must come "*for*, the law having (present tense, not past) a shadow of good things *about to come*" (again, from *mello*, which Kurt says means "about to be").

Kurt: *Do you now reject the truth that mello means "about to be, to be on the point of"?*

You have taught for years that it means this. *Do you now renounce this truth?* To continue to admit this definition means that Colossians 2 and Hebrews 10:1 proves that the Law had not passed.

So, again, we have *a present tense coupled with a future tense*. Yet, Kurt casts this evidence aside as insignificant. I have challenged him to give us the lexical, grammatical, contextual proof that justifies such bold rejection of the Greek, but he has adamantly refused. This is not solid theology.

I must note again that Hebrews 10:1 gives **the reason why Christ had to come again**, for salvation. It was, "*for* the law, being a shadow of the good things to come" (Hebrews 10:1). That word **"for"** gives the divinely mandated reason *why Christ had to return*. It was to fulfill the typological meaning of the atonement! Kurt ignored this, because *to admit this point is to abdicate his entire proposition.* The point stands, and Kurt is wrong.

TORAH'S NEGATIVE POWER

Kurt continues to claim: *"The lack of a mechanism to forgive does not equate with a negative power to forestall the grace of Christ's cross!"* This stands in stark contrast to Hebrews 9. Torah could not forgive nor give life. And, *as long as Torah stood valid, there was no entrance into the MHP!* **If Torah had no negative power, why couldn't man enter the MHP while Torah stood?** Why would entrance into the MHP only come when Torah was

186

removed? Torah *did* prevent entrance into the MHP, and that is a negative power, Kurt's obfuscatory denials notwithstanding.

If Torah died at the cross, and no longer had any negative power to prevent entrance into the MHP, yet the saints did not actually enter the MHP until AD 70, **why could the saints could not enter the MHP until AD 70?**

If removal of Torah was soteriologically irrelevant, then what was the "curse" from which Christ delivered those under Torah? Remember that I gave a list of passages, with exegesis, that described the negative power of Torah. I challenged Kurt to address those passages. He ignored them.

KURT'S DICHOTOMIZATION OF TORAH– MATTHEW 5:17-18 ISRAEL'S CEREMONIAL LAW OF THE FEAST DAYS NOT FULFILLED UNTIL AD 70!

In regard to Torah, Kurt claims, "Only the religious and ceremonial law was totally abrogated" at the cross. This is patently false.

Kurt divides Torah in a manner unknown to the Jews. He says: "Indeed, while the Old Testament was done away, most of the law *still exists* and condemns men of sin just as much as it ever did." Is that what Jesus said in Matthew 5? Clearly not. Where did Jesus even hint at such an idea in Matthew 5? Jesus said, "Not one jot or tittle shall pass until it is all fulfilled." Kurt says, no, that is wrong! Kurt says: "A few jots and some tittles will pass, but *most* of the jots and tittles will remain!" Kurt denies the words of Jesus.

Kurt has adopted the Sabbatarian view that the ceremonial law passed, but most of the law remains valid. Let's see if "the law" can be dichotomized as Kurt suggests.

TORAH'S OWN DEFINITION OF "THE LAW"

The Law of Blessings and Cursings (Deuteronomy 28-30, 31) calls itself "the law," <u>no less than ten times</u> (cf. 28:61; 29:21; 30:10, etc.). And that "the law" contains provisions of wrath against Israel that were not fulfilled until AD 70, *when Israel ate the flesh of her own children* ((Deuteronomy 28:54-57). **And get this**, it would be in that day *when God would abandon His covenant with both houses of Israel (Zechariah 11:6-10)!* This *irrefutably* confirms my proposition.

This proves that the Mosaic Law did not pass until AD 70. The time when Israel ate the flesh of her own children is when "all things that are written must be fulfilled" (Luke 21:22).

187

Remember:

Not one jot or one tittle of "the law" could pass until it was _ALL_ (not *some*) fulfilled.

The Law of Blessings and Cursings- with provisions of covenantal wrath for violation of Torah– including cannibalism-- is called "the law."

The Law of Blessings and Cursings-- including cannibalism-- was fulfilled in AD 70 in the fall of Jerusalem.

Therefore, not one jot or one tittle of the Law- including the Law of Blessings and Cursings-- passed until AD 70.

Here is a corollary:

The Law of Blessings and Cursings- with provisions of covenantal wrath for violation of Torah– including cannibalism-- is called "the law."

The Law of Blessings and Cursings- with provisions of covenantal wrath for violation of Torah– including cannibalism-- was fulfilled in AD 70.

But, the time when Israel would engage in cannibalism in fulfillment of the Law of Blessings and Cursings– would be the time **when God would abandon His Covenant with both houses of Israel** (Zechariah 11:6-10).

Do you catch this? God said the time when Israel would eat the flesh of her own children, **in fulfillment of "the law"** (when all things written would be fulfilled" Luke 21:22) would be when God's covenant with both houses of Israel would be broken! *Not the Cross!* It would be when they ate the flesh of their own children– in AD 70. This is *prima facie* proof that "the law" remained binding until AD 70.

Consider again my question that Kurt so desperately tried to avoid: "If a law has been abrogated, are any of its penalties or promises still binding?" Zechariah clearly affirms that the penalties of Torah would remain binding until the time when Israel would eat the flesh of her children– AD 70.

The Law of Blessings and Cursings– *The Law*– was irrefutably still binding in AD 70. Kurt's proposition is falsified.

Jesus' and the Gospel's Definition of "The Law"

Matthew 11:13- " For all the prophets and the law prophesied until John." Jesus said the law prophesied. It did not simply command, it *prophesied*! *This is verified in Hebrews 9:6f where the sacrificial system was typological (prophetic).* Thus, when Jesus said not one jot or tittle of "the law" could pass, he was saying that not one jot or tittle of the entire OT corpus could pass until it was all fulfilled!

188

John 12:34- "The people answered Him, "We have heard from the law that the Christ remains forever?" Now, *no where* in "the law" *as defined by Kurt,* does it say Messiah would endure forever! This is found in the Psalms and the other prophetic books. Thus, the Psalms and prophetic books were "the law"– and not one iota of it could pass until it was all fulfilled.

Paul's Definition of "The Law"

In Romans 3:10-23 Paul quotes from Psalms and calls it "the law."
In 1 Corinthians 14:20-21, Paul quotes from Isaiah 28, and calls it "the law."
Thus, the Isaiah and the prophets were "the law"

HEBREWS 9:6F, *AGAIN*

Kurt agrees that the ceremonial aspects of Torah would remain binding until all that they foreshadowed (predicted) was fulfilled. He falsely claims that all of those types were fulfilled at the cross.

Consider:
Not one jot or tittle of "the Law" could pass until it was all fulfilled (Matthew 5:17-18; Including all typological aspects of the "ceremonial law," KS).
But, all typological aspects of the "ceremonial law" i.e. *the feast days of Israel*, were not fulfilled until AD 70.
Therefore, not one jot or tittle of "The Law" including the "ceremonial aspects" passed until AD 70.

Let me establish the minor premise. There were seven feast days in Israel's world. **These occurred in chronological order.** Those feast days were (Leviticus 23):
1.) Passover
2.) Unleavened Bread
3.) First Fruits
4.) Pentecost
5.) Trumpets (Rosh Hashanah)
6.) Atonement
7.) Tabernacles (Sukkot)

The first four feasts occur at the beginning of the (civil) calendar, in the spring. Furthermore, those first four feasts were fulfilled **in sequence**, in Jesus' Passion-Pentecost. (So, part of "the ceremonial law" *but only part,*

189

was fulfilled from Jesus' Passion to Pentecost).

The last three feasts occurred in the seventh month. But what does Kurt do? He anachronistically has the atonement *finished* at the time of Passover, *the first feast day*! He has the atonement *finished* **before** the Unleavened Bread, the First Fruits, and Pentecost! *Do you catch that?*

The first four feasts take place **before** the atonement! Note that Trumpets, Atonement and Tabernacles all occurred in the seventh month, i.e. at the "same time."

The Feast of Trumpets foreshadowed the Day of Judgment; *Tabernacles is the Feast of Harvest, i.e. resurrection.* The atonement *came between these two feasts*, and *Tabernacles celebrated the consummation!* Kurt, however, rips atonement out of its chronological, eschatological and soteriological sequence, and makes it *the very first thing fulfilled!* There is *no justification for this*. This is a theological invention.

Jesus said *none* would pass until *all* was fulfilled. Paul said *the prophetic aspects of "the ceremonial law" would stand until they were all fulfilled at the full arrival of the reformation– **which Kurt admitted was in AD 70!** So, the typological aspects of the ceremonial law would stand binding until AD 70, Kurt himself agreeing!

Watch carefully:

The (Ceremonial) Feast of Trumpets foreshadowed the Judgment Coming of the Lord. (i.e. Fulfillment of Deuteronomy 28-30!)
The Lord had not come in judgment when Paul wrote Hebrews 9:6f.
Torah would remain binding until all of the types of Torah were fulfilled (KS; Matthew 5; Hebrews 9).
Therefore, Torah was still binding when Paul wrote Hebrews, and would remain binding until the fulfillment of the Feast of Trumpets (i.e. the judgment coming of the Lord in AD 70).

Also:

The *(Ceremonial)* **Feast of Tabernacles,** *(Harvest)* *foreshadowed the resurrection* **(Matthew 13).**
The Harvest (i.e. the resurrection) occurred in AD 70 (Matthew 13:39-43; *KS agreeing*).
Therefore, the typological meaning of the Feast of Harvest was not fulfilled until AD 70.

Now watch – and I challenge Kurt as kindly as possible to deal with this: Not one jot or tittle of "The Law" could pass until it was ***all fulfilled*** (Matthew 5:17-18; _including all typological aspects of the "ceremonial law," KS).

The ceremonial Feasts of Trumpets and Harvest were not fulfilled until AD 70 at the time of the judgment/resurrection.

Therefore, not one jot or tittle passed from "the ceremonial law" until AD 70.

To negate these arguments, Kurt must prove that the judgment and the resurrection, ***occurred at the Cross–*** when he says the ceremonial law was removed and Atonement consummated! He clearly cannot do that. Thus, his proposition is falsified. But we are not done.

All of the feast days were **_Sabbaths_** (And both the civil and religious years began with the **_New Moon_**, Leviticus 23)!

Not all of the (typological) feast days (_New Moons, Feast Days, Sabbaths_) were fulfilled when Paul wrote Colossians 2:14f.

Thus, when Paul said that the _New Moons, Feast days and Sabbaths_ "are a shadow of good things about to come" this means that the present and future tenses (Colossians 2 / Hebrews 9-10), must be taken as objective present and future tenses. They cannot be distorted into past tenses!

So...

Not one iota of Torah could pass _until the Sabbath aspect of the feasts was fulfilled._

The "Sabbath" aspect of all of the ceremonial feasts was not fulfilled when Paul wrote Colossians and Hebrews–judgment and harvest- _the ultimate Sabbath--_ had not yet been fulfilled.

Thus, none of Torah had passed when Paul wrote Colossians and Hebrews.

Consider this in light of Hebrews 8:13. Kurt claims– "This verse does not say that the old was still valid or binding."

Well, if the ceremonial Feast of Trumpets and Tabernacles had not yet been fulfilled– **and Kurt admits they weren't**– then the ceremonial law _was not abrogated!_ Further, if the Feast of Trumpets and Tabernacles had not yet been fulfilled, **then the Atonement was not perfected either!** This is why the saints could not enter the MHP until AD 70 (as _explicitly_, not implicitly, stated in Revelation 15). Trumpets and Tabernacles had not yet been fulfilled– Atonement was not yet consummated!

191

If all of those ceremonial types were not fulfilled, ***then not one jot and not one tittle of the law had passed***. Since the judgment / resurrection– fulfilling Trumpets and Tabernacles– was at hand when Hebrews 8 was written, ***then Torah was indeed "nigh unto passing."*** My friend cannot escape the force of this argument.

Notice the perfect correlation with Luke 21:22:
Jesus: Not one iota of Torah would pass until it was all fulfilled.
Torah– The Feast of Trumpets and Tabernacles typified the *soteriological / eschatological consummation– inclusive of Atonement!*
Trumpets / Tabernacles (and thus Atonement) were fulfilled in AD 70.
Thus, all things written were fulfilled in AD 70– **Torah passed in AD 70.**
Kurt's proposition is falsified. *This is Covenant Eschatology in its purest form.*

THE NOT YET OF SALVATION– 1 PETER 1– KURT'S FALSE DEFINITION OF SALVATION

It is almost unbelievable to read my friend's comments on 1 Peter. He says that the grace and salvation the saints in Asia were anticipating was *deliverance from persecution.* Let's see.

Those saints had been begotten unto an incorruptible inheritance. That inheritance was reserved in heaven, and they were being kept through faith for that salvation, "ready to be revealed in the last times." *The salvation is the reception of the inheritance to be received at the parousia– not death!* Furthermore, *they would not be delivered from persecution*, as Kurt falsely claims. Peter emphatically says they did have to suffer more! ***No deliverance from persecution, Kurt!***

They were then, *although under persecution,* "receiving the end of your faith, the salvation of your souls" (v. 9). Notice again, *under persecution*, but *receiving* (*present tense,* not past), the salvation of their souls! Then, Peter says that the salvation they were anticipating had been predicted by the OT prophets (v. 10).

Kurt, tell us plainly, where in the OT did the prophets predict that the Asian Christians would have their physical lives spared from the Neronian persecution? Give us the verses! The fact is that the text says *the exact opposite of what Kurt claims.* They were not about to be being saved from persecution! They had to endure *more* persecution!

Note again: The salvation Peter discusses is the salvation ***promised in the***

OT, God's promises to Israel! Peter is concerned with Israel, and her soteriological promises (see 1 Peter 2:9f– the fulfillment of Hosea 1:10), at the coming of the Lord! He is not discussing the death of individuals, nor deliverance from persecution!

1 Peter 1 is an irrefutable falsification of Kurt's "salvation completed at the cross" paradigm.

I have responded to every salient point raised by Kurt, and falsified his claims.

I have, in every way possible, negated and falsified Kurt's affirmative.

I have further demonstrated the truthfulness of Covenant Eschatology.

Preston-Simmons Debate

When was Sin Defeated? The Cross or A.D. 70?

Simmons' Third Affirmative

This debate has now reached its end. A lot of ground has been traversed. We appreciate the reader's patience. I know I have learned a lot; I trust the reader has too. We also want to thank Don for his brotherly conduct and vigorous advocacy throughout this discussion. We hope and trust that truth and understanding have been advanced through this exchange.

As suggested by the title above, this debate has been about the defeat of sin. When and how was sin defeated? When did the saints first stand "soterilogicallly" (sic) complete before the throne of God, cleansed and made pure by the blood of Christ? The Cross or AD 70? I say the Cross. Don says AD 70. The difference in our answers reflects the difference between Preterism and Covenant Eschatology. Preterism itself has nothing to say about redemption; it is not a system of soteriology (study of salvation), but of eschatology (study of last things). Preterism adopts a "contemporary-historical" analysis of Revelation and other "end time" prophecies, affirming that these were fulfilled in the events that overtook the Roman Empire following the death of Nero, including the AD 70 Destruction of Jerusalem. Preterism honors the traditional teaching of the church and Bible regarding the time and manner of our salvation from sin, affirming that all was accomplished at the Cross. This is the view I have been defending in this debate. Covenant Eschatology, which Don had been defending, is not Preterist *per se*. Unlike Preterism, which is merely a school of eschatology, Covenant Eschatology is also a system of soteriology. Not content to merely explain end-time prophecies from a contemporary-historical perspective, Covenant Eschatology completely re-interprets soteriology, changing everything the church has always taught about when and how man was saved from sin.

For two thousand years the church has taught that salvation came *at the cross* and that Christ's resurrection was the *objective evidence* that the atonement was complete. *("And we declare unto you glad tidings, how that **the promise** which was made unto the fathers, God **hath fulfilled** the same unto us their* *children, in that he hath **raised up Jesus again**" Acts 13: 32, 33.*) Nowhere in the history of Christianity has the least suggestion ever been made that the fall of Jerusalem contributed anything to man's redemption from sin. Search the volumes of the Ante-Nicene Fathers; pour over the volumes of the Post-Nicene Fathers; traverse the long centuries of the Middle Ages; study the work of the Reformers. You will not find it taught anywhere, at anytime, by any Christian writer that man's justification was held in abeyance from the cross until AD 70 (or the second coming, if you prefer). You will not find it taught the saints continued under the debt of sin, or that the Old Testament was "valid, binding, and obligatory" after the cross. You will not find these things taught by the church fathers because they are *not taught by the Bible.* No one even ever heard such claims until Max King, who *stripped* the cross of its glory, and made AD 70 the focal point of salvation. Here is the chart we produced in our third negative. Please consider it again now.

Cross	Covenant Eschatology
?	Atonement - AD70
?	Justification – AD 70
?	Reconciliation – AD 70
?	Forgiveness of sins – AD 70
?	Legal admittance into presence of God with the veil – AD 70
?	Time of Reformation – AD 70
?	Spirits of just men made perfect – AD 70
?	Old Testament fulfilled and legally annulled – AD 70
?	Grace triumphant over law – AD 70

Virtually everything that the Bible teaches about the cross, Covenant Eschatology transfers to AD 70. Does the Bible teach that atonement was made at the cross? Don denies it. Does the Bible teach that reconciliation

195

happened at the cross? Don denies it. Does the Bible say we have forgiveness of sins in the cross? Don denies it. There is NOTHING in terms of man's salvation that my brother Don is willing to say arrived at the cross. According to Don, *nothing happened at the cross*. In the church in Ardmore, Oklahoma, where Don used to serve as preacher, there was even a big picture of Titus' siege of Jerusalem on the wall when you entered the sanctuary. Where other churches might have the cross, or a scene of Jesus praying in Gethsemane, instead we find the fall of Jerusalem! What does that tell you about the misplaced emphasis of Covenant Eschatology?

Covenant Eschatology's emphasis upon AD 70 is not limited to *when* justification arrived, but *how*. The King/Preston paradigm changes the very *manner* of our salvation from the *addition of grace* to the *removal of law*. The Bible teaches that men are under condemnation of the law as sinners. "The law" is not the Old Testament, but the moral law God has enjoined upon mankind as partakers of his image and likeness. When we violate God's moral law, we come under condemnation of sin and death. The moral law and the law of sin and death have always existed and always will. If the Mosaic law had never been enacted, men would still be in bondage to sin by the law. What mankind needed to find salvation was the *addition of grace* by the substitutionary death and atoning sacrifice of Jesus Christ. Where there is no law, there is no transgression (Rom. 4:15). Grace acquits where the law condemns. Therefore, ***grace presupposes the coexistence of law.*** Grace triumphs over law. However, Covenant Eschatology denies that grace triumphs over law. The King/Preston paradigm has it that the law must first be removed before grace can enter in. It is in essence a system of grace by absence of law.

Covenant Eschatology spiritualizes the resurrection, equating it with justification from sin. But inasmuch as the resurrection came at the *end* of the eschatological period, Covenant Eschatology must *postpone* justification until the time of the resurrection. In order to postpone the justification, Don is forced to strip the cross of its power, elevating law over grace. Grace *should have* arrived at the cross, but the mysterious "negative power" of Torah prevents it. It is only by removal of the law in AD 70 that grace and justification finally arrive. Thus, **Covenant Eschatology changes the entire theory and mechanism by which man is saved.** Don is very explicit that "forgiveness of sin did not arrive until AD 70". Don is also very explicit that it is *only* by removal of the law that man is justified: "The destruction of the

196

temple signaled that God's covenant with Israel was now fulfilled. He had kept his Word and, 'brought life and immortality to light through the gospel' (2 Timothy 19f). The 'law of life in Christ Jesus' (Romans 8:13), now stood triumphant over the law that was *'the strength of sin,'* (Romans 7:7f)[1]" (emphasis Don's). PLEASE NOTE: Don says the law had to be removed before sin was defeated! What Paul places at the cross, Don moves to AD 70! Here is another quote: "You cannot logically affirm the fulfillment of the resurrection in AD 70... and not affirm the end of whatever law it was that held the condemning power over man." Thus, according to Don, we are saved by the removal of law, not the addition of grace. The cross accomplished *nothing*, for it is not until AD 70 when the law is removed that sin is defeated.

King/Preston Soteriology & Eschatology

Resurrection = Justification = Removal of Old Law (AD 70)

"death is abolished when the state of sin and the law are abolished"

WHERE IS THE CROSS?

Thus, Preterism today is divided between two camps: one that views eschatology as having been fulfilled in the first century, but otherwise leaves the historical teaching of the church about the cross intact. The other (Covenant Eschatology) adds to Preterism a completely new system of soteriology, which changes both the time and manner by which mankind was justified. To help hash out the issues involving these competing systems, the debate has been framed around the question of when salvation from sin arrived, at Christ's first coming, or at his second? Let us review the arguments and evidence.

The Bible Teaches that the Debt of Sin was Expunged at the Cross

---

[1] Don K Preston, *Like Father, Like Son, On Clouds of Glory* (Ardmore OK, 2006), p. 109.

"And you, being dead in your sins and the uncircumcision of your flesh, hath he quickened together with him, having forgiven you all trespasses; blotting out the handwriting of ordinances that was against us, which was contrary to us, and took it out of the way, nailing it to his cross; and having spoiled principalities and powers, he made a shew of them openly, triumphing over them in it" Col. 2:13-15

These three verses are dispositive of the whole debate. The controlling verbs are all in the perfect tense, showing completed action in the past: *Hath* quickened; *having* forgiven; *having* spoiled. Those verbs that are not perfect tense, are either past tense ("took it out of the way…made a shew of them") or are the historic present, showing how the perfect work of the cross was accomplished in the past. "He *has done* this, by *doing* that." ("He has forgiven our sins, by *blotting* out the evidence of the law's debt…*nailing* it to his cross, *triumphing* over sin and death in it") The whole thrust of the passage is to place *all* redemptive work in the past, at the cross. Notice the language of Paul:

Dead in sins, Made alive in Christ
Trespasses forgiven, Debt of sin blotted out
The evidence of our indenture was taken away, Nailed to the Cross
Sin and death spoiled, Made an open show of
Triumphed over in the Cross

In Jewish society, when a man paid his debts, the debt holder nailed the written evidence of the debt to the door post of the debtor's house, showing he was relieved of its obligation. That is the image Paul evokes here. More than merely nailing it to the cross, however, Paul says Jesus went so far as to blot out its writing with his very blood! All that was written against us, the law's recital of our debt to sin, was erased and expunged *at the cross*. In light of these verses, there is simply no way to keep the saints under the debt of sin until AD 70…*and Don knows it.* In an unguarded moment, Don gave away the debate and admitted that the saints could enter the power of the cross before AD 70. In his first negative Don said,

"When a person, through faith, entered into the power of the cross, *they died to the Law!*"

To enter the power of the cross is to *leave* the power of sin under the law.

198

To be dead to the law is to be acquitted from the guilt of sin; it is to be saved and justified. But if they were already saved from sin as Don says, then *the coming of Christ for salvation was at the cross,* not AD 70. A small sampling of verses of the scores that might be cited, which confirm the saints were already in a present state of grace and justification include (please note the verb tenses):

Rom. 1:5 – "By whom we *have received* grace."

Rom. 3:24 - "*Being justified* freely by his grace through the redemption that is in Christ Jesus."

Rom. 5:1 – "Therefore, *being justified* by faith, we *have peace* with God through our Lord Jesus Christ."

Rom. 5:9 – "Much more then, *being now justified* by his blood, we shall be saved from wrath through him."

Rom. 5:10 – "For if, when we were enemies, we *were reconciled* to God by the death of his Son, we shall be saved by his life."

Rom. 6:14 - "Ye *are not under law*, but under *grace.*"

Rom. 6:18 – "Being then made *free from sin.*"

Rom. 8:1 – "There *is now no condemnation* to them which are in Christ Jesus."

Rom.8:2 – "For the law of the Spirit of life in Christ Jesus *hath made me free* from the law of sin and death."

Heb. 10:14 – "*For by one offering he hath perfected forever them that are sanctified.*"

The reader is urged to recall that when Don was pressed to produce *even one verse* that plainly teaches or states that the saints were under the debt of sin until AD 70 he could not do it. What does that say about the "scripturalness" of Covenant Eschatology?

```
         Don's  Box Number 1
              Verses?

              EMPTY!
```

Don was unable to produce a single verse that said the saints were under the debt of sin until AD 70. What if we approach the issue from the other direction? What happened when we asked Don to produce a verse that plainly states or teaches justification occurred in AD 70? This is an essential premise of Covenant Eschatology. Was he able to produce a verse? NO, not even one! proposition of Covenant Eschatology: the idea that the debt of sin somehow survived the cross and that justification did not arrive until AD 70.

The Bible Teaches that the Old Testament Terminated at the Cross

All of Christendom affirms that the Old Testament ended at the cross. Only among Preterists does the error exist that the Old Law was somehow valid until AD 70. Preterists fall into this error for several reasons. First, the disciples' question to Jesus on the Mount of Olives regarding the end of the "world" may also be translated "age" (Grk. aiwnoj), leading to the assumption is that it is the "Mosaic" age that is referred to. This is reinforced by the fact that the destruction of Jerusalem is the main focus of the discourse. However, when we recall Nebuchadnezzar's dream of the great image and four world empires (Dan. 2), we realize that the coming of Christ was in no way limited to Palestine and Jewry, but was a world-wide event that brought an end to the "world" as it has theretofore existed, in place of which grew up the world-monarchy and dominion of Christ. The visions of Daniel chapter seven are to the same effect, where the Jews and Palestine do not even make an appearance, and the whole vision revolves around the four world empires, particularly Rome and Nero. In light of these and other passages, the idea that "aiwnoj" in Matt. 24:3 refers to the "Mosaic" age is certainly debatable. To my view, "world" is the better translation, for it is not merely the Old Testament that was ending, but a old world-order. Of course, even if the Mosaic age was intended by the disciples, this would not prove that the law was valid until AD 70 in any event. Slavery legally ended in America with the "Emancipation Proclamation" but the actual institution itself endured until at least the end of the Civil War and the enactment of the Thirteenth Amendment several years thereafter. Thus, even though some outward forms of the Old Testament law and ritual lingered on after the cross, this is not proof they retained any validity with God.

A second reason Preterists have fallen into the error that the Old Testament was somehow valid until AD 70 stems from apologetic attempts to explain the burning up of the "heavens and earth" prophesied by Peter. Believing that the Matt. 24:3 refers to the Mosaic age, the natural tendency is to try to explain the "heavens and earth" of II Pet. 3:7-13 "covenantally" in reference to Israel and the Old Testament law and ritual. The mistake is quite natural, given the strong emphasis upon the fall of Jerusalem in Old Testament prophecy and the Olivet Discourse. However, a more mature reading of the Old Testament brings within our view *many* passages where the cataclysmic passing of the "elements" and "heavens and earth" have no covenantal aspect at all. As we begin to bring these passages into the equation, we realize that the symbolism of the "heavens and earth" is *always* socio-political, *never* covenantal. N.T. Wright, a favorite of Don whom he cites in his books, says that the prophets employ imagery of shaking the heavens and earth, not covenantally, but socio-politically and militarily. *"This language denotes socio-political and military catastrophe."*[1] Don himself says the same thing: *"It is emotive language, hyperbolically expressing the catastrophic end to a social order, the end of a kingdom."*[2] In fact, it is our belief that there is not one single occasion in the whole Bible where the "heavens and earth" refer to the Old or New Testaments – not one. In any event, the idea that the "heavens and earth" refer to the Old Testament fosters the error that the Covenant was still valid, since it was not until the eschaton that these "passed away."

A third reason is the tiny handful of passages where the verb tenses seem to say the law was gradually and progressively being replaced. Heb. 8:13, for example, says "now that which decayeth and waxeth old is ready to vanish away." Of course, this in no way implies that the Old Law was still valid or binding, but in our zeal to prove that the second coming referred to first century events, of which the fall of Jerusalem was one of the most significant parts, we tend to make this error.

These are some of the chief reasons Preterists find themselves wrongly arguing that the law was valid until AD 70. However, if challenged on the question we quickly find that the notion cannot be defended, and that we are on the short end of the stick every time. Don's empty box is a good demonstration of just how totally lacking that proposition is of solid, Biblical evidence. We asked Don if he could produce *even one verse* that plainly stated or taught that the first generation saints (Jew or Gentile) were bound and obligated to keep the ceremonial or dietary law, circumcision, laws

---

[1] N.T. Wright, *Jesus the Victory of God* (Minneapolis, Fortress, 1996), p. 361.

[2] Don K Preston, *Like Father, Like Son, On Clouds of Glory* (Ardmore OK, 2006), p. 33.

forbidding association with Gentiles, or any other Mosaic law other than the moral law against idolatry, fornication, blood, etc. We challenged Don to produce BOOK, CHAPTER, AND VERSE. He produced none.

Don's Box Number 3
Verses?

EMPTY!

Don has concocted all sorts of arguments from such varied sources as the Mount of Transfiguration, the Feasts of the Jews, and the Most Holy Place to try to "prove" his case, yet he cannot produce a single verse that actually supports what he is saying. This perhaps that is to be expected. If you cannot produce verses, what else can you but concoct arguments? It is kind of like trying to argue that the Constitution authorizes the federal government to nationalize health care. You can argue all you want, but just try to find it in the Constitution!

In his last negative, Don brought up Matt. 5:17, alleging that "not one jot or tittle of 'The Law' including the 'ceremonial aspects' passed until AD 70." According to Don, "None of the law would pass, until all of the law was fulfilled."[1] Thus according to Don, it is an all-or-nothing proposition: if even one law can be shown to be invalid or non-binding, then all the law was invalid or non-binding. This is Don's position and he has argued it a hundred times in debates and in his books. But here Don testifies against himself, for he is on record saying that key provisions of the law were invalid before AD 70. Don argues (correctly) that the land covenant was coterminous with circumcision; that when the law of circumcision ceased, the land covenant ceased also. Don put this argument together to defeat futurists, who claim the land still belongs to Israel, but it works just as well to defeat Covenant Eschatology. Don says Paul taught **"circumcision was invalid"** and that he "unequivocally condemned the religious practice of circumcision." According to Don, "If God removed circumcision, the sign and seal of the

---

[1] Don K. Preston, *Like Father, Like, Son, On Clouds of Glory* (JaDon Productions, Ardmore, 2006), pp. 190.

202

Abrahamic land promise, then the Land Covenant was null and void."[2] Don says **"When Paul wrote...circumcision no longer availed, God had abrogated that mandate."[3]**

There we have it. By his own admission, circumcision was invalid and "abrogated" and the "land covenant was null and void." Both of these institutions were integral parts of "Torah;" they are the foundation upon which the whole Mosaic institution rests. *Without circumcision and the land covenant, there is no Old Testament.* Don says "None of the law would pass, until all of the law was fulfilled." Since Don says that the land covenant and circumcision were "abrogated" and "null and void" it logically follows that "all of the law was fulfilled." Don's argument against futurists proves the undoing of Covenant Eschatology. This it is only fitting, since Covenant Eschatology is also a form of futurism when one considers that it attempts to put off until AD 70 (the future) what was so plainly accomplished at the cross (the past).

But let us not rely upon Don to show the falsity of Covenant Eschatology; let us notice that it was Jesus' *first coming* he declared would fulfill the law. Matt. 5:17 establishes this fact beyond dispute:

"Think not that I am come to destroy the law and prophets; I am not come to destroy but to fulfill."

Notice Jesus' words: "I AM COME TO FULFILL." Thus, the very verse Don uses to show the law was not fulfilled until the second coming, expressly states that it would be fulfilled in Jesus' first coming! You would have to be blind to miss it! "I AM COME TO FULFILL." First coming! Jesus, before he died, cried out from the cross **"It is finished!"** (Jn. 19:30; *cf.* Matt. 27:50), showing that he had *completed* the work his Father gave him to do. Luke even states "And when they *had fulfilled* all that was written of him, they took him down from the tree, and laid him in a sepulchre" (Acts 13:29). In Jesus' resurrection, the promised salvation from sin and death God made in the Garden (Gen. 3:15) was finally fulfilled (still first coming):

---

[2] Ibid, pp. 134, 135.

[3] Ibid, p. 180.

*"And we declare unto you glad tiding, how that the promise which was made unto the fathers, God **hath fulfilled** the same unto us their children, in that he hath raised up Jesus again" (Acts 13:32, 33).*

One jot or one tittle would in now wise pass from the law except it first be fulfilled. But Luke just said "God hath fulfilled." Therefore, Paul says:

"Let no man therefore just you in meat, or in drink, or in respect of an holyday, or of the new moon, or of the Sabbath days: which are a shadow of things to come; but the body is of Christ." Col. 2: 16, 17

A shadow ends where the body begins. Since Paul is telling the Colossians that they are free from keeping the law, it is axiomatic that the "body" had already come. "The body is of Christ" is Paul's way of saying that the shadow of the law ended with the body of Christ upon the cross. "This is **my body** which is broken for you" (I Cor. 11:24). "When he cometh into the world, he saith, Sacrifice and offering and burnt offerings and offerings for sin thou wouldest not, but **a body thou has prepared for me**...He taketh away the first that he may establish the second" (Heb. 10:5-9) Notice what the writer of Hebrew says:

God did not want animal sacrifices for sin
When Jesus came into the world (first coming), he declared God's displeasure with the ceremonial law
God prepared a body for the Messiah as an offering for sin
In that offering, the first covenant was taken away, that the second covenant might be established.

This is Christianity 101, folks! Only where Max King has corrupted the gospel could such basic, foundational doctrine be lost and obscured.

The Bible Teaches that Spiritual Resurrection Occurs at Conversion

Covenant Eschatology asserts that the saints were "dead in sin" until AD 70 when they were allegedly "raised" (justified) by removal of the law. But the Bible teaches that men receive spiritual resurrection when they obey the gospel and are baptized:

"And you hath he quickened, who were dead in trespasses and sins...Even

when we were dead in sins, hath quickened us together with Christ, (by grace ye are saved;) and hath raised us up together and made us sit together in heavenly places n Christ Jesus." (Eph. 2:1, 5, 6; cf. Rom. 6:3-6; Col. 2:13).

The tense in these verses is perfect, showing completed action in the past (*hath quickened, hath raised*). Jesus' resurrection was objective proof that the atonement was complete and the way into the fellowship and presence of God was restored. In Jesus, the saints entered the very presence of God and were seated together with Christ in heavenly places. Paul makes the same point in Colossians when he says God "hath delivered us from the power of darkness, and hath translated into the kingdom of his dear Son" (Col. 1:13). Notice again the perfect tense (hath delivered, hath translated). Out from under the power of sin, into the presence of God within the veil (*cf.* Heb. 10:19). Naturally, the writer is speaking figuratively and in contemplation of law, for we are still on earth and not actually personally present in heaven at all. But in terms of our legal and covenantal standing before the throne, we are admitted into God's presence by and through the death, burial, and resurrection of Christ. Jesus' presence in heaven is our presence in heaven. The spiritual resurrection, which Don keeps trying to postpone until AD 70, was already an accomplished fact when Paul wrote.

We have now examined the main propositions of Covenant Eschatology: 1) the law was valid until AD 70; 2) the saints were under the debt of sin until AD 70; and 3) the saints were loosed from the bondage of sin (justified/"resurrected") in AD 70. In each case, Don was unable to produce a single verse in his support. We have seen on the other hand that the traditional teaching of the church is supported by a super-abundance of scripture as we would expect. Can we take seriously a doctrine which consistently fails to produce verses to support its most basic tenants, while contradicting the most basic teaching of the historical Christian faith?

Daniel Nine 9 & 12

Daniel says that the Messiah would "confirm the covenant with many for one week" (the final prophetic week of the Messiah). He then states that in the midst of that week, Messiah would "cause the sacrifice and oblation to cease." The traditional view of this passage has it that the cessation of the sacrifice and oblation refers to the legal termination of the temple ritual, which was rendered null by the sacrifice of Christ. We have cited several prominent commentators to this effect. By this view, the "covenant" that is being confirmed is the New Testament and God's promise to bring in redemption by the Messiah. The first half of the final prophetic week of Messiah is Jesus' earthly ministry; the latter half of the week is Jewish war with Rome and the destruction of Jerusalem (by my view), though some believe that the final week reaches to the death of Stephen or the beginning of the Gentile mission. By my view, there is a gap caused by the "cutting off" of Messiah, during which he goes into a "far country to receive a kingdom and return" (Lk. 19:12). However, the "daily offering" (not "sacrifice and oblation") in Dan. 12:11-13, refers to the daily sacrifice for Caesar, which the Jews began to refuse in AD 66, and which Josephus says was the real beginning of the war. Thus, the "sacrifice and oblation" in Dan. 9:27 is not the same as the "daily sacrifice" in Dan. 12:11; different terminology is used and different things are signified. (Don's accusation that I have "falsified my position" based upon Don's asserted identity of these sacrifices, is therefore without merit.) The "abomination of desolation" that was set up 1290 days later refers to the Titus' legions assembling at Caesarea in preparation for the war. The 1330 days (40 day more) is the point where they actually made camp before the walls of Jerusalem on the 14th of Nisan, AD 70. Such, at least, is our view of the question. .

Don, who wants to keep the law alive until AD 70, says the "covenant" that is being confirmed is the Old Testament; the midst of the week he says occurred in AD 66; its end in AD 70. ("That final week ended in AD 70. Thus, *Torah ended in AD 70!*") Thus, by Don's view the week runs from AD 63-70, with the cessation of the sacrifice falling in the midst. The citation Don provides in proof of his proposition is to Josephus, *Wars*, 6:2:1. However, this passage refers to the cessation of the temple sacrifice in AD 70, not AD 66, during the siege of Jerusalem, just months before the city fell. Thus, Don's "midst of the week" does not occur in the middle at all! Not only that, there is no rational basis for making the final week of the Messiah begin in AD 63, for nothing of Messianic proportion or significance occurred at that time. Don is haphazardly throwing arguments together in an attempt to save the sinking ship of Covenant Eschatology.

Salvation Ready to be Revealed in the Last Time
Don argues that I Pet. 1:5 refers to salvation from sin. He chided us for saying that this passage describes salvation from the end-time persecution that would be revealed at Christ's coming. This is a theme that runs all through end-time prophecy; therefore let's take a closer look.

"Who are kept by the power of God through faith unto salvation ready to be revealed in the last time. Wherein ye greatly rejoice, though now for a season, if need be, ye are in heaviness through manifold temptations: that the trail of your faith, being much more precious than of gold that perisheth, though it be tried with fire, might be found unto praise and honour and glory at the appearing of Jesus Christ." I Pet. 1:5-7

The context here plainly shows that there was a time of persecution coming, which would precede the advent of Christ, but the saints' perseverance would result in praise and glory at Jesus' coming. Can there be any doubt that the "salvation" that would be revealed was Jesus destruction of the church's enemies? This is the very theme of Revelation and numerous related passages. Jesus' first coming was to deal with sin; his second coming was to put his enemies beneath his feet.

Hebrews 9:28	Hebrews 10:12, 13
"So Christ was **once offered** to bear the sins of many; and unto them that look for him **shall he appear** a second time without sin **unto salvation**."	"But this man, after he had **offered one** sacrifice for sin for ever, sat down on the right had of God; from henceforth expecting till **his enemies be made his footstool**."

1) Zechariah, the father of John, prophesied of Christ "he hath raised up an horn of salvation in the house of his servant David…that we should be saved from our enemies, and from the hand of all that hate us" (Lk. 1:69, 71).

2) At his second coming, Christ would show "who is the only Potentate, King of kings, and Lord of lords" (I Tim. 6:15).

3) Jesus would destroy Nero and the persecutors "with the spirit of his mouth, and shall destroy with the brightness of his coming" (II Thess. 2:8).

4) Paul told the Roman Christians suffering persecution by the Jews

"now is our salvation nearer than when we first believed...the God of peace shall bruise Satan under your feet shortly" (Rom. 13:11; 16:20)

5) When Babylon the Harlot was destroyed, the saints and angels proclaim "Alleluia; Salvation and glory, and hour, and power, unto the Lord our God...for he hath avenged the blood of his servants at her hand" (Rev. 19:1, 2).

6) Daniel said the "little horn" (Nero) would persecute the saints 3 ½ years, "until the Ancient of days came, and judgment was given to the saints of the most High" (Dan. 7:21-27).

These and many more passages all show that Christ's second coming was to redeem the church out of the hand of her persecutors, not save her from sin. Peter thus says, "Beloved, think it not strange concerning the fiery trial which is to try you as though some strange thing happened unto you: but rejoice, inasmuch as ye are partakers of Christ's sufferings; that, when his glory shall be revealed, ye may be glad also with exceeding joy" (I Pet. 4:12, 13). Christ's power and divinity would be displayed at his coming by the destruction of his enemies. The saints would share in that glory and rejoice in his salvation. "And when these things begin to come to pass, then look up, and lift up your heads: for your redemption draweth nigh" (Lk. 21:28).

Don's Argument from "Ishmael"

Don charges that we "refuse" to answer his argument about Ishmael dwelling in Abraham's household together with Isaac for a time. The implication of Don's argument is that this "proves" the law was valid until AD 70. However, Don is mistaken and his argument without merit. Ishmael's living his Abraham's household does not prove there were two covenants in force at one time. The fact that he was not cast out until Isaac was weaned speaks to the fact that there was a *grace period* for the Jews to obey the gospel of Christ before the nation was destroyed, not that the Old Testament was still in force. Whatever claim Ishmael had to inherit Abraham's house, ended the moment Isaac was born, not when Ishmael was cast out. Besides, it is the women (Hagar and Sarah) that represent the covenants in Paul's allegory (Gal. 4:21-31). Sarah was Abraham's wife long before Abraham took Hagar who bore Ishmael. Thus, if we were to press the allegory to its limits like Don, the New Testament would be older that the Old Testament, which it wasn't. So much for trying to prove one thing by analogy to another! Allegories and analogies can illustrate, never prove. That is a rule of logic.

Saints in Hades, etc.

Don says I contradict myself by saying that the saints on this side of eternity had received the atonement before AD 70, but the saints in Hades did not receive it until AD 70. I never said any such thing. Even when I shared the mistaken views of Don, I *always* believe that both living and dead received the atonement simultaneously. Nowhere at anytime have I said or implied otherwise. It has been Don's tactic throughout this debate to attribute statements to me that I have never said. He sets them up as straw-men so he can knock them down, attempting to make me look bad and himself look good. In his second affirmative alone he did it four times. In his second negative, he did it at least four times more (and he has done it many times along the way I have simply passed over without mention). Don claims I said "physical death was the immediate doom of sin." But I have never said or implied any such thing. Don claims I said that the "law of sin and death was nailed to the cross," but I have never said that either. He says I admit that Rom. 9:28 refers to the salvation of national Israel. I don't. I believe it refers to their destruction! And Don now claims that I say atonement accrued to one group at a time different than another group. Yet, I have never said any such thing. It is pretty sorry when you have to win a debate based upon what someone else has never said!

Argument from Hosea

All of Christendom knows that the general resurrection is from Hades; only among Preterists will you find a spiritualized model that equates resurrection with justification from sin. Don, needing to find some support for this unprecedented view, looks to Hosea 13:1 "When Ephraim speak trembling he exalted himself in Israel; but when he offended in Baal, he died." Verse 14 goes on to state "I will ransom them from the power of the grave; I will redeem them from death: O death, I will be thy plagues; O grave, I will be thy destruction; repentance shall be hid from mine eyes." Don puts these two passages together and, Viola! Max King's spiritulized resurrection! But there are major problems with Don's view. First, Hos. 13:1 is clearly *historically specific*. It does not speak to sin in general, from which the prophet is promising a coming day of justification by the gospel. Rather, the prophet is speaking to the historical situation of the Northern Tribes and their apostasy from God. "When Ephraim spake trembling he was exalted," that is, when the Northern Tribes lived in the fear of God they were exalted in Israel and under God's blessings. "But when he offended in Baal, he died" speaks to the apostasy of the Northern Tribes, which began with Jeraboam the son of Nebat and his successors. Thus, the passage does not have the general problem of sin in view and therefore is not prophesying a general resurrection by gospel justification. What the passage is actually teaching is the coming captivity of Israel (its divorce); the nation "dies" when it goes into captivity; all of its political institutions cease to exist. The resurrection thus speaks, in its first instance, to the political resurrection of the nation when the captivity returns (recall the valley of dry bones in Ezekiel 37). Homer Haily, the great Old Testament expositor says:

"It is a promise of God to the doomed nation that though they go into captivity and there suffer the pangs of travail and sorrow, yet God will redeem them; He will deliver them from their captivity. Their restoration would be as a birth; also it would be as a resurrection from the dead (see Ezek. 37). The pestilences and destruction of Sheol would be overcome. Hosea looks not to Christ's resurrection or to ours, but to the restoration of the people. However, the true significance of death's destruction and of Sheol's defeat was not made clear until Christ's resurrection, and the complete defeat of death will be consummated in our own resurrection from the grave (I Cor. 15:54, 55)."[1]

Thus, Don's first problem is that he totally divorces the passage from its historical context, just as he does the Isa. 27 and 59. His second problem, is that resurrection is not a spiritualized model equated with justification, but an actual resurrection from physical death and Hades ("Sheol," in Old Testament terminology). The Corinthians were already "washed, sanctified, and justified" (I Cor. 5:11) but were looking for a further resurrection from physical death and Hades. Paul thus says "O death, where is thy sting? O Hades, where is thy victory?" (I Cor. 15:55). Clearly, I Cor. 15 is about – and ONLY about – the resurrection from physical death and Hades. The idea of a spiritualized resurrection from the "grave of Judaism" is nowhere in the text. What would these Greek Christians living on the Corinthian peninsula know or care about a resurrection from Judaism?! The littlest bit of common sense and critical thinking would go a long way among Preterits, if only we

---

[1] Homer Haily, *Commentary on the Minor Prophets* (Religious Supply Co., 1993), p. 181.

would use it.

Argument from Zechariah

Another of Don's "irrefutable" arguments. Here Don cites Zech. 1:10, where the prophet speaks in the person of God, saying, he would "break is covenant" with Israel. Don applies this to AD 70, but the fall of Jerusalem by Titus is nowhere in view. Where the prophet actually places the end the covenant is the betrayal and murder of the Messiah, or cross:

"And I took my staff, even Beauty, and cut it asunder, that I might break my covenant which I had made with all the people. And it was broken in that day...And I said unto them, If ye think good, give me my price; and if not, forbear. So they weighed for my price thirty pieces of silver. And the Lord said unto me, Cast it unto the potter: a goodly price that I was prized oat of them. And I took the thirty pieces of silver, and cast them to the potter in the house of the Lord" (Zech. 11:10-13).

The reader will recognize immediately that this speaks to Judas Iscariot's betrayal of the Lord and the high priests and elders of the Jews murder of Jesus for blood money (Matt. 27:9, 10). Therefore, if this passage describes the end of the Old Testament, then that occurred at Calvary in AD 33, not AD 70. Don could not be more wrong.

Summary & Conclusion

The traditional teaching of the church has stood the test of millennia. Tens of thousands of scholars from every nation under the sun have poured over the scriptures, testing the doctrine of the cross. Each new generation of men has subjected the teaching of the church to the most searching examination. All stand united in one voice that justification from sin *arrived* at the cross. It was not until 1970 that is was ever suggested that atonement and justification were "postponed" until the fall of Jerusalem. Can it really be imagined that all of Christendom down through the long ages missed something so fundamental? We are not talking about eschatology, which is clothed in metaphors and symbols and therefore difficult to understand, but soteriology, the doctrine of salvation, communicated in the most open and express terms the apostles knew how so that it would be widely known and understood and so endure from generation to generation. The idea that it lay hidden until Max King uncovered it in 1970 is shocking to say the least. What thinking person can believe it? Our sincerest hope is that Preterists

211

will distance themselves from this atrocious error and return to the fold of the Cross.

Preston - V - Simmons Debate

Passing of Torah and the Completion of Salvation

Preston's Final Negative

A word of clarification for the readers. In Kurt's second affirmative he said that he had granted me 8000 extra words, as if he had magnanimously offered me extra space– with the implication that I needed that extra space to prove my point. Kurt's "offer" sprang from a misunderstanding on my part in regard to the length of his first three negatives. *In private correspondence, I apologized to Kurt for my misunderstanding.* Also, when Kurt wrote what he did in his second affirmative, I posted to him privately asking him to correct the impression that his "offer" would make on the readers. Regrettably, my friend did not see fit to correct this misunderstanding. It is important that the readers know that I have not taken, (nor did I need) 8000 extra words for my negative. I *clearly* do not need that extra space to rebut my friend's affirmative. The readers need to know that I have scrupulously followed the agreement that Kurt and I signed as to the length of our presentations. All of my negatives have been the agreed to 8000 word count.
(Don K. Preston)

My friend refuses to confront his self contradictions. He appeals to" 2000 years" of church tradition, as normative when ***that same tradition condemns his preterism!***
He claims the church has always taught that salvation was perfected at the cross. This is false. *The church has historically taught that salvation– purchased through the cross-- would be perfected at Christ's parousia (Hebrews 9:28).* And, the church has *never–**EVER**–* taught Kurt's claim that salvation was deliverance from persecution! ***Period***!

Kurt's selective use of tradition is embarrassing. I can imagine Kenneth Gentry or Keith Mathison gladly citing Kurt's appeal to tradition, to validate their claim that: "2000 years of church history about a literal return of Christ at the end of human history has stood the test!" And, **every scholar Kurt cited would reject his eschatology as heretical!** 2000 years of church history contradicts his eschatology! His adamant refusal to acknowledge his

213

self-contradictory, selective appeal to church history betrays his desperation to make some point, any point.

Kurt's statement that preterism i.e. eschatology, has nothing to do with soteriology is one of the most Biblically inaccurate statements imaginable! *It is just stunning! Nothing is more soteriological than eschatology: "As in Adam all men die, even so in Christ shall all be made alive" i.e. via resurrection, i.e. eschatology!* Kurt's denial illustrates that *he has failed to grasp the very essence of the Biblical story*. Hebrews 9:28 says Christ was coming– *eschatology*– to bring salvation– *soteriology*! Kurt is dead wrong. In light of Kurt's incredible claim, I contacted two major scholars with whom I correspond occasionally and asked them about Kurt's position. *Both reject Kurt's position!*

KURT'S ACCUSATIONS THAT I MISREPRESENTED HIM.
The Charge: Re: Romans 9:28– "He says I admit that Rom. 9:28 refers to the salvation of national Israel. I don't. I believe it refers to their destruction!"
The *Truth*: Here is my argument:
> **The salvation of Israel in Romans 11:26f is the salvation of Israel in Romans 9:28.**
> **But, the salvation of Israel in Romans 9:28 would be finished in a short time.**
> **Therefore, the salvation of Israel in Romans 11:26f would be finished in a short time.**

Kurt responded, *(Second negative)*: "I agree with Don that the "short work" in Rom. 9:27-29 refers to national Israel. God gave the nation a 40 year grace period in which to obey the gospel, and then destroyed the nation." Kurt now denies that he admitted that Romans 9 speaks of the *salvation* of Israel in AD 70. He says it speaks of their *destruction*.

Kurt is guilty of creating a "false either / or." This is a debater's trick. It is *not*, "If Israel was *saved*, then she was *not destroyed*," or vice versa. It is rather, the remnant was saved *AND*, the majority was destroyed at the same time! Kurt's admission that Romans 9 was fulfilled in AD 70 is a fatal admission. It means that Israel's salvation came then. And if Israel's salvation came in AD 70, then salvation for the nations came then as well!

The Charge: "I have never said that physical death was the immediate result of sin."

214

The _Truth_: Kurt – "Since physical death was the immediate doom brought in by sin, and bespoke the greater doom of eternal death that followed, it is from physical death that the promise of resurrection was given." (*Plow and Sword*, **October 2009. Read it for yourself!**).

The Charge: "Don says I contradict myself by saying that the saints on this side of eternity had received the atonement before AD 70, but the saints in Hades did not receive it until AD 70. I never said any such thing."

The _Truth_: Kurt has affirmed _repeatedly_ that the living saints **did** receive the full benefits of the atonement before AD 70.

Kurt on the living:

Colossians 2:12f: "The whole thrust of the passage is to place *all* redemptive work in the past, at the cross." (His emphasis).

Kurt offered **88 verses,** claiming that the past tense verbs prove *the pre-parousia reality* of salvation, justification and atonement. He said *the living saints* "were already in a present state of grace and justification." *Do not miss this fatal self contradiction!*

Kurt on the dead: "The souls in Hades could not enter heaven until they received the benefits of Christ's atoning blood" **(Kurt, SP, October, 2009)**. *However*, *in his first affirmative*, he claimed: "Thus, God *had acquitted them* (the souls in Hades, DKP) based upon reception of Christ's blood." (My emphasis, DKP).

So, on the one hand Kurt says the dead saints *did not receive the atonement until AD 70.* On the other hand, they had already been acquitted before AD 70.

Kurt said the atonement was completed at the cross, and the saints before AD 70 were "already in a present state of grace and justification." Yet, *he now says* he has never said that the saints, "this side of eternity had received the atonement prior to AD 70"! *Really?* **What then has been the purpose of this debate, if Kurt now says the pre-AD 70 saints did _not_ fully possess the atonement?**

Kurt says the pre-parousia saints were "in a state of grace and justification" *and "had received the atonement." Kurt repeatedly said Romans 5:10 proved the saints had received the atonement, and chided me for saying it was proleptic! He said it was finished! Yet, he now denies they had received the atonement! Which Kurt do we believe? Kurt, you can't say they*

215

had received it, and then turn around and claim they hadn't! That is a fatal self-contradiction that all can see.

If those pre-parousia saints *had not received the atonement*, as Kurt *now* claims, *when would they receive it? Well,* Kurt told us that the dead saints received the benefits of the atonement in AD 70, and he *now says* he has always said the living and dead would receive salvation at the same time!

Kurt *did, without question*, affirm that the living saints possessed the atonement and salvation prior to AD 70. And he *did, without question*, affirm that *the dead did not receive the atonement until AD 70.* So, he has the living saints receiving salvation before the dead saints. He has *not*, as he now claims, always said that the living and dead saints received their salvation at the same time. **Every reader of this debate– and Kurt-- knows this is a false claim.** His self contradiction is inescapable, undeniable and fatal.

Kurt has surrendered this debate by admitting that the living did not, in fact, fully receive the atonement prior to AD 70, and by now affirming that salvation was in AD 70 for the living and the dead! This is my position! Kurt has conceded!

The Charge: "Don claims I said that the "law of sin and death was nailed to the cross," but I have never said that either."
The _Truth_: *Kurt, (Second Affirmative)*: "He nailed the debt of sin to his cross, triumphing over the law of sin and death." Kurt (October, 2009, Sword and Plow): "This promise was made in veiled, poetic terms when God said that the woman's seed would bruise the head of the serpent, *signifying that Jesus would crush the power of sin and death by his cross and resurrection* (Gen. 3:15)." (My emphasis).

The facts are undeniable. My friend's desperation is such that he falsely accuses me of misrepresenting him. He denies saying **what anyone can see that he said!** I challenge *anyone* to go back to his presentations and read them objectively. **I did not, *in any way*, misrepresent what Kurt said.**
Kurt seemingly forgets what he says from presentation to presentation, and from article to article. He changes position from presentation to presentation, when caught in self contradiction. *(Four different positions on Isaiah 27 in this debate!)* So, in desperation, he accuses me of misrepresenting him. This

is sad.

Now note the following:
Kurt says that I say the atonement did not occur at the cross. *False! I have consistently argued that the atonement process was initiated at the cross.* He says my position is historically unknown. Well, in numerous formal debates, I have asked my opponents, "Is there anything Christ must do _to complete the atonement?_" *Almost invariably,* they have answered: "Christ must come the second time!" Kurt's claim that only proponents of Covenant Eschatology say the atonement was not perfected until the parousia is false. This is a historically validated view!

Kurt says: "There is NOTHING in terms of man's salvation that my brother Don is willing to say arrived at the cross. According to Don, *nothing happened at the cross.*"
This is a _gross_ mis-representation. Read my comments– or my books. You will know how false this is. In logic, what Kurt has done is called *poisoning the well.* You ascribe some view that is so outrageous, so radical, to your opponent, that people will be afraid to read what they have to say. This is a debater's _trick_, but, should not be part of honorable controversy. Kurt is so desperate to make a point, any point at all, that he is willing to make blatantly false accusations. This is *shameful.*
Kurt queries: WHERE IS THE CROSS, in Don's theology? My answer has always been, the cross is the very foundation of our faith. Without it, nothing else matters, and nothing else happened! But it was the *initiation* of the salvation process, with the parousia being the consummation. *This is what Hebrews 9:24-28 proves beyond disputation.* It is Kurt's claim in regard to Hebrews 9:28 that is *historically unprecedented!*
Remember Kurt's claim: "But if the cross did not *triumph* over the law at Calvary, if man had to wait until the law was *removed* to be justified from sin, then *nothing* happened at the cross"?
I responded with several points; Only one is reiterated here (See my second Affirmative):
If the marriage is not completed at *the very moment* of the betrothal, then *absolutely nothing* happened at the moment of betrothal! **Kurt totally ignored this.** Yet' Kurt admits that AD 70 was the consummation of the betrothal, bringing with it "a greater intimacy!" His "all or nothing" claim is false, **by his own admissions!**

Consider Kurt's remarks from *Consummation of the Ages (231):*
"The temple in Jerusalem was merely a figure of the true (Heb. 8:1-2). It was a shadow of the substitutionary death and atoning blood of Christ. In his death, the veil of the temple was 'rent in twain', signifying that the way into God's presence was opened by the death of Christ. The Christian thus had 'boldness to enter the holiest by the blood of Jesus (Hebrews 10:19f). Nevertheless, true to the already-but-not-yet character of the transition period between the cross and the coming of Christ, "the way into the holiest of all was not yet manifest, while as yet the first tabernacle was yet standing (Hebrews 9:8). The Christians' access to the presence of God was forestalled pending passage of the Mosaic age. Thus, the Hebrews writer calls Christ a High Priest of 'good things to come" (Hebrews 9:11; cf. 2:5; 6:5; 10:1). At the time of his writing, they were not yet come, but they were very near."
Amen and Amen! This is **great commentary** *because he proved it with scripture*! It is sad that my friend has abandoned the truth.

DANIEL 9 / 12

Kurt selectively appeals to "tradition" to prove that Torah passed at the cross, and later, the sacrifice literally ceased in the Jewish War. But, he offers us no proof, just tradition.

Note again Daniel 9:

1.) Kurt says I make the seventieth week run from 63-70 AD. **False!** Like him, I posit Jesus' death *in the first part of the week* (Daniel 9:26). *Had he read my books accurately he would know this.*

Jesus' Passion - Pentecost fulfilled the first four of Israel's typological feasts. *The second half of the week —which included Atonement-- fulfilled the last three feasts. Israel's feast days provide the key for the "gap" between the first part of the seventieth week, and the last.*

2.) Torah could not pass until all of it– *including the ceremonial feast days, KS–* was fulfilled. But, the ceremonial feast days would be fulfilled at the end of the seventieth week, in AD 70, per Kurt. Therefore, none of the Torah passed until AD 70!

3.) Daniel says Messiah would *confirm*, (*gabar*--Strong's #01396) **not MAKE** (*berith*) the covenant for one week. *This does not speak of making the New Covenant*, but of **confirming an already existing covenant**. Kurt ignored the fact that the NT says Jesus came to confirm the Old Covenant, and to fulfill it (Matthew 5:17-18; Romans 15:8).

4.) I offered the following, in light of Kurt's claim that everything in Daniel 9:24 was fulfilled at the cross (Except the destruction of Jerusalem):

218

Daniel 9:24 foretold the coming of *everlasting righteousness*– this is *soteriology.*

Paul and Peter were still anticipating the arrival of the prophesied everlasting righteousness (Galatians 5:5; 2 Peter 3:10-13)- at the Day of the Lord (*eschatology*)..

Therefore, unless Paul and Peter were anticipating a prophesied world of righteousness *different from Daniel*, then Daniel 9 was not fulfilled– and salvation was not consummated— at the cross.

Unless Kurt can prove that righteousness is unrelated to salvation, then the fact that Peter and Paul were still waiting the full arrival of everlasting righteousness proves that salvation was not perfected at the cross.

Kurt misapplied Daniel 9. He ignored what the text says. He distorted my views on Daniel 9. My position is verified, and his falsified.

HOSEA 13

Kurt seeks to refute my argument on the resurrection *by divorcing Hosea 13 from Paul's discussion in 1 Corinthians 15!* Do not miss this!

1.) Paul said the resurrection of 1 Corinthians 15 would be the fulfillment of Hosea 13:14.

2.) **Kurt denies this**, insisting that Hosea has nothing– *NOTHING*– to do with what Paul was predicting!

3.) Kurt's newly invented theology forces him to ignore what Hosea said, and to claim that Paul was wrong when he said the resurrection of 1 Corinthians 15 would be *the fulfillment of Hosea!*

4.) Why would Paul say the resurrection of 1 Corinthians 15 would be the fulfillment of Hosea, if, as Kurt claims, Hosea's prediction contains nothing remotely resembling what Paul was predicting? **Kurt's hermeneutic denies Paul's repeated statements that his eschatological and soteriological hope was *nothing but the hope of Israel!***

5.) This distorted hermeneutic forced Kurt to deny that Isaiah 27 and 59 had anything to do with what Paul predicted in Romans 11. Both of those texts– in spite of Kurt's denials– foretold the coming of the Lord in judgment of Israel for shedding innocent blood. Paul said the coming of the Lord in Romans 11 would be the fulfillment of those prophecies. But, Kurt says NO, this can't be, those prophecies had nothing to do with Romans 11! They were about the Assyrian captivity!

6.) I have pressed Kurt repeatedly to give us some exegetical or logical proof to explain why Paul cited those OT prophecies to justify his NT doctrine, when according to Kurt, those OT prophecies had *nothing whatsoever to do with what Paul was discussing*! This is surely one of the most illogical, false hermeneutics imaginable.

7.) Kurt appeals to Homer Hailey to support his false claim. Yet, Hailey would reject Kurt's view of the resurrection as **heresy**!

Look again at my affirmative on **the Spirit and resurrection.**

The promise of the Spirit was made to Israel *to raise her from the dead* (Ezekiel 37:10-14).

This "death" from which Israel was to be raised was not physical death, but *covenantal death* (Isaiah 24:4f; Hosea 5-6; 13:1-2). Living people were called *dead*, but they continued to "sin more and more" (Hosea 13:1-2). Biologically dead people cannot do this! This is *spiritual death*- alienation-as a result of sin (Isaiah 59:1-2--The sin that needed to be removed at the coming of the Lord, Isaiah 59:20f--Romans 11!). Sin brought death. Thus, forgiveness would bring resurrection (cf. Acts 26:17-18)!

This resurrection, *guaranteed by the Spirit*, would be *Israel's salvation* (Isaiah 25:8-9). This is the resurrection promise of 1 Corinthians 15 when sin, *the sting of death*, would be overcome (1 Corinthians 15:54-56– ***Romans 11:26-27)***. So:

1 Corinthians 15 foretold the resurrection (when sin would be put away), predicted by Isaiah 25.

The resurrection of Isaiah 25 is the resurrection of Isaiah 26-27 (and thus, Romans 11:26-27), which would occur at the coming of the Lord in judgment of Israel for shedding innocent blood.

But, the coming of the Lord -- at the resurrection to put away sin-- of Isaiah 25-27 / 1 Corinthians 15-- would be the coming of the Lord in judgment of Israel for shedding innocent blood.

Therefore, the coming of the Lord of Romans 11 to take away Israel's sin-- to bring her salvation-- is the coming of the Lord at the time of the resurrection, in judgment of Israel for shedding innocent blood, i.e. AD 70.

Thus, Israel was not cut off at the cross. God's promises to her were "irrevocable" (Romans 11:28), *and until His covenant promises to her were fulfilled she would not enter her salvation (Romans 11:26f) at the resurrection.* Kurt ignored this argument.

Please catch this: Kurt says we still have the earnest of the Spirit today. Well, the Earnest was the guarantee of the (future) reception of what the early church *did not yet possess*! ***Do you catch that?*** *The very existence of the Spirit as the Earnest was proof positive that what the Spirit was guaranteeing was not yet fully accomplished! The Earnest guaranteed the redemption of the purchased possession* (Ephesians 1:12f). The Spirit guaranteed therefore, the completion of the atonement and resurrection (which is *salvation*)!

If we today still have the Earnest of the Spirit, then from the cross to this day, we do not yet possess the atonement and salvation! You cannot argue for the continuing possession of the Earnest of the Spirit, without thereby saying that we do not yet possess son-ship, redemption and salvation! Do you see how self-contradictory Kurt's position is? On the one hand he argues that the saints before AD 70 had "received the atonement." But if this was true, they did not need the Earnest of the Spirit to guarantee their redemption! When confronted with the implications of that false claim, he then denies saying they had the atonement. But then, he says that they (and we!!) had the Earnest of the Spirit. But, ***the Earnest of the Spirit was the guarantee of the future reception of the atonement, son-ship, and redemption!*** The presence of the Earnest of the Spirit was indisputable proof that ***the work of salvation was not perfected!*** Thus, Kurt's claim that we still have the Earnest, falsifies his new theology!

ZECHARIAH 11

I shook my head in amazement and sorrow as I read my friend's comments on Zechariah 11. It is sad to me that he is so desperate to support his newly invented theology that he is willing to purposefully manipulate the text. Did you notice his convenient use of the ellipsis: "And I took my staff, even Beauty, and cut it asunder, that I might break my covenant which I had made with all the people. And it was broken in that day... *And I said unto them, If ye think good, give me my price...*" **This is just so sad!**

Kurt tries to make it appear that the "in that day" referent is to Judas' betrayal. ***Patently false***. It is referent ***back*** to vss. 8-10; "Let the dying die. Let those who are left eat one another's flesh. ***Then*** I took my staff...revoking the covenant...It was revoked ***in that day.***" The "***Then***" and the "*in that day*" are undeniable references *to the time when Israel would eat their own flesh in a time of war.* As Kurt knows, this was in AD 70. Thus, ***God revoked His covenant with Israel in AD 70.***

This raises the issue again: "If a law or covenant has been abrogated, are any

221

of the provisions of that covenant, i.e. promises or penalties (positive or negative) still binding?" Unbelievably, contrary to all logic and law, Kurt tried to tell us that just because a law has been abrogated does not mean that its penalties cannot still be applied! However...

The provisions of a covenant are not applicable if the covenant has been nullified. Kurt, and every logically thinking person, knows this. But, the provisions of wrath found in the Mosaic Covenant – eating their own flesh in time of war– were fulfilled in AD 70.

Therefore, the Mosaic Covenant remained binding in AD 70.

So, yes, *my argument on Zechariah is irrefutable*, and all Kurt's comments have done is to expose his regrettable desperation.

NOTHING BUT THE HOPE OF ISRAEL

I have made, and re-made the following argument. It remains a **HUGE EMPTY BOX!** This one argument is fatal to his paradigm:

Fact: "Salvation is of the Jews." That is, salvation was to flow *from Israel to the nations*. Paul said his gospel was nothing but the hope of Israel (Acts 26:21f).

Fact: Israel's salvation would be at the time of the resurrection (Isaiah 25:8-9).

Fact: The resurrection occurred in AD 70. Kurt agrees.

Now, Kurt's new theology *demands*, that we delineate between the salvation promises made to and about Israel, and create another salvation distinct from Israel.

Now, watch...

Kurt has said repeatedly that redemption and atonement was completed at the cross.

Kurt ignores the **indisputable fact that the atonement and salvation** had to do with **the fulfillment of God's promises to OC Israel.** And, salvation is inextricably linked to the fulfillment of Israel's feast days!

You cannot affirm the perfection of salvation at the cross without saying the resurrection occurred at the cross. You cannot affirm the consummation of salvation *without affirming the complete fulfillment of Israel's typological feast days*– and not even Kurt does that!

Do not fail to catch this! Israel was to receive her salvation (*soteriology*) at the end of her age in AD 70 (*eschatology*). This is *prima facie* falsification of Kurt's ill-informed statement that there is no relationship between

222

eschatology and soteriology. This is *bad* theology.

If Israel and Torah were cast out at the cross, then Israel was cast out **before, and without,** her eschatological and soteriological promises were fulfilled. But, Biblically, **until and _unless_ Israel received her salvation, *no one else could receive salvation!* Yet, Kurt has salvation given to individuals (and Gentiles!) before Israel received her salvation, and *without* Israel receiving her salvation!** Kurt destroys the Biblical pattern of: "To the Jew first, then to the Greek."

Kurt says Israel and Torah was cut off at the cross. **But, the resurrection is the time of Israel's salvation (Isaiah 25:8-9)**– the salvation that was to be, "To the Jew first, *then* to the Greek." Thus, how could "the saints" have received their salvation– as Kurt claims– before the resurrection *when that is the time of Israel's salvation?*

Kurt said not one word about this issue. His proposition falls on this single argument.

This is Covenant Eschatology confirmed, and Kurt falsified.

You must ponder why Kurt has totally refused to deal with the issue of *eschatology and Israel's promises.* He rips those promises from Israel and divorces them from the end of her age. He makes them apply primarily to individuals at death–not the parousia, where the Bible emphatically posits them-- and he says those promises have nothing to do with the end of the age! Kurt's abject refusal to deal with this proves he cannot deal with it.

KURT'S FALSE VIEW OF RESURRECTION

Kurt's view of sin and death is wrong, and leads to wrong conclusions. I have documented beyond doubt that Kurt says physical death was the immediate result of sin.

Kurt says Christ died physically, as a substitution for mankind. This **_demands_** that if Jesus' physical death was the focus of his substitutionary death, that *those in Christ should never die physically!* Yet, Jesus' physical death on the cross has not kept one single person in history from dying physically! I asked Kurt, *if Jesus died as our **substitute**– in our place--* why do those in Christ have to die physically? Kurt response? **An empty box!** The reason is simple. It falsifies his view of sin-death-resurrection!

I have documented that Kurt did claim that Christ defeated the law of sin and death at the cross. Yet he says that when a Christian sins they are subject to the law of sin and death. His view demands that the physical death of even the most faithful Christian is a demonstration that they are under the **power of sin– not the power of faith or of Christ's atonement!** Folks, this is *fatal* to Kurt. It is why he did not say one word in response.

MATTHEW 5:17-18

Kurt claims I contradict myself on Matthew 5 and the issue of circumcision. He mishandles my argument. I argued that circumcision was being annulled IN CHRIST, and for those **IN CHRIST**, the land promises were fulfilled! I was not arguing that Torah itself had objectively been annulled. My friend is grasping at straws to find any semblance of an argument.

Paul no where asserts that the unconverted Jews were wrong to continue circumcision. He pointed them to Christ, telling them their promises were being fulfilled in him and that the old system was about to pass, to be sure. However, Kurt cannot find a single text where Paul told unbelieving Jews that Torah had been abrogated! He did, however, warn them that the provisions of Torah would come on them if they did not obey Jesus (Acts 13:34f), which again proves my proposition!

My friend's desperation continues: "It was Jesus' *first coming* he declared would fulfill the law." This is false.

Kurt appeals to Matthew 27:50– "It is finished!" claiming Jesus had finished every thing the Father gave him to do. No, *for he had not yet come in judgment, as the Father had given him to do* (John 5:19f; 12:48f)! Jesus' *suffering* was finished to be sure, but clearly, he had not finished the work the Father had given him!

Kurt appeals to Acts 13:29-33, "When they had fulfilled all that was written of him, they took him from the tree." Once again, Kurt is grasping at straws and ignoring the text! The focus of the "all things concerning him," is undeniably *limited to his suffering*. It does not even mention his resurrection, yet, Kurt believes that Jesus' resurrection was an essential element of fulfilling the Law!

Acts 13 is not a comprehensive statement such as "not one jot or one tittle shall pass until all is fulfilled"! Kurt takes a passage that clearly limits the "all" in view, and expands it into a comprehensive "all" without justification. Context determines the extent of the "all things," and in the texts Kurt cites there are limitations on the "all things." But, *there is no such limitation in Matthew 5!* And Hebrews 9 proves that Kurt is wrong to limit the fulfillment of "all things" to Jesus' incarnation. Watch carefully.

Remember, Kurt says that all that had to be fulfilled was the ceremonial law. Of course, *now,* he even changes that position and says that all that had to be fulfilled was Jesus' death! Notice Hebrews 9:6f again.

Paul says Torah stood in meats, drinks, etc.. *This is referent to the feast days of Israel.* Those ordinances were still being practiced when he wrote, for, "these are parabolic of the present time" (Hebrews 9:8). Kurt once honored the Greek tenses. He now refuses to honor them. We have challenged him repeatedly to give us some grammatical or lexical justification for denying the present and future tenses. The echo in that **EMPTY BOX** is resounding!. Furthermore, those ordinances– i.e. The Feast Days– *would remain valid until **the time of reformation***. Let's rehearse Kurt's constant vacillation on the time of reformation:

Kurt initially said the time of reformation ***arrived at the cross***. But, this demands that man could enter the MHP from that point, so he retreated from that view.

Then, he said that the time of reformation _ended_– not arrived– at the parousia in AD 70. But, this would demand that after AD 70 there would be no access to the MHP. So, being entrapped, he changed his position *again,* admitting that **the time of reformation was completed in AD.** This is the view I have argued.

Of course, *this demands that Torah remained valid until AD 70,* so, Kurt abandoned all discussion of the time of reformation. Let's look again at the argument.

Paul: Israel's feast days were typological.
Those feast days (Thus, Torah) would remain valid until the time of reformation.
The time of reformation fully arrived in AD 70 (Kurt Simmons)!
Therefore, Israel's feast days (Thus, Torah) remained valid until AD 70.

Kurt says that *the shadow ends when the body (fulfillment) arrives. **Amen!** But, **the "shadowy" feast days were still valid when Colossians / Hebrews was written!** Thus, Torah was still valid.

I made extensive argument on Israel's feast days. Kurt said not one word in response! Yet, my arguments on the feast days **fill up Kurt's boxes!**

I challenged Kurt to deal with this, but, he ignored my argument on the feast days:
Not one jot or tittle of "The Law" could pass until it was *all fulfilled* (Matthew 5:17-18; *"including "all typological aspects of the "ceremonial law,"* KS).
The ceremonial Feasts of Trumpets and Harvest were not fulfilled until AD 70 at the time of the judgment/resurrection.
Therefore, not one jot or tittle passed from "the ceremonial law" until AD 70.

Kurt's new theology rips the atonement from its direct link with Trumpets and Harvest– *eschatological consummation*– and posits it at the *beginning* of Israel's festival calendar. *There is no justification for this, whatsoever*. Seventy weeks were determined to make the atonement. Kurt posits this at the beginning of the final week. Typologically, however, it belongs to the last half, the time of consummation.

Do not miss the importance of this argument! It is "un-get-overable" proof that Torah remained valid until AD 70. If Torah was removed at the cross, the ceremonial law was not fulfilled, *the time of reformation never arrived!* And there is still no access to the MHP!

GALATIANS 4– TWO SYSTEMS AT ONE TIME

Kurt *finally* said something about Galatians 4! But what he said was false. Ishmael and Isaac dwelt in the same house– *together*. The women and sons represented the two covenants. Hagar / Ishmael– represented the Old Covenant and the Old Covenant people who persecuted Isaac (the spiritual seed). *As a result*, Paul said "cast out the bondwoman and her son."
Kurt says– as if it answers anything I said– that it was Hagar that represented Torah. *YES*! That is my argument!
Paul said– in spite of Kurt's dust cloud-- that as a **direct consequence of fleshly Israel persecuting the spiritual seed**, "cast out the bondwoman (Torah!), and her son (Fleshly Israel)." Once again, that casting out was to be *for persecuting Christians*! There were no Christians before the cross! Since the casting out was to be for persecuting Christians, and the casting out was still future when Paul wrote Galatians, this proves irrefutably that Torah

(Hagar) and Israel, (Ishmael) had not yet been cast out.

This also proves, indubitably, that the two laws existed side by side until **the casting out of Israel for persecuting the church!** And, I asked Kurt if the pagans did not have Torah, while Israel did have Torah? Do you hear the echo in that *empty box?*

I stand with Paul that the Gentiles *did not have Torah*, while *Israel did have Torah*. That means, *prima facie*, that there were two systems in place at the same time. Kurt is wrong.

1 PETER: THE SALVATION READY TO BE REVEALED
Again, Kurt's desperation manifests itself.

Peter speaks of the eternal inheritance ready to be revealed at the parousia. Kurt ignores this and says that salvation was relief from persecution. In fact, he says, "Can there be any doubt that the salvation that would be revealed was Jesus' destruction of the church's enemies?"

1.) I proved that Peter said those saints had to suffer more. Kurt says the promise was no more suffering. Kurt is wrong.

2.) The salvation in view was, "The salvation of your souls" *foretold by the OT prophets*. I challenged Kurt to give us the OT verses that support his view. Total silence.

3.) Kurt insists that the salvation promised was the physical destruction of Christ's enemies. Well, 2000 years of tradition-- that Kurt keeps appealing to-- denies this!

4.) Kurt overlooks the fact that *the last enemy to be destroyed was death* (1 Corinthians 15:24f). So, if the promise was the physical destruction of Christ's enemies, **then physical death should have been destroyed!**

5.) Kurt overlooks the fact that *physical events were signs of the **greater spiritual realities!*** Thus, the physical event of the fall of Jerusalem was signatory of the greater spiritual reality of the destruction of Christ's *spiritual enemies*. This proves that salvation was not perfected until AD 70.

HEAVEN AND EARTH AND 2 PETER 3
Kurt denies the covenantal context of the destruction of "heaven and earth." He says, "There is not one single occasion in the whole Bible where the "heavens and earth" refer to the Old or New Testaments – not one." This is just sad.

Response: Isaiah 65:17f said that the Old Heaven and Earth would pass and would be "remembered no more." Now, watch... In his comments on Revelation 16:18, which describes the destruction of "Babylon" it says she would be "remembered before God." Kurt says of this word "remembered": "'Remembrance' is a uniquely covenantal term...Similar usage nowhere appears with reference to any nation of the Gentiles" (*Consummation*, p. 313). ***Well said!*** He then gives verses that prove that "remember" carries covenantal significance.

Well, in Isaiah 65, the Old Heaven and Earth would "not be remembered any more"! This demands that **the Old Heaven and Earth was a covenant heaven and earth.** But, that covenant relationship would cease! ***This is Covenant Eschatology established beyond dispute***. (See Jeremiah 3:14f-- in the Messianic kingdom, the Ark of the Covenant **would "not be remembered" anymore**). Once again, Kurt has falsified his own theology.

I have now refuted every salient point in Kurt's affirmatives, so, let me recall some of the arguments of this debate.

A BUNCH OF EMPTY BOXES!

#1 – I have offered *multiple* logical syllogisms. Kurt urged the readers to beware of my use of logic, and openly stated he had no responsibility to respond to anything I would present. This *after signing an agreement to answer my arguments without evasion!* Lamentably, when he has attempted to answer my questions– after much pressure– he has done nothing but obfuscate.

#2 – ISAIAH 27 AND 59
Kurt began by telling us that proper exegesis of Isaiah 27 and 59 is irrelevant. This alone should alarm any student of scripture!

Paul said that the coming of the Lord would fulfill Isaiah 27 and 59.

Isaiah 27 and 59 were predictions of the coming of the Lord in judgment of Israel for shedding innocent blood.

Kurt changed positions four times on Isaiah 27! This is unmitigated desperation.

Kurt never explained why Paul cited these prophecies, when, per Kurt, they had nothing whatsoever to do with what Paul was predicting.

#3 – DANIEL 9

I demonstrated that everlasting righteousness promised by Daniel 9 was still future when Paul and Peter wrote, thus demanding that salvation was not yet perfected. Kurt's response? **An empty box!**

#4– DANIEL 12

My argument: The power of the holy people would be shattered at the time of the resurrection– in AD 70.

The power of the holy people was *Torah*.

Therefore, the power of Torah was not shattered until AD 70.

Incredibly, Kurt claimed that Israel's "power" was *identical to the pagan nations*. I proved (First negative) that it was *Israel's covenant with YHVH that was her only power*. Kurt totally ignored this. **This argument alone falsifies his theology.**

 # 5 – I challenged Kurt to give us commentary support for his view of 1 Thessalonians 4– Just one! Resounding silence! *2000 years of church history knows nothing of his view!* On the other hand, Kurt challenged me to provide commentary support that Isaiah 27 applied to AD 70. I provided that proof, but instead of acknowledging it, *he ignored it!*

#6 – For all of his appeal to "2000 years of church tradition," **Kurt claimed that Jesus had to enter the MHP TWICE**. Hebrews 9:12 says he entered *ONCE*! *2000 years of church history knows nothing of Kurt's claim!* I challenged Kurt to produce even one commentary to support his claim. The result? **An empty box!** Kurt is wrong.

#7 – Kurt claims that the Transfiguration was not about covenant transformation and was a vision of Jesus' incarnation. I challenged him to prove this. Not a word of response! And, 2000 years of church history knows almost nothing of his claim. Kurt is wrong.

#8 – He claims 2 Corinthians 3 refers to the already abolished Torah. (Although keep in mind that Kurt is on record as saying that it was not Torah that was nailed to the Cross! **Do not forget this!**) Look at 2 Corinthians 3 again.

Paul, speaking of the passing of Torah says, "Seeing then that we have– present tense– such *hope*." Paul does not say the hope of the passing of Torah

229

had been fulfilled.

Paul likewise says that "in the reading of Moses, the veil is still present, but when one turns to the Lord the veil is taken away." Paul speaks here of a person *dying to Torah*, not Torah being already dead! Kurt turns the text on its head.

Paul said that the transformation "from glory to glory" the transformation from the glory of Moses to the glory of Christ and the New Covenant was being accomplished by the Spirit, through his personal ministry. **Kurt totally ignored these irrefutable facts** because they falsify his new doctrine.

#9 – THE GREEK TENSES

In his books, Kurt insisted that we honor the Greek present and future tenses of the process of salvation, *begun at the cross, perfected at the parousia*. I have challenged him ***repeatedly*** to give us any kind of lexical, grammatical, textual proof for *why we should now ignore these tenses*. The answer? **An empty box!**

Kurt presented 88 verses telling us we must accept the past tense objective reality of the finished work of salvation before AD 70. When pressed with the implications of this, he now denies ever saying that the living saints had received the benefits of the atonement before AD 70!

#10 – I challenged Kurt to tell us if he still accepts– as he affirms in his books-- the *lexical definition* of *mello*, as "about to be." His answer? **Empty Box!**

#11 – I have challenged Kurt with his inherently contradictory view that Torah *was* nailed to the Cross, but then arguing that Torah was *NOT* nailed to the cross. Response? **Total silence!**

#12 – Kurt claimed that Hebrews 8:13 did not mean that Torah was ready to pass, but, only the already dead external form of Torah was ready to pass. But, if Torah was already dead, and could no longer prevent entrance into the MHP, *but the saints still could not enter the MHP until AD 70, why* could the saints not enter the MHP? **Total, abject silence!**

#13 – I have asked repeatedly: If salvation was completed at the cross why did the dead saints have to wait until AD 70 to enter the MHP? **NO ANSWER!**

230

#14 – Kurt says AD 70 was "soteriologically irrelevant." Yet, he says, the dead saints could not enter the MHP until then. I asked him why the dead saints had to await that irrelevant event to receive their salvation. **In six presentations, he typed not one word of explanation!**

#15 – I asked: Is the forgiveness of sins and entrance into the MHP, *which would only come at the end of Torah*, necessary to salvation? Kurt refused to answer.

#16 – **The only thing**, that prevented man from entering the MHP was *sin, and by extension, Torah because of its inability to forgive (Hebrews 9:6-10)*. Kurt says the pre-AD 70 saints fully enjoyed forgiveness– although *he now denies saying they had the atonement!* I repeatedly asked, **if the separating barrier– sin and Torah-- was "completely removed"** at the cross <u>*what prevented them from entering until AD 70?*</u> He **refused to answer!** Why? Because the correct answer destroys his rejection of Covenant Eschatology.

#17 – **Kurt claimed that** removal of Torah was unnecessary for salvation. I asked: <u>***Why then did Christ die to remove Torah and apply grace?***</u> Hebrews 9 says as long as Torah stood valid, there was no entrance into the MHP. If, however, my friend's new doctrine is correct, the removal of Torah was not necessary for entrance into the MHP! Yet, Paul is clear that as long as Torah remained valid there was no entrance! Kurt's view contradicts Hebrews 9.

#18 – **Kurt claimed Torah had no "negative power."** I presented seven passages which speak emphatically of the negative power of Torah: *no forgiveness, the curse, no righteousness, no justification, no life, condemnation, death, prevention of entrance into the MHP.* I challenged Kurt to explain how these were not negative powers. Surely, if Torah truly had no negative power, Kurt could explain these passages for us, yet, **not one word of response!**

#19 – Hebrews 9 says there would be no entrance into the MHP *while the Mosaic Law remained imposed*. Revelation 15:8; 16:16f says there would be no access to the MHP until Jerusalem was judged. Of logical necessity, *the Mosaic Law remained imposed until the judgment of Old Covenant Jerusalem in AD 70.* I challenged Kurt to give at least some response to this.

Not a key stroke was offered!

#20 – Re: The salvation of Hebrews 9:28. Kurt says it was *deliverance from persecution*. I challenged him to document that this is the traditional view of the church. **The box remains empty**, because **his view is unknown in church history!**

#21 – I have shown (Hebrews 11:40 and 1 Thessalonians 4) that the living and dead saints would receive salvation *at the same time*– at the resurrection. Kurt says the living received the benefits of the atonement / justification before then. I challenged him to harmonize this with these verses. He then claimed he had never said the living saints received the atonement before AD 70! Of course, *all readers of this debate know that he did make that claim*. Kurt was simply desperate to escape the contradictions in his own statements.

#22 – I asked Kurt: Do you now renounce as false teaching, what you wrote in October of 2009, and the proposition that *just last November* you wanted to affirm concerning the resurrection and Hades?

The souls in Hades could not enter heaven until they received the benefits of Christ's atoning blood (Kurt Simmons, October, 2009).
But, the souls in Hades could not enter heaven until the resurrection in AD 70 (KS, November, 2009).
Therefore, the souls in Hades did not receive the benefits of Christ's atoning blood until AD 70.
Kurt refused to answer.

#23 – Hades was the place of separation from God, even for the righteous, until the time of the resurrection when sin would be overcome through forgiveness and salvation (1 Corinthians 15:54-56; Revelation 20:10ff). *Hades existed because there was no forgiveness of sin.*
Kurt believes that Hades was not destroyed until AD 70, and the souls in Hades did not enter their reward until AD 70.
In his Sword and Plow, October / November 2009, he said the saints could not enter the MHP "without the atoning sacrifice of Christ, so, the dead were sequestered in Hades until the general resurrection." (Notice that highly significant "<u>so</u>" in Kurt's comments). He still affirms– at least we *think* so! – that the dead saints could not enter heaven until AD 70 and the "general

232

resurrection." *This is crucial!*

The existence of Hades until AD 70 as Kurt affirms, is *prima facie* proof that *neither the living or the dead entered the MHP until the resurrection.* The living saints could not bypass Hades when they died before the resurrection. So, until the resurrection in AD 70 neither the living or the dead saints could enter the MHP.

Since Hades existed until AD 70 then Torah remained binding until AD 70! **Paul said there could be no access to the MHP while Torah remained binding!**

The destruction of Hades is when man could enter the MHP. *Hades and Torah were coexistent!* Remember Luke 16– "They have Moses and the prophets, let them hear them"! As long as Torah stood valid there was *no forgiveness* and thus, no entrance into MHP. As long as Hades–which existed because of *no forgiveness*-- remained there was no entrance into the MHP. Kurt says Hades was not destroyed until AD 70. Therefore, Torah remained binding until AD 70. (*Because Torah could not provide forgiveness!*) Kurt owed it to the readers of this debate to address this argument **without evasion**, as he promised to do when he signed the debate rules. But, lamentably, **Kurt's silence reverberates in this empty box!**

#24 – The ceremonial sacrifices foreshadowed entrance into the MHP.
As long as the sacrifices (The Mosaic Covenant) were imposed there was no entrance into the MHP.
There was no entrance until AD 70– Kurt Simmons
Therefore, the sacrifices (and the Mosaic Covenant) were imposed until AD 70.
Not a word of response!

#25 – I presented extensive argumentation on Israel's feasts days.
The ceremonial feast days were typological of the better things to come– including the arrival of salvation.
Kurt said that all types of the ceremonial law had to be fulfilled for Torah to pass.
The feast days were still typological (and unfulfilled) of those better things when Colossians and Hebrews were written.
The Feast of Trumpets and Harvest typified Judgment and Resurrection (the time of salvation) which Kurt posits at AD 70.
This demands that the ceremonial law remained valid until AD 70!

Kurt said not one word in response! There is no answer in Kurt's new theology. The feast days of Israel are *prima facie*, irrefutable falsification of Kurt's proposition and theology.

Twenty Five Empty Boxes!!

The contrasts in this debate could not be clearer, or more dramatic.

1.) **I have appealed to scripture alone**. Kurt has appealed to church tradition, yet that very tradition *condemns his preterism.*

2.) I have utilized proper logic. Kurt has openly eschewed logic, and could not even frame a proper syllogism without violating the rules of logic.

3.) I have relied on proper exegesis; Kurt actually said proper exegesis was irrelevant.

4.) I have answered Kurt's questions and arguments without evasion. Kurt persistently refused to answer my questions or my arguments, as demonstrated by the 25 empty boxes (there are more!). He even stated he had no responsibility to answer anything I said!

5.) I have relied on the emphatic words of scripture; Kurt has denied and manipulated the words of scripture.

6.) I have been *consistent* in my argumentation; Kurt has **repeatedly changed his arguments** from presentation to presentation, often denying that he said *what everyone knows he did say*. **He told us the pre-70 living saints *did possess the atonement*, then he denied *ever* saying that!**

My affirmative arguments and proposition stand indisputably proven, untouched by Kurt.

My negative arguments have falsified Kurt's affirmatives. His refusal to answer my arguments prove this. His offering of historically unprecedented arguments proves this. His open rejection of the emphatic statements of scripture proves this.

I appreciate my friend for engaging in these discussions, which allows the readers to see *the indisputable truth of Covenant Eschatology:* **The coming of Christ for salvation in Romans 11:25-27 occurred in AD 70 at the climax and termination of the Mosaic Covenant Age**.